T0279627

'Russ Williams's nationwide search for some of Wales's most enduring folkloric landmarks propels the reader on a colourful whirlwind tour through millennia of weird history and culture. From heartbroken saints and tree-bound skeletons to ghostly apes and the mischievous Mari Lwyd, here you'll find a treasure trove of Welsh myth and legend waiting to be cracked open.'
Delyth Badder, folklorist and author of *The Folklore of Wales: Ghosts*

'A thoroughly entertaining romp through Welsh places and stories. Russ Williams is a gifted storyteller with a real knack for bringing places and old legends to life.'
Claire Fayers, children's writer and author of *Welsh Giants, Ghosts and Goblins*

'A winsome walk through the highlights reel of Welsh folklore. Russ Williams takes us on a journey of discovery filled with humour and heart. A must-read for those who believe in the magic that lives just outside their front door.'
Owen Staton, storyteller and host of the *Time Between Times Storytelling* podcast

'A personal road trip in search of the weirdness of Welsh mythology. A delicious blend of academia and anarchy, Russ retells Welsh folk tales in our time through the life and humour of a 21st-century Caernarfon boy.'
Peter Stevenson, storyteller and author of *Illustrated Welsh Folk Tales for Young and Old*

'Walk with the author in the footsteps of giants and dragons, wizards and ghosts, up and down the length of Wales. And in the process discover a bit more about where we all came from. A special book about a special place.'
Sarah Woodbury, author of *The Last Pendragon* saga and *The Lion of Wales* series

Where the Folk

Russ Williams

2024

www.uwp.co.uk

British Library Cataloguing-in-Publication Data

A catalogue record for this book is available from the British Library.

ISBN: 978-1-915279-70-5

The right of Russ Williams to be identified as author of this work has been asserted in accordance with sections 77 and 79 of the Copyright, Designs and Patents Act 1988.

Every effort has been made to contact copyright holders. However, the publisher will be glad to rectify in future editions any inadvertent omissions brought to their attention.

Cover artwork by Jonny Hannah
Typeset by Agnes Graves
Printed and bound in Great Britain by Bell & Bain Ltd, Glasgow
The publisher acknowledges the financial support of the Books Council of Wales.

I Nain Dre.

Contents

CROSSING THE THRESHOLD: THE WESTERN COASTS

Freedom to Live:
The Rugged North

'I think it's important to remember history because we can learn from it, and these stories and their morals are just as important as those lessons from history. Knowing these tales and their links to various locations makes visiting these places far more enriching. We don't have to believe in it, but it can teach us something, right?'

Sarah Woodbury

Preface

On the surface, this is a travel book in which I visit places across Wales associated with old legends, folktales and urban myths. In it, I take you from the bustling south-east to the stormy western coasts, then up to the rugged mountains of the north. Along the way, I meet some very interesting people and learn way more about my home country than I ever could have – argh, I sound like I'm introducing my latest 'Great British Road Trip' show.

I don't really know how it happened, but – well, I do know how it happened, actually – it was lockdown and I decided to go for a walk, then I went on another, and another, then I started actively seeking out places I could go that feature in Welsh folktales. I would seek out the tales that have had the most influence on Welsh culture, as well as any that stood out for being particularly bonkers. Then I started writing a blog about my walks and interviewing people whose lives revolve around these tales: writers, historians, museum curators, folklorists, academics and various 'folkies' who dress up like dead horses and go drunkenly galloping round town asking people for money in the name of charity and tradition.

Eventually, I sent out a few emails to some publishers, having not even started writing a book at that point, and by some miracle, after all those years of pitching what I considered to be polished-out masterpieces, Amy Feldman of Calon Books actually got back to me and said 'Okay, let's do it!' So now here I am, writing the preface for my first traditionally published book.

In any case, I really did go on an adventure that had all the makings of a Great British Road Trip. I'm talking about seeing places in my home country that I never knew existed, meeting a whole cast of wonderful, interesting and often eccentric characters, and learning more about my own culture and heritage than I could ever have hoped for. So, you see, although to the untrained eye the opening paragraph of this preface may have sounded like a bit of a cliché, the truth of the matter is, it really did happen that way!

But I did say that this was but a travel book 'on the surface'. What I meant by that is that I did try to dig into the origins and meanings of these tales as well. Often on my adventure, I found myself with more questions than answers: where did this story come from? Who told it first? Who the hell thought it was appropriate for children? In my search for answers, I found myself crawling deeper and deeper down a sort of 'folklore rabbit hole', and just when I thought I had reached the warren, all I found was another junction of winding tunnels. Though I did learn a lot about folktales while I was down there, I now have first-hand experience of why you shouldn't go poking around at the roots of folklore and mythology.

So come, join me as I make my way from the Welsh capital to my sleepy hometown in the hills and find out where you need to go to find the wackiest, the most epic and the most influential Welsh folktales around ...

Russ

Acknowledgements

For helping me put together my first traditionally published book, I would like to thank Abbie Headon, Alun Hughes, Amy Feldman, Angela Brushett, Anne Abel, Danny Hanks, David Moore, Dean Powell, Dr Julie Coggins, Edward Perkins, Ellie Townsend Jones, Gemma Alcock, Gwyn Jones, Helen, Jeff or Geoff, John 'Black Boy' Evans, Lewis Turner, Mari Hanks, Mr Jones Hanes, Peter Stevenson, Rhodri ap Hywel, Sarah Woodbury, Sian Roberts, Mam, Dad, Sophie and Kriss.

Diolch o galon.

YNYS LLANDDWYN
CAERNARFON
DYFFRYN NANTLLE
YR WYDDFA
BEDDGELERT
COED FELENRHYD
DINAS DINLLE
NANT GWRTHEYRN
HARLECH
CANTRE'R GWAELOD
DEVIL'S BRIDGE
N
W
E
S
FISHGUARD
NARBERTH
CASTELL CAREW
ST. GOVAN'S
PENNARD
LLANTRISANT
FERNDALE
CARDIFF
CAERPHILLY
CAERLEON

INTRODUCTION:
'Stori Nain!'

'Ah, stori Nain!' Dad would exclaim whenever he was told an unlikely story. Stories like the one about people camping up on a mountain and coming back either totally bonkers or as talented poets. Or the one about the floating island, of the lost civilisation drowned by the sea or of the bottomless lake leading down to the Welsh Otherworld. Stories of witches and giants and heroic kings, dragons and mad doctors, angry Welsh ladies, ghostly women of every colour of the rainbow, giant beaver monsters, vampire furniture and pirate-fighting monks.

Nain is the word we northerners, or *Gogs* (from the Welsh word *gogledd*, meaning 'north'), use for 'grandmother'. And that's exactly what a lot of these stories are: tall tales passed on by different generations, collective memories that change and evolve to fit the time and political climate of each narrator.

The *Mabinogi*, considered the oldest and the most influential collection of Welsh legends, told around campfires for generations beforehand, were not written down until around 1050–1225, when they appeared in the *White Book of Rhydderch* and the *Red Book of Hergest*. By then, they were full of political propaganda, modernised to suit the reader of the time. Indeed, the mere act of putting them into script in the first place altered them dramatically, for these were oral tales meant to be heard, not read.[1] But ignore that for now – keep reading!

These tales don't have to be great national epics to be passed on by generations – it happens on a local level, as well. I'll give you a personal example of how these things start: my own grandfather, or *taid*, told my cousins and I when we were young that an elephant lived in the garage that contained the local hearse in my home village.

I'm not sure if his aim was to keep us away from the hearse, but his story obviously had the opposite effect. One time, I swore blind that I had seen the elephant's foot after I peered under the doors whilst lying flat on my stomach, my eyes seeing what they wanted to see. We still call that place *cwt eliffant* (elephant hut) to this day, as do my cousins' children, who never even met my grandfather. Alright, fair enough, it's not exactly a folktale, but in terms of how they're passed on and why, that's essentially how it works.

Throughout history, people have used folktales to explain the inexplicable, to warn the next generation of dangerous places and to put them off immoral or selfish pursuits. However, we live in a digital age, where science and technology are the new gods; how much room is there for these tales in today's society? On a national scale, the most treasured of these legends remain big players in the arts, but to find out just how much the Welsh have carried on this oral tradition of storytelling and of how much influence these stories have on Welsh culture, you really need to get out there and talk to the locals themselves.

That's what *Where the Folk* was going to be about; however, I began seeing patterns in some of the tales, similarities with myths from other cultures, certain recurring themes … could there be more to these tales than meets the eye? Could they have less to do with our society as a whole and actually represent something more … personal? I also very quickly realised that there is an absolute abundance of them. I would visit somewhere with one story in mind and would leave having learned of three more – Wales is absolutely brimming with old legends and folktales. I had opened Pandora's Box.

I could never have fitted them all in, so I had to be selective in my approach. As such, I strived to provide this book with not only an equal geographical coverage of Welsh folktales, but I also picked out the ones that I, personally, believe to have had the greatest influence on our land and culture, plus I threw in a few hidden gems for good measure.

So come join me, dear reader, on a twenty-first-century quest of epic proportions … and bring a raincoat, just in case.

Call to Adventure:
The Bustling South-east

I

Where the folk's
the party at?

It was 1 January, and I promised myself that I was going to get out more this year. This year being 2020. I began by climbing over my neighbours' fence to go hang out with them. They had just returned from China, where they work for half the year teaching English. Then I came down with a nasty cold, which set off my crippling health anxiety something awful. Around the same time, a client at work was hospitalised with an undiagnosed chest infection.

As soon as I was better, I tried again. In a bid to allow myself more time to be sociable, I applied for my first ever Monday-to-Friday job. As a Family Mediator, I would 'help prevent youth homelessness in the County of Caerphilly' by helping families resolve their ongoing issues and disputes.[1]

I spent one day in the office, then was told that I was to work from home until further notice. That's as far as I got before suddenly, almost overnight, the whole world went into something called 'lockdown'. This was something big, like one of those things that you will never forget, something that changes everything while at the same time changing absolutely nothing at all. We could all sense it at the time.

I graciously accepted lockdown in those first few weeks, making the most of all my extra spare time stuck at home to get back into my writing, but by now things are getting tense. I feel like one of those SeaWorld orcas, forever circumnavigating my enclosure. I'm beginning to confuse my stories with actual memories, even arguing with my housemate one night after I got frustrated when he didn't remember being with me on one of my fantasy adventures. 'It's alright, Russ. Put the knife down, mate …'

In a bid to stay sane, I have formed an unhealthy relationship with a tiny black kitten named Loki, who takes the phrase 'climbing the walls' far too literally. Don't get me wrong, he's lovely and everything – well, actually, he isn't, he's a little gremlin – but I need more than that. Maybe it's time to take advantage of that five-mile limit we've been allowed by the Welsh Government ... Putting on my shoes, the concrete feeling notably hard beneath my feet, I follow the railway tracks through an eerily silent Cardiff and make my way to the city centre.

Cardiff, which has a population of around 362,400,[2] didn't become the Welsh capital until 20 December 1955, but had existed as a busy, multi-cultural city (one of the first in the UK, with around 100 languages being spoken here) way before that. This was mostly thanks to Tiger (now Cardiff) Bay and its role in the success of the British Empire.[3]

From a tiny trickle on top of a mountain in the Bannau Brycheiniog (Brecon Beacons), the River Taff snakes its way down the south Wales valley, through the city and into the bay, which made it easy for our imperial ancestors to transport coal down from the mines to the docks, where it was transported all around the world. Cardiff was booming.

The British Empire came to an end and for a long time the bay fell into a state of economic decline. Then, thanks to one of the biggest industrial projects in Europe to date, it was revitalised and now boasts numerous bars and restaurants, the Wales Millennium Centre and our national Senedd. But it wasn't just the bay that received a make-over: the Welsh Government pumps a lot of money into Cardiff (as a lot of people living outside of the city will tell you), and it seems that the city is always expanding.

Looking around, I think about how much I love living here. It's obviously much bigger than Caernarfon, where I grew up, but I find in Cardiff that I can disappear into the crowd without the place ever losing that 'small-town feeling'. After living here for a while, you start bumping into people you know, you see the same familiar faces in house parties, you get to know the names of the buskers and the homeless, and if you're eccentric enough, you might even be immortalised by your own Facebook appreciation society.

With the smugness of a capitalist reassured by the jackhammering of urban development, I make my way towards the Millenni– the

Principality Stadium, now transformed into a makeshift hospital for use during the pandemic. It's the focal point of the Welsh capital, I'd say, with many attributing its success to its proximity to the city centre. Any rugby fan will tell you that you'll never find a more conveniently placed stadium. It all seems very quiet in there today, mind.

Turning the corner, I head up my favourite watering hole in Cardiff. Womanby Street was once the site of one of the city's lingering slums. Today, it's full of pubs and nightclubs, none of which are particularly 'mainstream' (aside from Wetherspoons and the back end of Revolution) and mostly cater for those who prefer an 'alternative' night out. If you like modern chart stuff accompanied by loud stag and hen parties, you go to St Mary Street or Mill Lane; if you want live rock, ska and reggae accompanied by hipsters and potheads, you come here.

It's one of the oldest streets in Cardiff, with its name apparently deriving from the Norse word *houndemammeby*, which means 'huntsman' or 'hound keeper's dwelling'. However, there is no evidence to suggest that there were ever any Vikings here at all. Alternatively, and it would make more sense for the name to have directly originated from this, you've got the Teutonic word *womanby*, which translates to 'the abode of the foreigners'.[4]

Ironically, years later, during the Industrial Revolution and thanks to its close proximity to Tiger Bay, it became a busy street full of bars, brothels and slums, occupied by immigrants from all over the British Empire. Abode of the foreigners, indeed. Jones Court, just around the corner, was built by the marquess of Bute in 1830 to house imported labourers for the expansion of Cardiff docks, and is the last remaining example of the fifty-plus housing courts which quickly degenerated into slums that once existed in the Welsh capital.[5]

The Horse and Groom, one of the oldest pubs in Cardiff, was said to be haunted by a poltergeist. In 2013, it became Fuel Rock Club, one of the most popular venues here on Womanby.

At the top end of the street, directly opposite Cardiff Castle's clock tower, lies Clwb Ifor Bach. Standing outside the music venue, which is closed during this lockdown period, I'm taken back to a sixth-form history lesson with Mr Jones: 'I implore you to go to Cardiff, boys! Yes, for the degree, but more than that ...' A tiny glint appeared in his eye as his mind wandered off somewhere and he said, '*Iesu*, the times I've had at Clwb Ifor Bach! You've got to apply, boys, if only to experience Clwb Ifor as a student!'

I had heard about Clwb Ifor Bach before then, but I was never quite sure what it was. It is a place known to many Welsh speakers across Wales, even if they have never been there themselves. I was sold, and now I, too, have very fond memories of student nights at Clwb Ifor, or 'Welsh Club', as most English speakers call it.

Formerly a British Legion club, it was founded by Cymdeithas Clwb Cymraeg Caerdydd, chaired by Owen John Thomas of Plaid Cymru, in 1983 as a place for Welsh speakers to hang out and promote Welsh music and culture.[6] Today, however, it is a club for everyone, not just Welsh speakers.

But as I stand here today, seeing the name 'Ifor Bach' doesn't conjure up images of people snogging, dancing and vomiting into urinals. Instead, I see a desperate man scaling the walls of Cardiff Castle. I see secret tunnels and a roomful of shimmering treasure guarded by living stone eagles. And, no, I haven't taken anything.

You see, everyone knows Welsh Club, but not everyone is familiar with the twelfth-century leader from whom the famous nightclub got its name. Fewer still know about the legend of the treasure hidden in Ifor Bach's tomb, itself lying in a secret tunnel somewhere beneath the city, guarded by two (some say three) stone eagles within which dwell the spirits of Ifor's most loyal bodyguards.

Ifor Bach (Ivor the Short), or rather Ifor ap Meurig, was Lord of Senghenydd in the twelfth century. Senghenydd is an area found within the county borough of Caerphilly, not far from Cardiff. The Normans had already conquered England, as well as most of Wales, but Ifor Bach held tight in Senghenydd.

The Norman lord of the area back in Ifor Bach's time was William Fitz Robert, second Earl of Gloucester. Gloucester had his eyes on Ifor's land, but Ifor was not a man to be crossed. Apparently, he scaled the walls of Cardiff Castle using his bare hands and seized the residing Earl and his family. He then took them all to the woods of Senghenydd, where he refused to let them go until they gave back the land they had taken from him, with compensation.

Mind you, during Ifor Bach's reign, the castle was not the Disneyesque structure we know it to be today. Rather, it was a Norman keep, mounted on a man-made hill that still stands in the centre of the castle grounds today.

It is also said that Ifor Bach built a castle on the site of what is now Castell Coch, found at Tongwynlais, some five miles from Cardiff centre, and that he reputedly hid his treasures in a nearby secret tunnel that leads all the way from there to Cardiff Castle. When he passed away, he was buried somewhere deep within this castle, within a secret chamber.

Worried about being disturbed in the afterlife, legend has it that he turned two (or was it three?) of his men into stone eagles, positioning them near the entrance of his burial chamber so that they could guard him for the rest of time. I have no idea at which point he became a magician, but he did. Apparently, one night, two thieves found the chamber but were scared off by the eagles.[7]

I find the idea that there may be some hidden tombs containing lost treasure somewhere in the outskirts of Cardiff to be thrilling. As such, perhaps overcome with fresh air, I make the decision to head up to Castell Coch and explore nearby Fforest Fawr, imagining scenes reminiscent of *Indiana Jones*.

And so, the next day, I disturb the slumbering Griff. That's my little red Fiesta, by the way, so named because I bought it at Griffin Mill up in Pontypridd and because my female friends insisted that a car should have a name. In any case, Griff coughs and sputters to life, brakes creaking from weeks of neglect, and we head northward, out of the city.

Finding Castell Coch is all too easy. Many people see it on a daily basis on their commute to work, glancing up at it as it watches over Cardiff from the forested hill above the village of Tongwynlais, directly above the A470, which is the main artery into Cardiff from the valleys and, well, anywhere north of the valleys. I turn onto Coryton roundabout before taking the exit to the roadside hotel. From there, I make my way over numerous hefty speed bumps before arriving at Tongwynlais.

It's a typical Welsh village, but it has the advantage of being only a stone's throw away from the capital. There's a pub, a few shops, a football club, a rugby club, a golf course (which used to be the site of the Castell Coch vineyard, but the wine didn't really sell that well; be sure to check out the negative newspaper review they have on display at the castle should you ever go!) and a library. The Taff Trail, which follows the Taff all the way from Cardiff Bay to its origins in the Bannau Brycheiniog, also passes through here.

Going down to first gear, I make the steep climb to the top of the hill to Castell Coch, praying that I don't come across a horde of stumbling ramblers or a stubborn driver along the way. Parking's free by the way – just be sure to pull your handbrake all the way up!

Castell Coch (which translates to 'Red Castle') truly is a wonderful sight. That's because it's a nineteenth-century Gothic Revival castle; a Victorian folly, designed to be pleasing to the eye. Between the trees, I can see the entirety of Cardiff, along with nearby Garth Hill. Some of you may already know Castell Coch by sight from the CBBC show *The Worst Witch*.

Contrary to what some Ifor Bach enthusiasts claim, it is believed that the first castle to ever stand at the site was actually built by the Normans some time after 1081 in order to defend the newly captured town of Cardiff. I looked it up: turns out that the Normans took Cardiff around the same year. It was the sixteenth-century historian Rice Merrick (Rhys Meurug) who claimed that it was built by Ifor Bach, a claim that most historians have since dismissed.

The castle was shortly abandoned, with its motte (the fabricated hill or mound used as the base for a castle) being reused by Gilbert de Clare as the basis for a new stone fort (1267–1277), which was eventually destroyed in a Welsh rebellion in 1314. Then, in 1760, the ruins fell into the hands of John Stuart, third Earl of Bute, as part of a marriage settlement. After that, John Crichton-Stuart, the third Marquess of Bute, inherited the castle in 1848 and turned it into what we see here today.

Sadly, the castle is shut until further notice, what with the pandemic, but it is essentially a Victorian summer frat house complete with ceiling murals, a distinct theme for each room, elaborate sculptures and gender-specific bedrooms. And that's exactly what Castell Coch was in its heyday: a summerhouse for some of the richest Victorians in the world that was rarely used.

It is said to be haunted by the so-called 'White Lady'. The story goes that a woman died of a broken heart here after her son drowned in a nearby pond. Her spirit can often be seen wandering the castle, searching eternally for her lost child. It is even said that Lady Bute, who decided to live in the castle with her daughter following her husband's death, was eventually driven away by the White Lady.[8]

The surrounding woodland of Fforest Fawr, sometimes referred to as the Taff Gorge Complex, are among the most westerly natural beech woodlands in the British Isles.[9] Indeed, there is a somewhat ancient or medieval aura to the place; it is easy to imagine Ifor Bach and his men hiding between the trees, ambushing unsuspecting Normans.

It was nice getting out of the house, and it just goes to show that you don't have to go far or spend much to have a good time. I should do it more often … not what I had in mind when I said I was going to get out more this year, but there you go.

2

Where the folk
can I find
a hungover ghost?

'Maybe you should meet up with Rhod? It would be good to socialise, don't you think?'

'Yeah. Yeah, that sounds like a good idea. I'll get in touch with him. Thanks, Marion.'

Marion's my line manager. Staff well-being is her top priority during the pandemic and she's concerned about the two single men working from home. That'll be me and Rhodri ap Hywel, the only guy I know who has retained the Welsh 'ap' who isn't a politician or a dead prince.

'Ap', or 'ab', means 'son of', by the way. Those who trace their Welsh ancestry far enough will eventually find that their family name disappears altogether, as this was once the widespread traditional naming system here in Wales. Then Henry VIII's Act of Union (1536) sought to anglicise Welsh culture and, from then on, any Welsh surname would have to be used in its anglicised form in any legal documents, and so the tradition fell into decline. In recent years, however, some Welsh people have gone back to using this original naming system.

In any case, I get in touch with Rhod and we make plans to walk up nearby Garth Hill together. I remember reading a rather quirky story from Garth Hill that went something like this …

It was a warm, moonlit night in glorious midsummer, between midnight and one in the morning, to be precise. A man was staggering home over Garth Hill after a night out in Cardiff. As he brushed past the fern, the seeds fell off and got all over his coat and boots. He was plastered so thickly in the stuff that his hair actually glistened in the moonlight as he made his way home that night. Once home, he fumbled at the door with one eye shut for a while, then went inside and found that his mam and sisters had already gone to bed. He curled up to sleep downstairs, next to the fireplace so as not to wake them up.

When he got up in the morning, they acted as though he wasn't there. He thought that they must have been winding him up for getting home so late, so he apologised and said, 'Sorry, my lovelies, I won't be late again!'

At that, his mam and sisters stopped in their tracks and looked around in bewilderment.

'What's wrong? You look like you've seen a ghost!'

That time, they both screamed and legged it clear out of the house. Confused, the man happened to scratch his back as he watched them running off, and that's when, dislodging the fern seeds, he became visible again and it all made sense. For you see, it's a well-known fact, apparently, that fern seeds turn you invisible ...[1]

Now, at this point, it might be worth mentioning that the Garth is a mushroom picking hot-spot, according to local youths. Every year, from September to November, students, local teens and ageing hippies flock to the hill to harvest the psychedelic fungi. Mind you, the story's set in the middle of summer, so it may have been a bit early for that ...

This particular anecdote featured in Marie Trevelyan's book, *Folk-lore and Folk-stories of Wales*, published in 1909. It is said to have derived from a local boy who claimed it to be a story his grandfather once told him, who in turn claimed it involved a friend of his. He must have been one of the boys who were at the pub with the invisible man earlier that night.

At the foot of Garth Hill lie the villages of Gwaelod-y-Garth and Taff's Well. Taff Well Park is most famous for being home to the only thermal spring in Wales. For hundreds of years, people would come from all over Europe to bathe here, but today, the spring is nothing more than a murky puddle with a few bubbles in the middle, fenced off from the public and often littered with crisp packets and cans of lager.

I meet Rhod outside the pub at Gwaelod-y-Garth. 'Alright, Russ?'

If Rhod were more laid back, he would be horizontal. We had only spoken briefly before this, and most of that was work talk. By the time we made the steep climb up past the pub then up the dirt track to the foot of the hill, I had learned that he lives near Caerphilly, plays for a band called Vertigo Flo and loves nothing more than a walk and a pint and talking about 'all the old Welsh princes'. He also identifies as an 'urban explorer', a term I am not familiar with.

He stops and pulls out his phone. 'Here, look – so I go into old buildings and such, take a few photos, leave everything just as I found it. I upload the photos to this website, look – there's a whole bunch of us!'

'Cool! I've always wanted to go into like an old asylum or something. Is it legal?'

He grimaces and puts his phone back in his pocket. 'Some land owners don't like it, but some don't mind. You should ask for permission beforehand. These places are out in the sticks, old farmhouses in the arse end of nowhere, old mills, that sort of thing. Basically, it's between you and the landowner, but you should always ask first.'

'Have you ever been asked to leave by anyone?'

'Oh, yeah! I remember once, a whole group of farmers with dogs and shotguns were waiting for us outside. That was pretty gnarly, I have to say!'

Rhod is a few years older than I am, and I get the feeling that he has lived quite the life. He went on to tell me about the ghosts, banshees and secret tunnels of Caerphilly. 'You'll have to go and have a look for yourself some time!'

'I will.'

Garth Hill, referred to by locals as 'The Garth' or 'Garth Mountain', or Mynydd y Garth in Welsh, sits between the communities of Llantwit Fardre and Pentyrch. It offers great views of Cardiff and some of Rhondda Cynon Taf, and on a clear day, you can even see as far as Weston-super-Mare. At the Garth's summit sit a number of tumuli, being ancient burial sites dating from the early to mid-Bronze Age.[2] On the other side of the valley sits the Garth's sister hill, the Lesser Garth, herself scarred by limestone and iron ore quarries.

Now, there's a reason why Garth Hill is often referred to as a mountain and it involves another grandfather's bold tales. You may also be surprised to know that it is a fairly recent phenomenon. In 1995, Christopher Monger, a native of Ffynon Taff (Taff's Well), released the novel *The Englishman Who Went Up a Hill But Came Down a Mountain*, based on a story his own grandfather had told him. The book is based on the fictionalised village of Ffynnon Garw, which means 'rough well'.

Based in 1917, it tells of the time two English cartographers visited the place to measure what is claimed to be the 'first mountain inside of Wales'. The villagers love their 'mountain' and are disappointed when the cartographers conclude that it is in fact a 'hill'. Unwilling to be told by a pair of pompous Englishmen that their precious mountain is nothing more than a mere hill, the villagers set out to raise the summit by their own means.

Adapted into a film starring Hugh Grant, the story spread across the globe, and people have flocked to view the site ever since. They come to climb Garth 'Mountain' for themselves, but heads up – the mound upon which the trigonometrical point stands in the book and film is in fact that Bronze Age burial ground that I mentioned, so don't be fooled by this *stori nain*! Or *stori taid*, whatever.[3]

'Go sit by there, look.' Rhod takes my phone and gestures for me to sit on a small boulder overlooking the side of the hill. 'This'll be a nice shot, now. There you are, look – stunning picture!' He shows me the photo as I walk back over to him.

'Nice!'

'Pint?'

Heading back to the pub, our hopes are shattered when we are told that the place has shut early due to COVID restrictions (it was open when we passed earlier – no one really knows what's allowed and what isn't these days). So with that, we go our separate ways and head for home.

On the drive back, I wonder what else is sitting right at my doorstep and decide to make a conscious effort to see what's out there. Then, at home, I sit at my laptop to do some writing but soon find myself longing to share my discoveries and ever-growing knowledge of Welsh folklore with others.

Staring blankly at an empty Word document, I sit back in my chair and decide to write a blog chronicling my trips instead. I could take photos – that one Rhod took was nice – and I could include links to Google Maps, that kind of thing. Gives me something to do until things get going again, at least. But it needs a catchy title …

I look at the stack of books on Welsh history and mythology sitting on my desk. I've been reading up a lot about them since lockdown. It is strange where research for a work of fiction takes you; my cupboards are chock-full of notebooks filled to the brim with notes on the most random assortment of subjects you can imagine. One of the books catches my eye: *Welsh Folk Tales* by Peter Stevenson.

Welsh. Folk. Tales. Welsh locations. Where. Where Folk Tales … Where Folk … Where. Where? Where the … Where the Folk? Where the Folk! Yes!

3

Where the folk
can I hear the scream
of a banshee?

Lockdown restrictions are gradually easing up and I am now allowed to work from the Caerphilly office a couple of days a week, should I want to. Unfortunately, my new work bestie was allocated different days to me and no one else seems to have taken on the offer, so I often find myself sitting alone in an empty building. On my lunch breaks, I make the most of being out of the house and head to the town centre for a Greggs in front of the castle.

Caerffili, as it is known in Welsh, lies just seven miles north of Cardiff, but the difference in accents is unmistakeable. Should you head over Caerphilly Mountain from Cardiff and see the magnificent view before you as you descend on the other side, you really will get a sense that you have crossed some kind of threshold. You're in the valleys now. Or are you? I never can tell with the valleys – it seems that each person has their own idea of what constitutes being 'in the valleys' and where the boundaries lie.

Caerphilly is known for its cheese, really, which the town celebrates every year with a festival called the Big Cheese. There are food stalls, live music, plenty to drink and even a 'cheese race' in which people run around the castle with a block of cheese.

It has been suggested that Saint Ffili, Cenydd's second son, built a fort here and that is where the town gets its name: *Caer Ffili*, meaning 'Ffili's Fort'. Others, however, argue that the town was named after Philip de Braose, an Anglo-Norman Marcher lord.[1]

Behind me, on the square opposite the castle, stands a statue of

Tommy Cooper. He was born here, you see, then moved away when he was three, but he always considered himself to be a Welshman. On our walk, Rhod told me a rumour that there are some hidden tunnels beneath that statue that run under the town square, and said he would love to explore them one day. I'm telling you, since meeting Rhod, I find myself observing my surroundings with keener eyes. I can't help but be on the lookout for hidden clues from the past or quirky place-names and such. For example, the other day, while driving the back-roads of Caerphilly, I came across Heol y Bwnsi.

It's an unassuming country lane, really, found just over the border at Nantgarw. But the 'road of the banshee' surely has an interesting story behind it? I asked Rhod, who told me that it was actually his mate who re-discovered this place-name from an old map not that long ago. He showed his findings to the council and they agreed to revive the name.

Still, what's this about a banshee? Rhod told me that he had heard stories about the lane when he was growing up: 'That road, well, the whole of Mynydd Meio, really, is said to be haunted by a female spirit called "Shinny". She's said to appear either as a crippled old woman asking for help or as a seductive "femme fatale" type of thing. You should be alright as long as you ignore her and keep on walking, but stop and engage with her and she'll chop off your head. They say she used to wash decapitated heads in a nearby stream.'

I was intrigued, and had googled the ghosts and banshees of Caerphilly later that day. What I found was that Shinny was just the tip of the iceberg. I mentioned earlier that nearby Taff's Well has a natural hot spring. What I didn't know at the time was the story of the Grey Lady, who apparently dwells in said spring. The story goes that, in life, she would frequent the public baths, always turning up dressed all in grey. She was such a character, or weirdo, in other words, that people would talk about her for many years after she died. Then, one day, a local man went down to fill up a pitcher at the spring and the Grey Lady's ghostly hand came up from the depths and grabbed him by the wrist.

'Hold my hands!' she pleaded with him.

The man, understandably bricking it, did as she asked. He tried pulling her out, but to no avail. He asked her several questions during all this, but she just stared blankly back at him the whole time, saying nothing. Eventually, her fingers slipped from his grasp and she disappeared back under the water, wailing as she went: 'Alas, I shall remain in bondage another hundred years! And then, I must find a woman with steady hands that are stronger than yours, so as to hold me!'

I'm not sure of the origin date of this tale, but I'm sure a hundred years have come and gone by now, so please, if there are any sturdy-handed women out there … I dare you![2]

I also learned that, sometimes, you don't need to take to the back-roads to find myths, legends and tales of wailing dead women, for two of Caerphilly's most famous hags can be found right at the town's main focal point and tourist attraction: the castle, in front of which I'm currently sat, eating my sausage roll.

When the Normans arrived in the late eleventh century, Senghenydd stood its ground under Gruffydd ap Rhys, grandson of our old friend, Ifor Bach. Gruff was the last Welsh lord of Senghenydd and the place fell to Gilbert de Clare (aka the 'Red Earl') in 1266. Gilbert didn't exactly have it easy once he took control, mind.

In 1268, Llywelyn ap Gruffydd took over the northern territories of Senghenydd, which made Gilbert nervous. As such, having already established a fort at the site of Castell Coch the previous year, he began construction on Caerphilly Castle. But Llywelyn's forces attacked the site in 1270. Work on the castle resumed in 1271 under the rule of Gilbert's son, also called Gilbert de Clare. The finished article featured a ring of concrete walls, a first for British castles. At thirty acres, it is also the largest castle in Wales and the second largest in the UK, with Windsor Castle taking the prize.[3]

And so, from the White Lady of Castell Coch, we go now to the Green Lady of Caerphilly Castle. Gilbert's interests included war, power and control. His French wife, Alice de la Marche, niece of Henry II, on the other hand, was the total opposite. She was a liberal who enjoyed late nights and was by all accounts pretty woke. Needless to say, their marriage was strained.

Then one day, Gruffudd the Fair, Prince of Brithdir, came to stay. Alice was infatuated, and Prince Charming felt the same way about her, so the two had an affair. However, Gruff was a fair man in more ways than one and he just couldn't live with the guilt of it all. He confessed his sins to a local monk, who was fiercely loyal to the tyrannical de Clare and immediately grassed him up. Gilbert was livid and ordered Alice to be shipped back to France and for Gruff to be brought in. Nice guys finish last, I suppose.

But someone also tipped Gruff off, and instead of getting the hell outta Dodge, he instead went off on a murderous rampage, tracking down the monk who grassed him up and hanging him from a tree. Not long after, Gilbert's men caught up with him and he suffered the same fate. Over in France, news reached Alice of Gruff's death and, in classic folktale fashion, she died of a broken heart.

Even though she died in France, it is said that her spirit came back to haunt the ramparts of Caerphilly Castle. Some say that she's stuck there in purgatory for her sins, others that she is looking for her lover boy, others that she is still in shock. Whatever the reason, she's here, apparently, and people have reported seeing her for many years now. Perhaps the eeriest accounts describe how she has the ability to turn herself into ivy, and that if you spot her and she takes a liking to you, then she'll reach out to shake your hand before vanishing into thin air.[4]

Alice tends to keep to herself for the most part and doesn't go around scaring the pants off people by screaming like a banshee. One old hag who does exactly that, however, is the castle's other resident ghoul: Gwrach-y-Rhibyn.

There's an old Welsh saying that goes '*Y mae mor salw â Gwrach-y-Rhibyn*', which means 'She's as ugly as the Rhibyn Witch'. Although she often turns invisible when traversing the land, those who have seen her have hardly been subtle in their descriptions: 'wild, unkempt hair' … 'long, gangly arms and legs' … 'leathery, bat-like wings' … 'a hideous, ugly old woman with black teeth and pale skin'. Between this and the incessant wailing (she is sometimes heard calling out for her own loved ones, but she mostly makes an appearance to warn people of the death of a loved one, or of their own impending doom), you certainly wouldn't miss her if you did come across her.[5]

The old hag is known throughout Wales, in some shape or form, though I'm not sure if she is supposed to be just one supernatural being or if her name is more of a collective term for an entire class of monster. She is said to be a harbinger of doom, much like the Irish banshee, and is often seen hanging around people's windows at night, calling out the names of those who are about to die. She often calls out to people when the mist rises in the morning, hence her other name, 'Hag of the Mist'.

Some claim that she has one long, hollow tooth that she uses to drain the blood of children and slumbering babies. Mind you, others say that she has a soft spot for the young 'uns, perhaps due to the fact that she is sometimes heard mourning for her own child. In her defence, they argue that she has never actually killed a child, but does enjoy scaring the crap out of them and will drink some of their blood, but not all of it. They'll just be left feeling a bit under the weather, is all. Indeed, in days of old, if a baby got sick, people would often blame it on her.

The story of how she ended up at Caerphilly Castle comes from the 1700s, around the time people from all over Wales started coming here for the market. Apparently, she used to live in a nearby swamp, but a heavy flood forced her to flee into the town itself, where she scared the living daylights out of everyone by flying around, screaming like a banshee. Some of the local men tried to catch her, but she legged it into the castle and hasn't come out since.[6]

So what exactly is Gwrach-y-Rhibyn? Well, most scholars and folklorists tend to associate her with the *cyhyraeth*, Wales's answer to the banshee. The name derives from the word *cyhyr*, which means 'muscle' or 'flesh', but they are usually depicted as disembodied voices that call out and moan just before someone dies. They would always call out a total of three times, growing fainter each time. Apparently, they can even call out to Welsh people on the other side of the planet. In Glamorgan, they would often be heard just before a shipwreck would take place. They are also associated with floating corpse lights, which in turn are linked to Saint David, the patron saint of Wales, but we'll find out more about those later. Argh, maybe this is one of those 'chicken-or-the-egg' kind of things ...[7]

'Ruuusseeeell ...'

I freeze, sausage roll halfway into my mouth.

'Ruuuuuseeeeell ...' It's a woman's voice, distant and faint. 'Where aaare yooou?'

'Hello?' The hairs on the back of my neck stand up.

'Russseeell ... are you coming to this meeting or not?'

The penny drops. Reaching into my pocket, I take out my phone and realise that Marion's phoned me. Must have pressed against the screen and answered it without realising.

'Bloody hell, Marion, you scared me then!'

'What?'

'Never mind ... I'm on my way.'

4

Where the folk
can I travel back in time to catch witches, fairies and ghosts?

The invitation reads: 'To my beloved brother-in-law, greetings. Sir, I beseech you to welcome and protect the bearer of this letter, who I commend to you as known unto myself. Praye let your bondsmen and servants give this bearer all accord and shelter in your house as you would give yourself. I rest yours to be commanded. Your most humble servant and friend, Bussy Mansell.' It is dated the year of our Lord, 1645.[1]

I pocket the piece of paper and make my way through the gardens until I find myself standing before the great manor house itself. A path leads up through a flawless lawn and into a tunnelled porch, where a young man in tights stands ready to greet me.

'Good afternoon, my Lord. May I see thy invitation?'

'What? Oh, yeah ... here you are.'

I hand him my ticket – I mean, invitation – and he reads the back of it, which has the same text in Welsh, and then hands it back to me with a courteous bow. 'Thank you, my Lord. Please, step inside. One must be gut-foundered after such a long journey, pray truth! Where have thou come from today, my Lord?'

'Only Cardiff ... about half an hour or so.'

'Half hour? Thou must not have used a horse then, my Lord, oh no! Please, step inside, but do cleanse one's hands on the way in ...'

He points to the hand sanitiser outside the door. 'Oh yeah, sure ...'

I'm at Llancaiach Fawr Manor in Nant Caiach, just across the Caerphilly border in Merthyr Tydfil county borough. I have driven past the place a couple of times whilst out on home visits, but had no idea what to expect. Truth be told, although it might be handy for the blog, I'm here because I won a free ticket after taking part in a survey a while back. It was an online Zoom thing with a local politician and some people from the council. Only me and one elderly woman turned up for it. She won first prize.

So far, Llancaiach Fawr has proven to be a rather interesting place, if you're into the occult and the paranormal like I am, I mean. Turns out, people have been living in the area for thousands of years and the house is built on top of one of those earlier settlements. Off to a good start!

It was built for the Prichards, a well-to-do family who descended from none other than Ifor Bach. The Prichards lived through dangerous times, including a civil war. As such, the house is surrounded by strong walls which are over a metre thick. However, they also liked to entertain, as well as flaunt their wealth, so the inside was built to impress.

Like so many grand manor houses, however, Llancaiach Fawr fell into disrepair when it became a financial strain. Eventually, the last of the Prichards married into other affluent families and sodded off. For years it functioned as a farmhouse, complete with an orchard out back. Then the former Rhymney Valley District Council bought it in 1979 and refurbished it throughout the 1980s, opening it as a 'living museum' in the 1990s.[2]

Hence why the staff are all talking to me as though I have just got off the back of a horse. They remain in character throughout – it's hilarious! Normally they would run day tours, as well as ghostly night tours, but alas, although restrictions have eased off a bit, things are hardly back to normal just yet. Before the pandemic, you could get married here. They also held various functions and events, including ones on local folklore.

Llancaiach Fawr has been the site of numerous paranormal events over the years. Apparently, there's a ghost here who enjoys cooking up a Sunday roast. You can even go on tours where they use electromagnetic field meters, field effect sensors, electromagnetic pumps, direction and proximity sensors and all manner of ghost-busting equipment.[3]

Now, recently, with the blog, I felt that it could do with a bit more heart. As such, I've decided to reach out to members of the public. I posted on several social media platforms asking people for their own stories and one of the saner ones to reply was Ellie Townsend Jones of Llantrisant, who told me of an eerie encounter she had when she went on one of Llancaiach Fawr's ghost tours.

'There came a time when my son reached the age when he was old enough not to get too scared, think he was about ten or so, so we decided to go as a family; my ex-husband, my son and myself. Now, I don't go on these things as a believer, but I am curious and I find the whole subject matter to be very interesting.'

I can tell – Ellie's eyes light up as she begins narrating her tale. But there's something she needs to clear up first: 'I know others who have had similar experiences. Now, one interesting thing to note is that we associate ghostly encounters with what we've seen in horror films. In those, they are always there to scare us, to freak us out, to harm us, even. But I think you'll find that the majority of people will tell you that it's a rather benevolent experience.'

Her tone softens as she says this, as though to put me at ease, or to express sympathy for the vilified dead. 'So, anyway, you are taken around the building by a person who tells you all these stories as you make your way through the rooms. There must have been about thirteen or fourteen of us in our group. Now, I'm the type of person who likes to stand in the front, as you can imagine, but for some reason on this occasion, we stood at the back.'

'Right.' I love that about ghost stories; every detail is crucial, so that you've got everything covered for the inevitable interrogation at the end.

'Now, you call me "Ellie", but I was born at a time when people had very traditional Christian names and I was actually christened "Eileen". As this man was telling us about the room, I hear a voice whisper in my ear: *"Eileeeeeeen!"*'

Here come the goosebumps. You know, I always try to put my cynical hat on whenever I listen to a ghost story, but will always get sucked in and end up glancing over my shoulder. 'Eek!'

'And this voice came from the opposite side of where my husband

and son were standing. Then I felt someone tugging at the bottom of my coat. I turned to tell Robin off, but he was standing there with my husband, listening to the tour guide, who went on to tell us about the ghostly presence in the previous room ... the ghost of a child who would often interfere with people's clothing.'

'No! Did you tell them about your experience?'

'Afterwards, yes. Before the tour was done, I asked the tour guide if I could ask the group a question, and he agreed, so I checked if anyone else there was called Eileen. There wasn't. The guide then went on to tell us that they often lock up in pairs at the end of the night just in case someone is too nervous.' Mind you, this is a common safety procedure in many places, in case one of them has a heart attack or if there's an intruder, that sort of thing.

Heading upstairs, I walk through what looks like a courtroom of sorts and into a big room with a huge fireplace. Suddenly, a wooden panel in the wall slides open and out comes the same guy who greeted me on the way in, only this time he's wearing a different hat. 'Oh! My Lord, how can I help you? Did one of the servants let you in?'

I sigh inwardly and ask him, 'Yhm ... yeah, so ... so I'm writing about Welsh folklore. I saw in the museum on the way in that ...'

'You mean the coach house?'

'Yes, sorry ... the coach house. I saw that you've seen your fair share of spooky goings-on here?'

'Pray truth, you tell no lies. Here, behold these markings above the fireplace – they are to ward off evil spirits and *Tylwyth Teg* who come for our children, my Lord.'

Squinting, I can just about make out tiny carvings of a pentacle, that satanic star you see in horror films. I know that the *Tylwyth Teg* are fairies of sorts, but I don't know much about them. Turns out, the occupants of the house would carve these at various places to stop them and other evil spirits from entering.

Red was also thought to ward off spirits and many fireplaces were painted this colour. Offerings have also been found tucked away beneath floorboards: children's shoes stuffed with herbs, mummified bats and so on. That little courtroom that I walked through was not only used to settle local legal disputes, but also for holding witch trials.

Witch trials were mostly popular between the fifteenth and eighteenth centuries, with practising witchcraft being made a capital offence in 1542. Before then, most people who engaged in any magical, superstitious or healing arts were generally held in high regard by ordinary folk. People would turn to them for help with various ailments or to predict their future and would refer to them as 'healers' and 'helpers'.[4]

Then the Tudors changed the face of religion in Britain and attitudes towards them changed. All of a sudden, their practices were seen as satanic in origin, and they themselves were seen as a threat. Paranoia swept throughout the Christian world and thousands were executed, but to be fair, the hysteria didn't hit Wales quite as badly as the rest of Europe. To be honest, Wales held relatively few witch trials, really. There were only thirty-seven persecutions in total, and even then, only five of those were executed, three of whom were a trio of siblings from my hometown of Caernarfon, who, in 1622, were blamed when a local girl had a stroke. By comparison, around 500 people were executed in England during this time.[5]

That being said, there is an abundance of stories about witches here in Wales. You've got Dolly Llewelyn, the Queen of the Pembrokeshire witches; Old Moll, the Romani witch of Llanrug who left out poisoned apples for children; the Old Hag of the Black Mountain; and Poor Hannah, who according to legend was burned alive in a cave on the Great Orme in Llandudno. There's the Llanddona Witches, Dark Anna and the aforementioned Gwrach-y-Rhibyn ... the list goes on.[6]

Indeed, although witch-hunts were never big here, witches themselves did have a major part to play in Welsh folklore and people most certainly did partake in what some would refer to as 'witchcraft'. Many of the tales often involve a cave or sacred site and some cannibalistic old hag of some sorts ... stories to keep children away from places they shouldn't be playing, perhaps.

Visiting Llancaiach Fawr gave me a glimpse into just how important folklore was to the people of Wales. It affected how they viewed the world and how they lived out their daily lives, and people are still drawn to this fantastical world today.

I'm interested to learn more about the influence that *Tylwyth Teg*, in particular, have had on Welsh folktales over the years. Until today, I had no idea that people actually left them offerings and took measures to keep them out of their homes. For this, with lockdown restrictions slowly lifting, I'm going to need to head to the beach …

5

Where the folk
can I find a genuine fairy-tale castle?

Once upon a time, in a small castle by the sea, there lived a cruel warlord. One day, in the midst of a bloody war, a messenger arrived with a proposition from a neighbouring prince. The prince was willing to give the warlord anything he wanted if he were to win a battle for him.

When all was done and dusted, much to the prince's horror, the warlord chose his beautiful daughter's hand in marriage to be his reward. The prince had no choice; he stuck to his word. Reluctantly, the princess agreed to marry him and a great feast was held. On the night of the celebration, as the party reached its peak, the guards heard music playing from outside the castle walls.

Upon closer inspection, they saw a band of fairies, clapping and dancing to their music and waving flaming torches. To their further surprise, the fairies asked if they could join the party. I'm not sure how I would have reacted, but the evil warlord, blind drunk, told his guards to tell them to get lost. Big mistake. Using magic, the fairies conjured up a terrible sandstorm that buried the castle and everyone within, leaving behind nothing but dunes and ruins.

As always, there are a few different versions of this tale floating about. Some say that the wedding guests all managed to escape, that the prince was actually the king of the northern kingdom of Gwynedd, others that the fairies arrived just as the evil warlord was about to rape his new bride, or that the fairies had secretly been friends with the princess all along, but the basic narrative remains the same.

Built in the twelfth century during the Norman invasion of Wales, the exact date that the castle was abandoned is unknown, but it would have been some time in the fourteenth century according to reports concerning the state the structure was in by then. Some believe that a huge storm might have passed through the area, but the general consensus is that the site was gradually enveloped by sand dunes over time. So where can you find this genuine fairy-tale castle, then? Try Pennard, on the Gower Peninsula.[1]

Pennard, formerly Llanarthbodu, is a small village with a population of around 2,000 residents.[2] A mere seven miles from Swansea city centre, it takes me about an hour and a quarter to get there from Cardiff; just a straight run down the M4 then through Swansea city centre. From there, I pass through the Mumbles and onto the peninsula itself. 'You have arrived at your destination.'

Pennard Golf Club, otherwise known as the 'links in the sky', is an eighteen-hole course known for its magnificent views of Three Cliffs Bay and Pennard Sand Dunes. Parking up in one of the bays, I get out and walk over to a pair of chatting women and their bored children. They look posh, but approachable. I ask them where the best place to park would be if I were coming to see the castle, which is located on land owned by the golf club. Glancing at all the other cars, I spot Mercs, BMWs, and Jags ... looking at Griff, I suddenly feel like Del Boy turning up for clay pigeon shooting.

'You can't park there!'

'I gathered that, that's why I'm asking!'

They tell me about a National Trust car park down the road. It grants access to the Wales Coast Path, which follows the entirety of the Welsh coastline. They add that I could also cut across the golf course, but I opt for the coastal path.

'Are you meeting anyone there, or ...?'

'No, no ... just me.' Looking for fairies. On my own.

From the car park, I join the coastal path and head towards Three Cliffs Bay, drooling over the smell of someone's barbeque as I go. I think it's coming from the retirement home that sits right next to the cliffs. Admiring the view, I think to myself how nice it would be to retire here. Then I spot the eroding cliffs and quickly change my mind. Probably a bit out of my price range, in any case.

'Yhm … sorry, excuse me … I feel a bit daft, but … I came here to see a castle. Know where that may be?'

'Castle? Why, no …'

'Excuse me, you seen a castle around here?'

'Why no, no I haven't …'

I begin to doubt whether I have come to the right place. The only route I can see is a steep path heading down to the beach. Then I spot it. Fair play, from here, it doesn't look like much of a castle, more like a pile of rubble. I must endure a steep climb up the dunes to reach it, dragging my feet through the sand and getting lost twice in the maze of different trails along the way.

Eventually, I emerge on a field covered in golf balls. Then it dawns on me. Looking up, I see that I am standing directly on the driving range, just a few feet away from the hole itself. 'Shi–!' ducking my head, wishing I had a helmet, I run to the other side.

Once at a safe distance, I look up and spot my fairy-tale castle, peering over the dunes. It sits right on the edge of the cliff, overlooking the mouth of the Pennard Pill stream and Three Cliffs Bay. It was built in the early twelfth century after Henry de Beaumont, the Earl of Warwick, conquered the Gower Peninsula. It was a timber 'ringwork' castle, which was the earliest form of Norman castle in Britain.

The Braose family then rebuilt the walls in the thirteenth and fourteenth centuries. During this time, they also introduced a stone gatehouse and built the nearby church of St Mary's. However, invading sand dunes caused the site to be hazardous and difficult to get to, and the place eventually fell into ruin. A survey from 1650 describes the site as being 'desolate and ruinous and surrounded by sand', and by 1741, most of the south wall had collapsed.

From then on, it became nothing more than a muse for budding Victorian artists. No doubt, tales of fairies would have arisen from this time, seeing as Welsh romanticism was catching the imagination of rich English tourists, hook, line and sinker, and it would have been foolish not to make full use of a ruined castle that was seemingly abandoned for no reason. Indeed, there is no record of any battles ever being fought here. The place was somewhat 'restored' during the course of the twentieth century and the site is now protected under

UK law as a Grade II listed building.[3]

So what about these 'fairies', then? *Tylwyth Teg* play a big role in Welsh folklore and we are guaranteed to come across them again. *Stori Dylwyth Teg* is Welsh for 'fairy tale'. Growing up, the term *Tylwyth Teg* was very familiar to me, but I knew nothing of fairy lore, really. They appear in many stories, with different variations of them found all over Wales. As well as this, a number of other Welsh ghosts and ghouls can trace their origins to them.

Here on the Gower Peninsula they are called Verry Volk, from the English term 'fairy folk', referring to fairies in general. I would not go calling one a 'fairy' to its face, mind, for Welsh fairies are nothing like the delightful, winged godmothers that we are all familiar with – they're hard as nails!

The origin of the term *Tylwyth Teg* can be traced back to a fourteenth-century poem by Dafydd ap Gwilym. Most Welsh people describe them as beautiful, fair-haired beings who kidnap human children in the middle of the night, replacing them with 'changelings' known as *Plant Newid* ('changed children').[4]

Parents would claim that their children were developing fine one minute then suddenly became mute and start displaying some pretty odd behaviour the next. Interestingly, some scholars believe that *Plant Newid* were, in reality, autistic children, with many tales of *Plant Newid* placing them as being of the age in which autistic traits become apparent. Mind you, this is all just a theory.

Tylwyth Teg were said to live underground in Annwn (or 'Annwfn' – the spelling differs across sources), the Welsh 'Otherworld'. There, they danced and made fairy rings all day in a tropical paradise. Others argue that they are not ruled by Arawn, the king of Annwn (nor Gwyn ap Nudd, who was later associated with the Welsh Otherworld) at all, but rather by Queen Mab, a fairy goddess mentioned in the work of Shakespeare.

It was said that Annwn could only be accessed via magical rifts, portals or through the various lakes dotted around Wales. This is why so many folktales are centred around bodies of water. Stories of beautiful women emerging from lakes accompanied by magical creatures are plentiful here, and even the well-known Welsh goddess Rhiannon, on whom Fleetwood Mac based their hit song, shares similarities with these Lake Women.

Some tales claim that iron is the *Tylwyth Teg*'s kryptonite, or the female of their kind, at least. In tales referring to them as *Bendith y Mamau* ('Blessing of the Mothers'), they ride flying horses and go out on 'fairy raids', flying through the night sky like some sort of Evil Santa. It was customary to leave out a bowl of milk for them so they would leave you alone, for, unlike Santa, a visit from a fairy raid was certainly not desirable.[5]

However, there must be some bigger supernatural forces at play here at Pennard Castle, for fairies are just the tip of the iceberg. A tale that concerns the origins of the castle, as opposed to its ultimate abandonment, tells of a wizard who built it overnight all by himself to protect him from invading Normans. For good measure, he also conjured up everyone's favourite old hag, Gwrach-y-Rhibyn. This is reminiscent of the story of Ifor Bach's apparent ownership of Castell Coch, whereby the Welsh lay claim to a Norman keep.

There is also the story of the maiden who who died by suicide jumping off nearby Penrice Hill (similar to the White Lady of Castell Coch), landing in the lake below. She apparently did so after avenging the murder of her lover. It is said that anyone who encounters her will go mad.[6]

Ghosts, fairies, witches and warlocks: Pennard Castle has it all. Not that I actually saw any of those things while I was there, mind. Would anyone care to spend the night here to find out if there is any truth to these tales? In fact, don't do that, I don't think the members of the 'links in the sky' would be too happy. But it's probably as close as you'll ever get to an actual fairy-tale castle.

I came here to learn more about the *Tylwyth Teg*. However, as I leave the sunny Gower and head for home, I find myself with more questions than answers. I wonder why there are so many different types, why are they so closely linked with other Welsh ghouls, and how many other natural phenomena they were blamed for over the years. And the modern-day image of fairies is so positive; they couldn't all have been that bad, surely?

Unsatisfied, I decide to learn more about one of the most popular and nationally recognised versions of *Tylwyth Teg* … for that, I need to head inland, into the valleys.

6

Where the folk
is the propa'
Lady of the Lake, 'en?

The details of the following tale are hazy. Truth be told, I'm not even sure if I've come to the right place to tell it. Llyn-y-Forwyn, or the 'Maiden's Lake', in Ferndale, is said to be the home of the ghostly enchantress Nelferch, who, at one point, married a local man. The story of their encounter varies depending on who you ask, ranging from a happy-ever-after to one of murder and evil spirits.

To add further confusion, Llyn y Fan Fach, located some forty-six miles away in the Black Mountains, also claims to be the haunting ground of a so-called 'lady of the lake' who married a local boy. As do Llyn Barfog, Llyn Eiddwen, Llyn Syfaddan, Llyn y Morwynion, Melin Wern Millpond, Llyn Du'r Arddu, Llyn Dwythwch, Llyn Cororion, Llyn Coch, the Pool of Avarice, the Taff Whirlpool … the list goes on.

Many of these 'Lake Maidens' are accompanied by herds of cattle, with one story attributing them to the origins of the Welsh Black. Like the *Tylwyth Teg*, they are also associated with Annwn (I'm sticking to that spelling from now on). In fact, some people refer to them as *Gwragedd Annwn*, which means 'the wives of Annwn' and actually consider them to be *Tylwyth Teg*, of sorts. As mentioned before, lakes (or bodies of water in general) are regarded as tears between our world and the supernatural Otherworld here in Wales, and a lot of folktales are centred around them.

But we can't go to all those lakes, so let's stick to Ferndale for now. Ferndale (or Glynrhedynog in Welsh) is located deep in the Rhondda Valley, in the county borough of Rhondda Cynon Taf. North of the town lies the end of the line for the bus service from Cardiff. To get here, I drove up the A470 through Pontypridd, birthplace of Tom Jones and the Welsh national anthem. Turning off the A470, I headed into the Rhondda Valley through Porth, then took the turning to Tylorstown.

The Rhondda Valley paints a picture of a Wales that everyone in the world is familiar with: narrow streets of densely packed terraced houses, an abundance of churches and chapels, social clubs and community halls. There are rugby pitches, floodlights, ironworks and old mines, the ghostly remnants of the Industrial Revolution, and as a backdrop to all this, you've got miles and miles of rolling green hills. Unlike Caerphilly, there's no debate that we're in the valleys now (or *cymoedd*, in Welsh).

The valleys accent is renowned across Wales and the world; ask someone to do an impression of a Welsh person and they'll more than likely do the valleys accent. Either that or they'll do an Indian accent, for some reason. I lived in a nearby village back when I was going out with a girl from Ferndale, and the place certainly left a mark on my dialect following my relatively short time there. Phrases like *cwtsh* ('cuddle'), 'I'll do it now in a minute', 'by 'ere', 'by there' and 'is it?' are all part of my vocabulary now, and my mongrel accent certainly confuses a lot of people.

There is a strong sense of community in the valleys; family is very important to the people here and most would never just uproot and leave, despite years of economic strife following Thatcher's reign of terror. Indeed, there remains a strong sense of abandonment by both the Senedd and Westminster. Go for a pint in one of the social clubs and it won't be long before someone says something along the lines of 'None of the money makes it past Cardiff, mun!' and it is very clear that people's concept of time is divided into two eras: before and after the mine closures.

High up in the hills above Ferndale sits the tiny hamlet of Llanwonno (Welsh: Llanwynno), which mainly consists of St Gwynno's Church and an old pub, the Brynffynon Hotel. But the place is mostly recognised for being the final resting place of legendary athlete and cross-country runner Griffith Morgan (1700–1737), otherwise known as Guto Nyth Brân (English: Guto Crow's Nest), from the name of his parents' farm near Porth.[1]

The tales of Guto's running abilities are legendary; there is one about him chasing down a hare as a young boy (not to mention various horses, foxes and even birds). Some claim that he ran to Pontypridd and back, a distance of around seven miles, by the time his mother's kettle had boiled. Others boasted that he could blow out a candle and be in bed before the light went out. *'Argh, stori nain!'*

Guto was trained and managed by local shopkeeper Sian o'r Siop (English: Sian from the Shop), the pair splitting the prize money they won in competitions. They eventually fell in love and Guto retired from running. However, when a rival runner known as the 'Prince of Bedwas' came on the scene, Sian convinced Guto to come out of retirement to beat the newcomer in a race (which had a prize equivalent to £180,000 in today's money, astonishingly). Guto covered the twelve miles from Newport to Bedwas Church in just fifty-three minutes, but it was too much for his body to handle; he collapsed and died in his lover's arms that day and was buried at Llanwonno Church.

He is celebrated in the nearby town of Mountain Ash on New Year's Eve in an event known as the Nos Galan Road Races, in which runners from all over the world race through the local streets. The race finishes near the bronze statue of him found on Guto Square.[2]

But I digress – I'm here for the Lady of the Lake. Peter Stevenson's *Welsh Folk Tales* (2017) offers a straightforward narrative: a local farmer falls in love with a young woman who lived beneath the lake, where she tended to her herd of milk-white cattle. The locals would often hear her singing to her cows in the morning. The pair married and lived happily ever after at Rhondda Fechan Farm.[3]

However, several websites tell a much a bolder tale, such as this one: one day, a local farmer took his pony down to the lake for a drink. That's when the beautiful-but-mysterious Lady of the Lake appeared. She told the bewildered young man that her name was Nelferch and that she lived beneath the lake's surface with her family and her herd of white cattle. The farmer immediately fell head-over-heels for her and, using his trusty Welsh singing voice, won her affection by serenading her one night.

But she had one condition if they were to marry: that if they should argue three times, she would return to the lake with her cattle, never to be seen again. Other versions state that the condition was that she would leave should he hit her a total of three times. Desperate to marry her, the farmer agreed to her condition.

They lived happily for a while, then one day, Nelferch let the fire go out in their home, and the man raised his voice, or struck her, depending on who is telling the tale. She reminded him of his promise and he apologised; then, a few months later, she spilled a milk churn, and an argument ensued. Sternly, she warned him that he only had one more chance left. Another year passed by, then one night, a fox slaughtered some of their lambs and the farmer blamed his wife for not locking the young animals away.

This time, before he had time to apologise, she vanished before his very eyes, along with her mysterious white cattle. From that day on, the farmer would return to the lake in search of his wife, spending the rest of his days pining for her love, eventually going insane with grief.

A rather different version altogether claims that the maid of Llyn-y-Forwyn was the unfortunate victim of a deadly love triangle. She was due to marry and on the eve of her wedding, her groom-to-be pushed her into the lake. He told everyone that she ran away, then he married the other woman instead. It is said that her spirit still haunts the lake to this day, with numerous people claiming to have heard terrifying shrieks and wails over the years, with some even going as far as saying that they have seen a half-naked girl emerging from the water, wet hair hanging lankly over her face like the little girl from *The Ring*.[4]

There is even an account of a young local boy drowning in the lake at the start of the twentieth century when attempting to rescue his mate, who had fallen in. His family was convinced that it was Nelferch whom had taken him for her own, impressed by his act of bravery. Some even reckon that you can hear the voices of their singing children beneath the surface, if you listen carefully.[5]

Parking up, I make my way through Darran Park towards the lake, passing a sculpture of a dragon along the way. Llyn-y-Forwyn lies right at the back of the park, near the edge of the woods. At present, there is no plaque offering an account of the attributed tale, but there is a wooden sculpture of Nelferch. Sadly, she's been left charred following an act of arson. Standing by her side, I turn to observe the lake and soak in the silence.

Other lakes hold claim to the sequence of events said to have taken place here, such as Llyn y Fan Fach. This version of the tale provides far more details and the reasons why Nelferch was struck are also different. It tells of a romantic young poet named Rhiwallon (in some versions, he's called Gwyn) who, one day, sees a herd of milk-white cows grazing on the hills near his home. He goes to investigate and sees that they belong to a beautiful young girl. She stands in the lake, plaiting her gorgeous red hair. Stuttering, he offers her some of his stale bread to break the ice. She smiles at him, tells him that he needs to try a lot harder than that, and disappears.

He asks his Mam to prepare some fresh bread, then takes it back to her the following day. Unimpressed, she laughs at his efforts and vanishes once more. Third time lucky, Rhiwallon's mam's bread eventually manages to impress her, and she agrees to marry him, under the condition, of course, that he doesn't strike her three times …

Time passes, the pair get married and they have three sons (Cadwgan, Gruffudd and Einion), whom she teaches all about the medicinal properties of water and the curative nature of herbs. Then, one day, the melancholy Nelferch (although, in some versions, the mysterious lady of the lake remains nameless) tells the mother at a christening they attend that the child will die before his fifth birthday, and Rhiwallon strikes her.

Further on down the line, the couple find themselves at a wedding, during which Nelferch bursts into tears, claiming the marriage would never last, and Rhiwallon hits her a second time. Then, when she laughs at a friend's funeral, happy that the person was now free of all earthly worries, Rhiwallon hits her for the third and final time. She whistles for her cattle to follow and she leads them all back into the lake, never to be seen again.

After that, Rhiwallon raises their three sons alone, until one day, their Mam reappears, urging them to use their botanist skills to care for others. Together, they develop cures for aches, pains, melancholy and depression, becoming the most famous healers in all of Wales; the 'Three Physicians of Myddfai'.[6]

Their story is a fascinating one in itself. Their first appearance dates back to the thirteenth century, when Rhiwallon and his three sons were doctors to Rhys Gryg, Prince of Deheubarth. By all accounts, the brothers treated Rhys when he was wounded in battle, though he died of his wounds shortly afterwards. Despite this, the family continued to follow the profession in the direct male line until 1739, when John Jones, the last of the physicians, died. Along with tales from the *Mabinogion*, the *Red Book of Hergest* also contains instructions for preparing herbal medicine, all attributed to the same family under the title Meddygon Myddfai.[7]

As I leave Ferndale, I cannot help but ponder over one thing: this obsession with the number three that I'm picking up on. At Llyn y Fan Fach, it took three attempts to impress the lady of the lake; she and her husband had three sons and, of course, she put forth the condition that she should not be struck nor quarrelled with three times. Interestingly, numerous stories in the *Mabinogi* also focus on this number, not to mention countless other folktales from around the world, with the main character's success or failure undeniably determined in the third attempt. I kept asking myself what the reason for this could be.

As well as reaching out to members of the public for my blog, I also emailed various experts: folklorists, historians, authors and such. And I was lucky enough to speak with Peter Stevenson, the man whose book inspired me to get out there and do this in the first place.

On the subject of the number three, he had this to say.

'All over the world, there's a fascination with different numbers … there comes a point in a story when you've got to give your hero a set of tasks to complete. So how many? A hundred and one? We'd be here 'til next Thursday! Eleven? Okay, that would still take all day. Let's just do three, shall we? In any case, from a storyteller's perspective, it's a really handy number! You can't reach a consensus with two, there needs to be a third. If it happens once, might be coincidence. Twice, you get suspicious. Three times? Something's wrong … so it works pragmatically.'

Ask a simple question, I guess … but Peter's answer reminded me that these tales were formed through oral storytelling and that it's important to keep that in mind to avoid going down that folklore rabbit hole. In relation to differing names and such, stories travel and people adopt their favourites, changing the location, the nature of the monsters and throwing in some real locals as they do so. This, in turn, explains why there are so many different versions of the *Tylwyth Teg* throughout Wales.

I think of how different the various 'ladies of the lakes' are to the other types of *Tylwyth Teg*. Whether they are kidnapping children or burying castles in sand, *Tylwyth Teg* are usually up to no good. The Lake Women, however, are generally seen as morally superior to us humans. In these tales, it is our own nature that is the cause for concern. Or the nature of a certain type of man, at least. Like so many fairy tales from around the world, the Lake Women of Wales serve as a warning. Mind you, I'm not sure if the idea of 'give him three chances' still stands today.

But my biggest takeaway is how easy it is, when considering the fantastical, to get distracted by mysticism and to follow a train of thought that takes you away from reality. More often than not, there is a simple explanation. Speaking of which …

7

Where the folk

can I get vampire furniture from?

'Where have you been today, then?' Gwyn, my housemate, landlord, old school friend and pandemic captor, asks with a smile.

'Vampire hunting.'

'What?'

'Well, hunting for vampire furniture, to be precise …'

Most people, when picturing a vampire, think of a pale-skinned dreamboat with bloody fangs, a black cape and slick hair with a receding hairline. They think of bats, wolves, garlic, or wooden stakes. Not the Welsh, though. Here in Wales, vampires come in the form of antique chairs and four-poster beds.

Legends of blood-sucking vampires have been popular throughout Europe for hundreds of years. Then, when Europeans established colonies in other countries around the world, myths of undead ghouls travelled with them, essentially going viral. Throughout history, stories of vampires have often coincided with plagues and epidemics. But they were more than just stories – some people actually took measures when burying their dead, like sticking bricks into the mouths of plague victims so they couldn't bite anyone should they ever wake up.

All this was a product of a general lack of knowledge regarding decomposition. As a corpse's skin recedes, teeth and fingernails can look as though they've grown longer. Then, as the internal organs break down, a dark fluid can sometimes leak out of the nose and mouth, thus completing the blood-sucking vampire look.

For most of us, the thought of being buried alive is our worst nightmare, but we live our lives safe in the knowledge that the likelihood of this happening is very small. However, for our ancestors, thanks to this lack of medical knowledge, the risk was all too real. People took to attaching bells and strings to headstones so that, in the event of being buried alive, the poor sods could tug the string and ring the bell to get someone's attention. So it turns out that it's not only in boxing that people can be 'saved by the bell'.

Then Victorian romanticism transitioned vampires from bloody, bloated corpses into the sexy fiends we recognise today, thanks to novels such as Bram Stoker's *Dracula* (1897). Before that, in 1852, the Irish actor and playwright Dion Boucicault wrote of a vampire who climbed Yr Wyddfa (Mt Snowdon). In any case, time went by, medical and technological advances were achieved and paranoia over the undead subsided. Today, despite no one having claimed to have seen a real one for a while, vampires are still very popular in almost every form of media and have been for a very long time, as well as being a popular Halloween costume.[1]

But despite their global popularity, vampires never really made it big here in Wales. Unless we're talking about vampire furniture, that is.

It is said that, on a Friday evening sometime in the early 1700s, a Dissenting Minister (being a minister for a nonconformist church as opposed to the main established church at the time, the Church of England) was making his way to Breconshire on a grey mare when he stopped to rest for the night at an old farmhouse in Glamorgan.

He spent the morning sat on an armchair in his room, reading the Bible. But he must not have slept very well the night before, because he nodded off, and when he awoke, he saw that his left hand was bleeding. Washing off the blood at the basin, he found a strange-looking bite mark.

Despite this, he delivered a sermon later that day and decided to stay another night at the old farmhouse. He didn't sleep too well on the second night either, mind, as it felt as though a dog was gnawing at him all night. Lighting a candle in the darkness, he lifted his shirt to find his ribs dripping with blood. In the morning, he was horrified to discover that his horse had similar bite marks on its neck. He decided to issue a complaint, telling the landlady 'Madam, I believe a vampire walks in your house!'

She told him that the same thing had happened to two other ministers who had stayed there before him. He asked her about the house. Apparently, the previous tenant had been an old antiquarian who was not exactly keen on ministers or men of the faith in general. For this reason, he had returned as a vampire upon his death.

Several ministers had attempted to exorcise the creature. Once, a dignitary of the Church of England gave it a go, only to be bitten on the left hand and leg. But despite their efforts, it refused to leave the library. As such, when the place was converted into a farmhouse, the library, complete with all its dusty books and nick-nacks, was sealed up. However, a few items of furniture were left behind in the rest of the house, including the armchair and the bed in the minister's room.

The Dissenting Minister advised her to get rid of the furniture altogether, probably wondered why the hell they didn't tell him all this in the first place, and then left, never to return. It is said that the vampire only left the house when the furniture was sold at auction to some poor unsuspecting sap who, as it turned out, quickly grew wise to the demonic qualities of his new decor (what he did with them is anyone's guess).

That was in the early 1700s. Fast-forward to 1840, and a certain Elizabethan chair is advertised by a local auction house as a 'Vampire Chair'. The buyer wants to complete a set of similar chairs that he is already in possession of. However, after a while, he places his new purchase in the far corner of the room, away from the others. He does so because guests complained that they were always scratching their hands until they bled whenever they sat in it.

Eventually, the entire set of chairs is sold for a high price to a rich merchant, whose family would later complain about scratches on their hands when sitting in one chair in particular. When the merchant died, the chair was sold to a lover of antique furniture, whose name is not on record. He, by all accounts, loved the chair and had no qualms with it, and the trail ends here.[2]

I wonder if there's a dusty room somewhere in Cardiff full of demonic furniture, draped in cloth and locked away for humanity's sake. Perhaps they are on display in some museum of the occult somewhere, behind a pane of glass next to Annabelle and Robert the Doll, Hollywood's favourite haunted dolls. Or maybe some desperate family manage to burn them in a dramatic showdown worthy of a *Poltergeist* sequel, never to speak of the incident again …

… or perhaps they never even existed in the first place; the story derives (in print, at least) from Marie Trevelyan's 1909 collection, *Folk-lore and Folk-stories of Wales*. She said that vampires were dead men doomed to an eternity of serving Arawn, the king of Annwn under the watchful eye of the Cŵn Annwn, the ghostly white hounds of the Otherworld.

She said they would visit the mortal world at night to drink the blood of the living, their souls forever tied to the furniture they owned in life, a far cry from the traditional vampire legend that we are all familiar with. There is no other mention of vampires in Welsh mythology and no further proposed link between vampires and Annwn.[3]

'So … bed bugs?'

'Huh?'

'The furniture … bites … it was obviously bed bugs, right?' Gwyn has put down his book now and is looking up at me intently.

He's probably right; much like the vampires of lore, perhaps, too, the strange bites and rashes attained from sitting on Vampire Furniture can be explained rationally. I decide to check out what bed-bug bites look like – large spots, nothing more – they certainly do not match the description in the story. But it gets me thinking about what I had already read about vampires; that they were often associated with plagues and epidemics. As such, I take a look at what was going on in south Wales in that respect between 1700 and 1850.

Turns out, there were several huge epidemics of numerous diseases in this region in that period, from influenza to cholera to typhus and typhoid.[4] I have a quick look at the symptoms of each disease and the only one that mentions a rash of some kind was typhoid, but again the description doesn't match.

There has only been one other account of Vampire Furniture in Wales and it took place here, in Cardiff. Apparently, during the reign of James I (1603–25), a family in Cardiff owned a four-poster bed bought at a bankruptcy sale. Proud of their new purchase, the couple placed it in the master bedroom. Then, when her husband went away, the lady of the house let their infant son share the bed with her.

On the child's first night in the bed, the woman found him to be restless. On the second night, he suddenly let out a violent cry and did not stop crying for the remainder of the night. In the morning, his mother sent for a doctor, who prescribed him with something which ensured that he rested more easily (God only knows what that was).

On the fourth night, the boy let out another painful scream. A few moments later, he was dead. On his throat was a large mark with a red spot in the centre that was oozing blood. When the doctor examined the body, he couldn't figure out what had happened, but apparently it looked like he had been drained of his blood with a straw.[5]

It is said that the family never got rid of the bed and that it stood unused for generations, described by the family as 'an uncanny piece of furniture'. This suggests that, somewhere in Cardiff, Vampire Furniture may very well still be at large …

Again, the account leaves us hanging. Numerous Google searches into 'vampires in Wales', 'vampire beds in Cardiff', 'vampire furniture Wales' and so on came up with nothing but a handful of articles on the above two accounts, none of which had anything to add. There was a bizarre moment when I was shown a link that said 'buy vampire beds today at eBay'. Naturally, I had to check it out, and was presented with an assortment of *Twilight* bed sheets and *Buffy the Vampire Slayer* scatter cushions.

I also checked out the websites of several local antique dealers and second-hand furniture stores – no mention of Vampire Furniture anywhere. I even popped into a couple of them to ask the owners directly. Needless to say, they looked like they had better things to be doing. Mind you, one of them did tell me that any auction houses or antique dealerships from that time would have been situated on or around Queen Street, the city's main shopping district, and would be long gone by now.

When I was talking with Gwyn, I had just returned from rural Glamorgan, having been on the lookout for the old farmhouse from the story of the Dissenting Minister. It had originally been a dower house, you see, before the vampiric antiquarian had moved in, and some online research hinted that it might be located at the small village of Llanmaes.

To get there, I had gone up the A4232 (commonly referred to around here as the 'Concrete Road'), passing the towering blocks of flats which look out over Cardiff Bay as I went, then turned off just before reaching the M4. Along the way, I spotted what seemed to be the ruins of a monastery or small castle of sorts; I passed the layby too quickly to stop, so I made a vow to go on my way back.

Once at Llanmaes, I spotted a young girl scurrying around a heap of second-hand books in a bus stop. I pulled up beside her. The phone box next to the bus stop was crammed with literature, from children's books on dinosaurs to Penguin classics.

'Alright?'

'Hey ...'

'Bit random, like, but I'm writing a blog on Welsh folklore. Know anything about Vampire Furniture?'

'Yhm ...'

'... wouldn't think so, gauging by your reaction ... is there a big house around here? I'm picturing like an old manor house kind of thing, maybe a farm...'

'Oh! That'll be down there ...'

'Just straight down there?'

'Straight down there, yeah!' she said with a smile.

'Thanks!'

Just down from there, I passed a row of beautiful cottages, each with a unique name, like the Old Church House, the Quarry House ... there was one named after a pub, I think. Then I saw it – the one everyone must have been on about – it was huge and yellow and had a gated path leading up a well-kept garden. I parked ol' Griff up on the side of the road and wandered back on myself, trying to have a good look at the house without seeming as though I was scouting it in preparation for a burglary.

That's when I saw an elderly man in full walking gear emerging from a nearby hedge. 'Alright? I'm writing a blog on Welsh folklore. Know anything about Vampire Furniture?'

'Vampire Furniture?' he repeated with enthusiasm, as though he knew something about it.

'Yeah!'

'Nope. Sorry.'

I wandered around some more, eventually coming across an old, faded map of the village pinned up on a notice board outside the church. Squinting, I just about made out the names. According to the map, I had the right house.[6]

For a moment, I considered going up there and knocking the door, but decided against it. Might be a bit strange, having a total stranger knock your door and ask if you know anything about Vampire Furniture that you and some guy on the internet believe can be traced back to your house – I decided to head back to Dracula's Castle instead.

Parking up in the layby, I realised the ruins were actually situated at the far end of a cemetery, with a standard-looking church at the other end. Ignoring the church, I took a few snaps of the ruins then went and made my way back to Cardiff.

I realise now that the ruins were those of Llantrithyd Place, an old, sixteenth-century manor house. The Aubrey baronets were lords of the manor and of the nearby village of Llantrithyd for centuries, but the family died out in the 1850s.[7]

And the 'standard-looking' church that I had dismissed? St Illtyd's Church, one of the most famous church complexes in Wales and the site of Cor Tewdws, a Celtic monastery and the oldest college in all of the United Kingdom. The church building is one of the oldest in Wales and is a Grade I listed building which has often been referred to as the 'Westminster Abbey of Wales' due to its architectural beauty.[8]

I clearly have no eye for architecture. Funnily enough, the candlesticks in the church are dedicated to none other than folklorist Marie Trevelyan (1853–1922), who, it turns out, hailed from the area. Indeed, one does speculate whether Marie Trevelyan was just jumping on the Victorian romanticism bandwagon when she wrote about Vampire Furniture. Wales was lacking in the blood-sucking department and needed to catch up. Either that, or somewhere out there, perhaps right here in Cardiff, Vampire Furniture still exists …

8

Where the folk
did the 'Mad Doctor'
go to burn the baby
Welsh messiah?

High up on the hill above the town of Talbot Green and its busy shopping centre sits an older town with an interesting history, a great deal of which is shrouded in mystery and lore. Apparently (though widely debated), the rude hand gesture the 'V-sign' was invented by the famous local longbowmen, the same men who helped make the three ostrich feathers the symbol of the Prince of Wales. A former vicar once said that he has been called out for more blessings and exorcisms to this town than anywhere else in his career. Women accused of witchcraft were put on trial there and the great-but-eccentric Dr William Price cremated his son up on the hill, an act that would ultimately lead to the revival of cremation in the United Kingdom.

Can you tell where it is yet? That's right – or not, I actually have no idea what you're thinking – I'm heading up the steep, winding road that takes you to Llantrisant. The 'Parish of the Three Saints', as its name literally translates into in English, pays homage to Saint Illtyd, Saint Gwynno and Saint Dyfodwg. Saint Illtyd was said to have been King Arthur's cousin and served him as a soldier in his youth. He was also one of the 'triumvirate', being the three men to whom Arthur gave custody of the Holy Grail, the other two being Cadoc and Peredur. Because of this, some scholars have tried connecting Illtyd with Sir Galahad.[1]

I pass by the Cross Keys Hotel and head up a short hill to the centre of town. Back in the 1800s, the Cross Keys was used for 'petty sessions', in which women accused of witchcraft were put on trial. As I wait for other cars to pass, my satnav hollering at me to 'go straight', I see the famous statue of Dr William Price that I came here for.

He stands on the Bull Ring, being a commercial square and the main focal point of the town. Back in the day, they used to hold bull-baiting events here, a pretty grisly sport in which they tied a bull to a large stone. The farmers then brought their terriers down and the one who bit and held onto the bull's tongue the longest, won. They put a stop to it in 1827, not due to animal cruelty, but because the local constabulary just couldn't handle the drunken rabble any more.

Dotted around the Bull Ring are numerous pubs, cafes and restaurants and an antique toyshop. Here you can also find O'Sullivan's Brasserie, a restaurant with a rather bizarre menu. Expect python and llama stew, buffalo steaks, kangaroo – anything but the expected, really.

Heading down the other side of the hill, I'm presented with a view of the common. Beyond this stretch of wild land lies the Royal Mint, which produces all of our British coins. I descend a little then take a right and park up at the free car park before heading back up the hill on foot.

It's a steep climb and isn't made any easier by the fact you have to climb up onto people's front doorsteps at times to avoid traffic, but it's not far. It being lunchtime, I decide to pop into the Butchers Arms Gallery & Coffee Shop, a rather quaint-looking former coaching inn tucked away behind the much larger Bear Inn. It's busy inside, the air thick with the smell of coffee beans and freshly baked cakes. The walls are adorned with locally made goods, from art and crafts to jams and chutneys. I'm greeted by the loveliest group of women, one of whom takes me to my table.

'The stuffing's fresh, made today … can I recommend the turkey and stuffing?'

'Sounds lovely, I'll have it in a sandwich, please.'

'With salad?'

'Go on, then. And a pot of tea, please. And one of those coffee and walnut cakes!'

'And a coffee and walnut cake … righto! So, are you just visiting town, then?'

'I am. I'm writing a blog on Welsh folklore.'

'Oh well, you've certainly come to the right place for that, let me get you a leaflet.' She wanders off and comes back with some information on Llantrisant, complete with a brief history of each building of interest. She also hands me a little hand-drawn map of the town and guides me through it: 'That's where they filmed *The Indian Doctor* back in 2010 ... and that'll take you right up to the Billy Wynt.'

The people in the pubs of Llantrisant could argue all night and day about what the Billy Wynt once was. What you can see there today was erected as recently as the 1890s, when they built a folly out of the ruins of the stones that were already there. Some say that it used to be a windmill (*wynt* is a mutated form of *gwynt*, the Welsh word for 'wind'), but others argue that it was a Norman lookout tower.

When I leave the cafe and cross the road onto the Bull Ring to snap a photo of William Price, one of a trio of friends calls me over to them. It's only Ellie, the lady who had a ghostly encounter at Llancaiach Fawr. 'Bloody hell, Ellie! How are you?'

She introduces me to her friends. After telling me all about growing up in Llantrisant, they start pointing out various places of interest and then give me a series of confusing and heavily debated directions. But the one place I simply have to go to, they all agree, is the museum up at the Guildhall. I assure them that I will go just as soon as I had my pic and they go on their way.

Dr William Price had a profound impact on British culture in his lifetime. He was also a right character and lived a very bizarre and exciting life. It would make for a great film, let me tell you. Actually, whilst on the subject, Robert Downey Jr apparently based his portrayal of Dr Dolittle on him, hence his dodgy Welsh accent in the film.[2]

Climbing up the steep cobbled street known as Yr Allt, I take a left and find the Guildhall, with the remains of Llantrisant Castle behind it. There is a set of stocks outside and, in the distance, you can see the hill where the great doctor cremated his son. Heading inside, pausing to put my mask on, I'm greeted by a group of curators who scarper into position as I head inside. 'Please, sit down!'

I feel as though they are about to sing 'Be Our Guest' from *Beauty and the Beast*. They put me in a chair in front of a television then look on eagerly and with great anticipation as I am treated to a ten-minute video that tells me everything about the town's history. They proudly point out anyone they know who's in the video, smiling with astonishment as though it's the first time they're seeing it.

After that, they take me to see the silver mace of the Freemen of Llantrisant then promptly usher me downstairs. There, a lovely lady shows me everything they have on Dr William Price, which includes a replica of his outfit, his surgical instruments, old photos and a stained glass image of him that was found in a skip, amongst other things. I tell her about my blog.

'Whether what?'

'Where. Where the folk.'

'Weather? What about the weather?'

'No! "Where" the folk … it's a pun on where the f–'

'Oh, right! Ha-ha! Brilliant!'

Before I leave, she encourages me to speak with Dean Powell, manager and a 'Freeman of Llantrisant', whatever that means. 'Wait right here, I'll go get him.'

'Alright …'

When Dean comes out, I mention my blog and he tells me that he is something of an expert on the subject and that he has written several books, pointing out *Dr William Price: Wales's First Radical* and *Ghostly Tales of Llantrisant* on the shelves behind the till. Turns out, he also does ghost tours around town. I ask him if he's free for a chat and he takes me into his office.

'Cup of tea?' One of the female staff members pops her head in.

'Please. Milk, no sugar.'

Dean is a Freeman of Llantrisant, a title handed down to him by generations going as far back as the fourteenth century. Today, the title mainly gives Dean the right to graze cattle and horses out on the common. Sheep have never grazed here, meaning that both the flora and fauna are quite unique, making it a Site of Special Scientific Interest. Throughout the years, however, the title of Freeman came with a lot more privileges (and responsibilities).

'So where does the name come from?'

'… in 1346, the traders of the town were given a charter by the Lord of Glamorgan. It gave them the right to charge traders from outside Llantrisant for the right for trading in their market. As such, they became known as the "Free Men of Llantrisant".'

The Freemen have been very much involved in the town for many years, and one other tradition they upkeep is that every seven years, they 'beat the boundaries' of the old borough which is a seven-mile walk, in a tradition called the 'Beating of the Bounds'. The event usually attracts around 15,000 people each year. There are numerous rocks dotted around the boundaries of the town. These days people just do the walk but, traditionally, the local Freemen's sons would be picked up and their bums bounced on top of the rocks in a somewhat bizarre ritual. Dean reckons it was so that they would never forget where the town boundaries were.

'1346 was a big year for Llantrisant. Because the Freemen were given this charter, they needed somewhere from which to govern and administer the town as best as they could, so this building was erected the same year. We have the stocks outside; now, any child who comes here today often thinks "Oh well, because I've got small hands and feet, I could have pulled myself out of those stocks easily and ran away", but then I get to tell them that, in fact, if you were a child, then they would have nailed one of your ears to the stocks as well, to make sure you didn't escape! I'm sure Llantrisant was full of kids with ripped earlobes!'

'Eek!'

'The third reason why 1346 was such a big year for Llantrisant is that was the same year that the local longbowmen fought for the Prince of Wales at the Battle of Crécy, in northern France. We have a long tradition of longbowmen in this town, and they fought gallantly in that battle, by all accounts, despite being outnumbered three-to-one. At the end of the battle, the Prince of Wales himself took the emblem off the chest of the enemy king, King John of Bohemia, and it was the three ostrich feathers that now signifies the Prince of Wales.'

'Yes, well, I was astounded, to be honest, to hear just how much influence the archers of Llantrisant have had on Welsh culture. There is also the claim that they came up with the famous "V-sign" ... is there any legitimacy to this?'

'Ah well, you see, according to some historians, there is no legitimacy to Welsh archers being at that battle, at all. Some deny the claim that we were even there, but I think I would go with the evidence that we were there. They say that in the battle, any of the French who caught a Welsh bowman would chop his two fingers off to stop him being able to use his bow and, of course, those Welsh that weren't caught couldn't wait to "give them the two fingers" to show them that they still had them. I love the idea that we were that quirky, but whether or not there is any legitimacy to it, I don't know. As it often happens, myth and legend become part of history.'

Indeed, the intertwining of history and myth is very prominent here in Llantrisant, which brings our conversation to the great man himself.

'I was about seven or eight when I learned about a doctor who lived in the same town as me who went on top of a hill in the middle of winter and set fire to a baby. I was in awe. Most books created this kind of clownish, buffoonish, idiotic image of a man, that he was some bizarre, eccentric "Welsh wizard" who danced naked around flames and walked mountains in the nude and things. So I thought; there's got to be more to the man than this.'

Dean, who clearly idolises the man, wanted to change people's perceptions of him, and before writing his book, he gave lectures on the life and times of Dr William Price, in which he focused more on what happened before that fateful day up on the hill.

'He was an excellent surgeon who graduated at the Royal College of Surgeons in London when he was only twenty-one, and this despite the fact that he grew up in an impoverished farmhouse on the outskirts of Caerphilly with a father who was a schizophrenic and a vicar who could never hold a living. He didn't have a penny to his name. At twenty-one, he's a surgeon, a midwife and a pharmacist – he's got all these qualifications! He comes back to Wales and proposes a healthcare system that would undoubtedly influence people like Aneurin Bevan when they wrote up the NHS a hundred years later.'

There's a twinkle in his eye as he goes on listing Dr Price's achievements.

'He becomes part of a "culturist group", is what I'd call them … Lady Llanover is one of them, she's the one who really stamped her authority on the national costume of Wales, and Lady Charlotte Guest is the other, who translated the *Mabinogi* into English. And they respect each other and fight for the same cause.'

'Wow!' I shake my head and take a sip of my tea. That was a genuine 'wow' by the way – I literally came here because of the whole cremation thing. I hope he doesn't ask me anything about him …

'But he's more radical than them, and quite militant. So he joins a Chartist movement who are desperately trying to penetrate parliament with six points of reform which becomes The People's Charter. He becomes the leader of several thousand men for the Charters' rising.'

'He spends quite a bit of time in France. He's a left-winger, he goes on long drinking binges with Karl Marx in London, apparently. When he comes back to Wales he is involved in the re-establishment of the National Eisteddfod in 1861. But more than anything, he is an obsessive disciple, I suppose, of Iolo Morganwg and his ideas about Druidism and the thought that Wales was the centre of some "Druidic ideal". He latches onto it, and he obsesses over Druidism. He becomes the "Archdruid of Wales", a title that he gives himself – huge ego! He wears flamboyant costumes, all these red waistcoats, specially minted brass buttons with goats' heads on them, green trousers and tartan shoals, a fox on his head.'

This is the image that comes to mind for me whenever I hear Dr Price's name. It is how he is presented in his statue on the Bull Ring, with outstretched arms.

'He has a lot of women in his life, but he doesn't marry any of them – he doesn't believe in marriage, he believes that it enslaves women. He's a bit of a feminist, I suppose. He often came to the defence of some poor unmarried mother who was being shouted at from the pulpit. Which is ironic, because I wouldn't be surprised if he was the reason she ended up there in the first place! There were a lot of women and a lot of children …'

I pull the face my grandmother used to make whenever she was given a bit of hot local gossip, then take another sip of my tea. He tells me that Dr Price didn't come to Llantrisant until he was seventy-one years of age, and that at eighty-three, he married his housekeeper Gwenllian Llewelyn (in a Druidic marriage), who was fifty-one years younger than him. They had a son whom they considered to be the 'Druidic messiah' and wanted to give him a name that people would remember. Naturally, they settled on Iesu Grist.'

'Jesus Christ.'

'Precisely! Within five months, the baby dies, and he decides to cremate him because that's what the Druids did. Before you know it, you have three hundred people gathered up on the hill wondering what on Earth is going on. The police come and kick the casket over. The baby rolls out onto the field and it causes a riot. They try to set fire to Price, but in the end, he's dragged away and taken to the police station next door to the Guildhall. The baby's remains are put in a box and kept in a cell there. The trial takes place a few weeks later. Dr Price defends himself brilliantly in the trial and is found not guilty on both charges and because of all the media coverage, Price becomes a celebrity. He does cremate the child eventually, and it goes ahead peacefully.'

Is my mouth open? I think it is …

'He dies at ninety-two in the arms of Gwenllian, drinking a glass of champagne. His own cremation was well-documented – Gwenllian sold tickets, in fact, and a good 20,000 people turned up for it.'

Dr Price: a legend in death as he was in life. A feminist, a vegetarian and outspoken critic of smoking, he was ahead of his time in many ways. And, as with most popular and eccentric people, his legacy includes many anecdotes that are far too fantastical to be true, though he certainly wasn't very orthodox and was quick to call out other medical practitioners as a 'bunch of poison pedlars'.

Take, for example, the time he treated a man for his alcoholism. Price gave him some liquid to drink and got him to vomit into a bucket. But Price had thrown a toad into the bucket beforehand and told him 'Well, that's the trouble – that toad was growing in your stomach because you're an alcoholic!' which put the man off drink for life. Another story tells of a woman who was having problems with her chest. Price put a lump of beef on her breast, which tempted a worm to come out through the skin. It is a combination of these urban myths and the man's real escapades that makes Dr Price a legend in his own right.

I leave Llantrisant feeling as though I've made myself a whole new group of friends. While elated, I decide to get in touch with Ellie to thank her for today and ask if she knows of anyone else from Llantrisant that I could speak with.

'Are you covering the Mari Lwyd at all?' she asks.

'Got to have a Christmas special, I suppose.'

'Well then, I've got just the pair for you ...'

9
Who the folk
dances with Mari?

Picture the scene: you're sitting in front of the fire with your family some time between Christmas and New Year's Eve when you hear the jingling of bells coming up the street and voices chanting: 'Well, here we come, innocent friends, to ask leave, to ask leave, to ask leave to sing ...'

You peer out from behind the curtains and see a crowd of people gathered outside your house clad in strange outfits, including two blokes dressed as Punch and Judy. Their leader is a man grappling with an elaborately dressed horse skull mounted on a large pole, himself hidden beneath the cloth. The demonic mare stops outside your front door and challenges you to a Battle of Rhymes called a *pwnco*, in which two individuals take turns singing verses until one admits defeat.

The dead mare sings that she should be given access to your house and you must sing back to her why she should bugger off instead. Succeed and she leads the crowd onwards to the next house. Lose, and she will burst into your home and cause all manner of havoc, snapping her skeletal mouth at you and scaring the life out of your children while the man beneath the cloth does his best to keep her under control. In the meantime, the crowd raids your pantry and drinks all your booze.

This is the old wassailing folk custom of the Mari Lwyd, a tradition that Llantrisant Folk Club revived and has been keeping alive since 1980. I have come for a chinwag with Pat Smith and Anne Abel, two leading members of the club, to discuss this strange, re-emerging custom. We're sat in Pat's living room, with Ellie on her way to join us.

'Sugar?'

'No thanks, Pat, I'm sweet enough! So there's Mari, on your sofa ... tell me about the decorations and what they mean.'

'Well, the bells are there so that you can hear her coming. People think "Oh Lord, here comes the Mari Lwyd!" Scared the kids to death, back in the day. And the ribbons are there just to make her look pretty. Now, the colours of Llantrisant are black and gold, so originally, our Mari only had black and gold ribbons, but she's acquired more over the years.' She shakes Mari about, jingling the bells.

'I put some extra ones on to make her look more ... jolly,' Anne adds. 'She also has a rosette that she got when she went to a gathering of Mari Lwyds over at Chepstow.'

'A gathering of Mari Lwyds? So how many of them are there?'

Anne shifts in her seat. 'Right, well, let's get one thing straight – this is a "skull-and-pole horse", and it's a "long pole". There are horses with shorter poles, so depends what you mean, really. This one is held above the head – you never have the carrier's head inside the skull.'

'So the taller the better, for Mari!' exclaims Pat.

'You hold her, go on ...' Anne urges me.

'Right, okay ...' I pick her up and carefully lift her above my head, wary of damaging her as well as Pat's ceiling. 'Oh yes, she is heavy, isn't she!'

'Now, you would have to hold that above your head ...'

'For how long?'

'Oh, we'd be out for hours,' says Pat, handing me my tea. 'When we go out with her on the Sunday Solstice, the Sunday before Christmas, we leave at midday and we don't get back until about five o'clock, so whoever's got the horse is under her all that time.'

'See, now this is one thing that confuses me – I originally thought the Mari Lwyd went out at Christmas, then I was told it was New Year's Eve ...' I dip my tongue into my tea then immediately pull it back out. I really need to stop using my tongue as a thermometer.

'It doesn't matter, it's the turn of year, she can go out any time from Halloween,' says Pat.

'The story goes,' Anne explains, 'that back in the day, during the winter, the local men didn't have any work, they didn't have much

55

money. So what they did was they went from house to house, essentially begging, but using the *pwnco*, where they'd say something along the lines of "Here we are outside your house, we are marvellous, give us a drink!"'

'… and then you'd say something like "You can't come in, you're horrible, bugger off!", but eventually they'd get a drink, regardless.'

'… but the more houses they visited, the drunker they got, so the church didn't like it. It was too much fun. The modern-day version that Patti and them reintroduced in the seventies – this horse was made in the seventies – involves going around collecting money for charity. The only time we do the *pwnco* is at Chepstow Festival.'

'… because people around here don't know the *pwnco* anymore, see!'

'I don't know it. It's done in Welsh, of course.'

'Yes, well, I was going to ask about that, actually … how much engagement do you get from the public?'

'People don't remember the *pwnco* because the Mari Lwyd tradition died out in this area,' Pat explains. 'My father remembers it as a child, used to scare him to death! It died out everywhere, really. The only place it didn't die out was at Llangynwyd, in Maesteg. And it still goes on there, as far as I know, on New Year's Day. The Cardiff Welsh Dance Team have a horse and they take it there for that.'

'Now, a *pwnco*, to my understanding, is a "Battle of Rhymes" of sorts …'

'It is, yes, they hire a poet for it. When we go round the pubs here, we sing …'

She goes on to sing several verses of a *pwnco* in Welsh, which I shall roughly translate for you. Mind you, north and south Walian can differ greatly, so here's my Gog interpretation:

Well, here we come, dear friends, to ask for your permission to sing,

Mari Lwyd is here, dressed in her ribbons, giving light to you on this night and asking for your permission to sing,

Mari Lwyd is coming to the pub to ask for money and beer,

Well, tap the barrel, clear out all the beer and we'll all have a good holiday …

'That's the version we sing at the pubs, but if you do it round the houses, you never know what they'll come back at you with.'

'And would people genuinely be trying to beat the horse in a *pwnco*, then?' I ask.

'Oh, yes, very much so. But what happens these days is that I wait outside with the horse and we'd have a few musicians with us, a couple dressed as Punch and Judy ...'

'Stock characters,' Anne explains.

'And do they ever change?'

'Well, you've always got the Merryman ...' – Pat looks up at the ceiling and begins listing the different characters – '... the fiddler. Then Punch and Siwan, Siwan always being a man dressed as a woman.'

'Then I lead the horse inside,' says Anne. 'Because the person can't see very well, you see, and we go around all the tables. But I'm always on the lookout in case people get scared and what have you. Children are often worried by it. But if they look interested, we engage with them. Now, most people know that when you go under the horse, you adopt the spirit of the horse, and some people can do it better than others. PJ was the best, wasn't he?'

'Oh, yes!'

'PJ was brilliant. The last time we went out with PJ, he ran across a field acting like a horse!' Anne chuckles. 'It's like theatre – you go under that horse and you *become* the horse. I remember once we went to a shopping centre and he sat amongst a display of teddy bears. Ha-ha! And another time, there was horse-racing on at the pub, and he got up and began racing around the room like one of the horses.'

'When you say that you adopt the spirit of the horse, does that mean Mari Lwyd herself, or just a generic horse? I mean, has Mari got a personality?' I ask.

'Oh, yes, very much so, yes. Very mischievous. That's part of the fun. It's great when you've got a whole bunch of horses getting together. We rest Mari's head on unsuspecting people, we try drinking their beer ... although, you've got to do it within reason. For the most part, people like us being there, but we have had people say, "Get that filthy thing off me!" and that sort of thing.'

'No way.' I take a sip of my tea. Too cold now. *Damia fo!*

Pat suddenly stands up and goes to get out some photos of the club's outings with Mari, pointing out various characters as she goes through them: 'Some of these people aren't with us any more. He's not with us, she's not with us … David Pitt!'

'Aww, David Pitt!' Anne puts her hand on her heart.

'Who's David Pitt?' I ask.

'David makes flat-pack Mari Lwyds for schoolchildren,' Anne explains. 'I mean, it's not easy to get a skull these days, what with health and safety and what-not. So, David has a cardboard skull that looks just like the real thing.'

'You know, I don't think we spoke about the Mari Lwyd once in school, growing up,' I say, scanning the ceiling for memories.

'That's because you're from north Wales!' says Anne.

'Is it a southern tradition, then?'

'Yes. Mainly Glamorgan.'

'Well, not entirely …' says Anne. 'It's spreading, and was traditionally done in Pembrokeshire, as well. There was a big folk revival in the 1970s, a lot of it comes from that.'

'Tell you what, though, I can see why it died out in places, what with all the young people leaving – you've seen how heavy she is – we're struggling now and not sure what to do …' Pat shakes her head despairingly.

'What's your plan?' I ask, throwing back the last of my lukewarm tea.

'It really is a struggle,' Anne laments. 'There was a woman, wasn't there? A woman, down the Guildhall, but we didn't catch her name …'

She then looks me up and down and asks, 'Do you want to do it?'

'Me?'

'Yes!' Pat exclaims, loving the idea. 'You're tall, you're strong, you're a nice young man …'

'I'm tall, at least,' I say with a shrug. 'I see now – you were sizing me up when you had me lifting her up earlier, weren't you? Well, it's nothing I've done before, but never say never, I suppose!'

'Now, would you like to know how our Mari was made?' Anne asks.

'Yes, please!'

Reaching into a bag she has by her feet, Anne takes out some notes. Back in 1978, a friend of theirs named Ian Jones, the man who made their Mari Lwyd, had a neighbour who owned a slaughterhouse. Through him, he obtained a horse's head. What he did next required a strong stomach: according to Anne's notes, he cleaned the flesh off, then buried it, knowing that the residual flesh would disappear over time. Also, this way, the skull would not become brittle. It was buried in manure for twelve months, then put in hot water so that the maggots rose up to be removed.

He next devised the internal structure, putting a pole up the horse's head and building a handle to pull the jaw. He then gifted the skull to the folk club, where Pat decorated it, though she did complain that a few maggots remained. Ian was a member of the folk club and carried the Mari for a number of years. He loved misbehaving and causing mayhem with the horse and once got kicked out of the Penny-Farthing (a pub in Llantrisant) because everyone had left and he didn't want to leave. According to Anne, he knew that to carry the horse was to become the spirit of the horse.

'Is there any maintenance involved? Or once you've done that, you're sorted?'

'That's all you need to do. Just don't drop it.'

'Right. Let's get back to basics a little: where does the name "Mari Lwyd" come from, then?'

'Ah, well, that is the question!' says Pat. 'She's the Grey Mare, the Grey Mary ... no one really knows.'

'One theory I've heard is that it comes from the English tradition of the "merry lude",' I suggest, raising my brow.

'Hmm ... no.' Anne puts a stop to that one. 'One popular theory, that I don't really buy into, is that it refers to the Virgin Mary. But this isn't a Christian tradition. But why "Mary"? Who knows. I tend to go for "Grey Mary", myself. Now, I want to tell you about something else Mari and some other hobby horses do, as well, and that's visiting someone's house when they are ill to cheer them up. When I had my brain haemorrhage, Mari came to see me.'

'Oh wow, that's lovely!'

'It was quite scary when I first saw her, to be honest.'

'It's the "Magic of the Mari", see,' Pat says with a smile.

'I love me a hobby horse, I do!' says Anne.

'Yes, I can tell.' That's when the doorbell goes and in comes Ellie. 'Well, thank you very much for speaking with me tonight, ladies. And thank you for the tea. And thank you, Ellie, for setting all this up. Shall we take this party to the pub?'

And off to the pub we went, to ask leave, to ask leave to drink and be merry.

10

Where the folk
can I find a good,
old-fashioned hero?

A new year is upon us and, while others flock to the gym, I stay at home as usual, for I have bigger aspirations for *Where the Folk* this year. It's picked up momentum as of late and my mum is no longer my top fan, though she is still the first to like each post. I mean, I'd hardly call myself an influencer, thank God, but there's clearly an audience out there who want to read about it. Now I think I need to include a few belters, some of the classics. I mean stories with a good, old-fashioned hero lead, epics that withstand the test of time.

In 1949, Joseph Campbell wrote *The Hero with a Thousand Faces*, in which he discusses a theory he had that all the classic 'hero tales' of every culture on Earth share common themes and follow the same narrative structure. The themes delve deep into our psyche and represent humankind's deepest fears and desires, the trials and tribulations of daily life and our sense of place in the universe. In terms of narrative structure, he suggested that most stories can be broken down into three acts.

Act One concerns the protagonist's 'Call to Adventure' from their normal, everyday life. This is the bit when they run away from home or get told that they are the 'chosen one', the only person who can save everyone. In Act Two they 'Cross the Threshold' and enter the 'Belly of the Whale' if you will, leaving their mundane (or even miserable) life behind and entering unknown and often dangerous territory. Here they overcome various obstacles that often require them to have a few tricks up their sleeves. Then in the third and final act, they apply everything they've learned to their new life, having achieved their goal and grown as an individual. Follow this formula and you've got yourself an instant classic.

I decided to see how Campbell's theory of the Hero's Journey applies to Welsh legends. For this, I'm heading to Caerleon, not far from Cardiff. As I make my way down the M4, following brown road signs adorned with Roman helmets, I am taken back to a family holiday I went on many years ago, before moving down south. I simply cannot say 'Roman helmet' and not think of the time we visited the Roman baths on that trip and I got my brother to pose with a gladiator's helmet on his head (you're allowed to do this by the way), which was comically too big for him at the time.

'Leave him alone,' Mam said, tutting pitifully. 'I wonder if he'd do the same to you!'

Steadying my digital camera, I glanced over at Dad, who was creasing up in the corner. 'If we're anything like him, then I'm gonna go with "yes he would" on that one!'

Chuckling to myself, I switch my indicators on and descend the slip road. Caerllion, as it's known in Welsh, sits along the banks of the River Usk, some five miles north-east of Newport. Most people know it for its Roman amphitheatre and fort, a site of significant archaeological importance. Built not far from an old Iron Age hillfort, it was the main headquarters of the Roman legion *Legio II Augusta* from around the year AD 75 right up to AD 300. But they didn't call the place Caerleon, they called it Isca, after the River Usk. Its modern name probably derives from Old Welsh for 'fortress of the legion', emerging in AD 800, when it was referred to as Cair Legeion guar Uisc.[1]

Geoffrey of Monmouth reckoned that the site was first founded by the mythical king of the Britons, Belinus. He also claimed that King Arthur himself held court here, with Caerleon being something of a capital city for the legendary king. This would make the place the 'original Camelot', if you will.[2]

There are three main places of interest here when it comes to the Roman history, I'd say, with remnants of old walls dotted about elsewhere. You've got the Roman baths, the Roman Legionary Museum and the amphitheatre. I decide to head to the amphitheatre first. What remains of it today is a broken circle of large grassy mounds, so don't expect a seat.

Geoffrey of Monmouth claimed that the amphitheatre is actually the remnants of King Arthur's Round Table. In reality, it was a stone structure aligned with wooden stands where up to 6,000 Romans would gather to watch gladiators fight to the death, be it against each other or against various apex predators from around the world.

Clambering up one of the 'stands', I use my coat as a blanket and tuck into my packed lunch, imagining what it would have been like munching away whilst watching the entertainment all those years ago.

I've come here because Caerleon was the location of Arthur's court in the story of 'How Culhwch Won Olwen'. Known also as '*Culhwch ac Olwen*', this is an ancient Welsh tale that features in Lady Charlotte Guest's translation of the *Mabinogi*. The earliest printed versions of this tale feature in fragments in the *White Book of Rhydderch* (*Llyfr Gwyn Rhydderch*), *c*.1350 and a complete version is in the Red Book of Hergest (Llyfr Coch Hergest), *c*.1400, though it didn't have a title back then.[3]

Now, when I said I was going to find you an epic tale, I wasn't lying: '*Culhwch ac Olwen*' is by far the longest of these ancient Welsh prose tales and ticks all the boxes of Joseph Campbell's 'Seventeen Stages of the Hero's Journey'. Well, most of them, at least – it's important to note that not every myth or legend in the world follows the cycle in its entirety.

Act One

The Call to Adventure, or leaving equilibrium: Culhwch (whose name means 'narrow sow') is born and his mother Goleudydd dies in childbirth. He is raised by his father, King Cilydd, son of Celyddon. Eventually, Cilydd remarries and Culhwch's new stepmother tries to pair him up with his stepsister.

Refusal of the Call: But he's not really into that kind of thing, so his evil stepmom puts a curse on him as punishment. The curse declares that he can only marry the beautiful Olwen, daughter of Ysbaddaden Pencawr, a giant of such proportions that he needs men by his side at all times just so they can lift his heavy eyelids up for him with the use of massive poles. He's also a bit of a ... protective father, let's say.

Supernatural Aid: Cilydd warns Culhwch that convincing Ysbaddaden to let him marry his daughter won't be easy and that he needs the help of his cousin, King Arthur. Though Arthur isn't a magician, he is considered capable of achieving impossible things. Culhwch heads to Caerleon to see his cousin, who agrees to help him. Arthur also enlists six of his finest warriors to the cause, namely Cai, Bedwyr, Gwalchmei, Gwrhyr Gwalstawd Ieithoedd, Menw son of Teirgwaedd, and Cynddylig Gyfarwydd, each one equipped with his own unique set of abilities and skills. But that's not all: Arthur recruits over a hundred men, dogs and horses for their heroic band, with many well-established names from both Welsh and Irish mythology mentioned, including Gwyn ap Nudd, leader of Annwn and of the infamous Wild Hunt.

Crossing the First Threshold: With all the boys present, Culhwch and his allies head to Ysbaddaden's court.

Act Two

Belly of the Whale: Culhwch, along with cousin Arthur and his mates, arrange a meeting at the giant's court. Luckily, Olwen also takes a fancy to our Culhwch, but her father insists that he can only marry her if he completes a set of forty (or thereabout) near-impossible tasks. Culhwch is committed to the cause now. Being given a set of impossible tasks is also popular in ancient mythology.

Road of Trials: These would be those forty impossible tasks Culhwch et al. need to complete so that he can marry Olwen. For this, they travel to various locations all over Britain and Ireland, though not all of them are recorded in the tale. Along their way, they encounter witches, giants, the magical boar Twrch Trwyth, and all sorts.

Meeting with the Goddess: This would be Olwen, so in this instance Campbell's steps are out of sequence. But remember, Campbell himself was very clear that not every tale follows each step to a T.

Woman as Temptress: Usually this concerns a femme fatale who serves as a distraction for the hero from his ultimate goal. Some online versions describe the Black Witch in this tale as something along those lines, but in the *Mabinogi* she is described as a 'hag'. Perhaps, then, this step doesn't quite fit in here, but let's not forget that the whole story revolves around Culhwch's infatuation.

Atonement with Father: Culhwch eventually wins the girl, which gains him his father's respect. Furthermore, he also manages to complete all the tasks given to him by Olwen's father, thus impressing him, as well.

Apotheosis: Many people are killed or injured in this tale, but Culhwch's infatuation pushes him onwards.

The Ultimate Boon: Ysbaddaden hands over his daughter's hand in marriage, but one of Culhwch's many helpers suddenly rushes forward and kills the evil giant, beheading him. Later that night, Culhwch has his way with Olwen – getting the girl and thus achieving his ultimate boon.

Refusal of the Return: So Culhwch doesn't necessarily refuse to go home once the job's done, but he did refuse to give up on a seemingly hopeless quest that took him years to complete.

Act Three

Magic Flight, or the journey home: A lot of Welsh tales end abruptly, with journeys either being round trips, or they simply skip the bit when they ultimately have to go back home. This tale ends with Culhwch in bed with Olwen, and with Arthur and the others heading home.

Rescue from Without: This happens more than once in '*Culhwch ac Olwen*', but there's always another legendary hero nearby to save the day.

Crossing the Return Threshold: Culhwch goes back to Ysbaddaden's court and goes home with his true love.

Master of Two Worlds: Culhwch returns to his normal life in the end, but a hero, with the girl of his dreams in his arms. The attraction is all, or at least mostly, to do with the curse, but at least he's happy.

Freedom to Live, or a new equilibrium: The hero gets the girl and lives happily ever after.[4]

Like I said, a classic. It'll be interesting to see if I can spot similar narratives in other Welsh tales moving forward. In his book, Joseph Campbell also discusses how different cultures have influenced each other's folklore and traditions over the years. For the Welsh, he reckons that it was the Irish who had the biggest influence over our narratives, even giving us King Arthur. The Irish hero *Cú Chulainn* has a fairly similar adventure to that of Culhwch's, in which an impossible task is presented to him.[5]

But it's not just the Irish who have influenced our stories. Campbell also talks about the 'Wild Women' of Russian folklore, who were often found near bodies of water, would marry local mortal men and leave forever when crossed too many times. They also loved to dance and people would also leave out food for them as peace offerings. Sound familiar?[6]

Mind you, Campbell would turn in his grave if he heard me rambling on about the origins of folktales, for, as he reflects in his book: '… it is never difficult to demonstrate that as science and history, mythology is absurd. When a civilization begins to reinterpret its mythology in this way, the life goes out of it, temples become museums …'[7]

Stuffing the rest of my sandwich into my mouth, I pick up my coat and awkwardly stumble down the grassy mound to the middle of the amphitheatre. I don't recall doing that being so difficult when I was here with my family all those years ago … taking centre stage, I consider Joseph Campbell's theories.

He described mythology as psychology being confused with history and biography. He believed legends to have been heavily inspired by people's dreams and underlying thoughts, passions and fears. Essentially, that myths and folktales are simply representations of our daily struggles, worries, fears and ambitions.

We don't hear or read about good, old-fashioned heroes at all – we are the good, old-fashioned heroes! Gladiators, not spectators. Whether the helmet fits, or not.

11

Where the folk did King Arthur, his sleeping army and the giant caveman go?

Camelot, the Knights of the Round Table, Excalibur, the Holy Grail ... everyone knows about King Arthur. He is the epitome of a legendary hero, a base model for all great kings, leaders and all those knights in shining armour who once protected the Britons from homeland enemies, Saxon invaders and the supernatural forces of the Otherworld.

Most scholars and historians agree that King Arthur probably wasn't a real person. Mind you, there may well have been a rogue warlord around in the fifth or sixth centuries whose life may have inspired the legend. Where the legend hailed from is widely debated, with the Welsh, Cornish and English all laying claim to a Brenin Arthur, Arthur Gernow and a King Arthur, respectively.

Furthermore, numerous locations are rumoured to be his final resting place or former court. Many of them share the same prophecy: that one day, Arthur and his boys will come back from the dead to save us all from a foreign invader.

Geoffrey of Monmouth's *Historia Regum Britanniae* (1138) introduced us to some of the common themes of Arthurian legends. He depicted Arthur as being a British king who faced off against the Saxons. It is in his version of events that we were first introduced to Uther Pendragon, Arthur's dad, whom some later attributed to Merlin. We were also introduced to Arthur's wife, Guinevere (Welsh: Gwenhwyfar) and the legendary sword, Excalibur. Geoff proposed that his final resting place was in Avalon, a legendary island. Whether Geoff came up with the whole thing or that he adapted the character from earlier works or oral narrations is unclear.[1] It was the twelfth-century French writer Chrétien de Troyes who later added Sir Lancelot and the Holy Grail and other things to the mix.

Like I said, there are numerous places claiming to be Arthur's final resting place, where he and an army of slumbering knights wait in a deep sleep, guarding treasure and waiting for the day when they may rise again and take Wales back from her oppressors. One of those places is Dinas Rock (Welsh: Craig y Ddinas), in Waterfall Country, on the edge of the Bannau Brycheiniog National Park.

The area comprises four rivers, which wind their way down through tree-lined gorges over a series of waterfalls before joining up to form the River Neath. Nowhere else in Wales has such a rich diversity of cascades and waterfalls. Dinas Rock itself is a large, rocky outcrop of carboniferous limestone that rises between the Afon Mellte (Afon is Welsh for river) and the Afon Sychryd, on the border between the counties of Powys and Neath Port Talbot. Its name (*dinas*: city) refers to the Iron Age earthworks that sit on its summit.

Several short caves descend into Dinas Rock, including Ogof Pont Sychryd, Ogof Bwa Maen and Will's Hole, the latter also being referred to as 'Arthur's Cave', extending just under 400 metres (1,300 ft) below Dinas Rock. It is down there that legend states King Arthur and his men lie in wait. According to rumour, two men discovered the hidden chamber and were subsequently chased away by the knights. This account is reminiscent of that of Ifor Bach's underground tunnels.[2]

It takes me just under an hour to get there from Cardiff, heading up the A470 before turning up the Heads of the Valleys road. Along the way, I recall the time that my mate and I came walking here and saw a couple furiously going at it on one of the boulders in front of the falls. Not gonna lie, this walk probably won't be as exciting as that!

Following the river, I arrive at Dinas Rock. The formation stands right next to the car park and, as a result, many photos don't do it justice. Arriving early in the morning, with the sun rising behind it, it reminds me of when I visited Uluru in Australia, somehow. The car park's already full and rock-climbing enthusiasts are busy scrambling up to the top.

There are two walking trails leading away from the car park. I take the Sychryd Trail first, a quick, twenty-minute stroll along the river through a narrow, wooded gorge to another rock formation known as *Bwa Maen* and the Sychryd Cascades.

Back at the car park, I somehow manage to twist my ankle walking on the gravel and spend five minutes sitting on Griff's bonnet wondering if I'll be able to do the other walk at all. Luckily, the pain subsides and I head on my way, along the Sgwd yr Eira Trail.

A two-hour hike, there and back, you can either climb up alongside Craig y Ddinas and follow the path along the hillside, or go along the river past the old gunpowder works and what a fellow hiker referred to as 'Looney's Lake', a popular local swimming spot. The trail takes you to the famous Sgwd yr Eira waterfall (translation: Fall of Snow).

Once there, you can climb down a natural path that takes you into an alcove behind a curtain of water. It's a popular spot, and difficult to snap a photo without other people in the frame. It falls into the Afon Hepste, forming a large pool before snaking down what is referred to as 'Devil's Glen'. All manner of supernatural beings are said to inhabit the glen, from ghosts to *Tylwyth Teg*. Indeed, looking down at it from the trail, the place does look like something out of a fantasy film. The path leading through the alcove behind the waterfall was once used by local farmers when moving their sheep and cattle from one side of the river to the other.

A lovely walk, but my search for Arthur's cave doesn't end here. A few days later, I head in the opposite direction and make for Herefordshire. King Arthur's Cave is located at the north-western end of Lord's Wood in The Doward, near Symonds Yat. This limestone cave, which lies about four miles north-east of Monmouth, in the Wye Valley, has a very interesting history, but admittedly lacks any connection to King Arthur, whatsoever. A red herring, but worth a look, nonetheless.

The cave sits on a hillside above the River Wye and consists of a double inter-connected entrance and two main chambers. It is protected as a nature reserve by the Herefordshire Nature Trust. At first, I wasn't sure if it was eligible to be covered, seeing as the border lines are quite blurry in this area and I might be stealing an English tale here, but I decided to come, regardless. The cave has an interesting history and it's located in a beautiful area within the Forest of Dean, with plenty to see around it, including a large Iron Age hillfort.[3]

I manage to go on a long walk past a quarry and down a rocky gorge then through fields of bluebells and back to the car park, missing the cave completely. I find it eventually though, tucked away below a rocky outcrop not a five minutes' walk from the car park. There's a small hillfort sitting at the top, hidden amongst the trees.

Nobody is certain how the cave got its name, but it has long been the focal point of local superstition and urban legends. It has been linked to King Vortigern, or Brenin Gwrtheyrn, in Welsh, and in 1700, the skeleton of a 'giant human' was found here, which was subsequently lost when a local surgeon named Mr Pye took the skeleton with him on a voyage to Jamaica and the ship was never seen again.[4]

Later, in 1871, Reverend (and Sheriff) William S. Symonds (whose name was attributed to the aforementioned Symonds Yat) led an excavation of the cave after he learned that a group of miners had recently raided the small system. They found hyena bones, lion bones, brown bear, red deer, rhinoceros, Irish elk, reindeer and horses, all dating back to the Late Pleistocene period. There was evidence that the bones had been crushed up and, eventually, tools were found, which hints that people used to live there. Either that or it was the giant, of course.

In the years that followed, they unearthed elephant bones, oxen, beavers, badgers, wolves and even mammoths. The cave was then either called 'The Bear's Den' or 'The Lion's Cave'. In the years between archaeological digs, several people set up home there, and a photograph of one such couple can be found on the information board in the car park.[5]

So, I found the cave, but no legendary king and an army of slumbering knights, not that I was holding my breath. But I'm keen to know more about King Arthur's Welsh roots, and for that, I've reached out to an American. Sarah Woodbury hails from Oregon and has written more than forty novels, with over a million books sold to date, all of which are set in medieval Wales and are based on Welsh history and mythology, with much of her own imagination thrown in to form modern works of fiction. Sarah first visited Wales when she went to university, but her Welsh heritage goes way back – she is even a descendant of Welsh royalty.

Sarah fell in love with Wales and has been writing books on our history and mythology ever since. She and her husband also have a YouTube channel named 'Making Sense of Medieval Britain', with over 150 videos all about Welsh history. I got in touch with her because she seems particularly interested in Arthurian legends, and it was a good thing I did, for she certainly has a thing or two to teach me.

'You know Taliesin?' she asks.

'Taliesin? The bard? Yeah, I know of him …'

'Right, so Taliesin is basically Merlin. He isn't called Merlin, but he fits within a lot of the lore. He was writing around the sixth century. To give a sense of the timeline, the Battle of Mount Badon, which was a great victory for King Arthur, was around the year 500. Taliesin was writing shortly after that. His tales of Arthur are very mythological, blending pagan and Christian elements. In one, Arthur leads a group of warriors into the Welsh Otherworld, even though he's Christian. My husband and I are giving a talk next Thursday to a university class and one of the things we will talk about is how he was a Welsh hero that the English stole, very deliberately.'

'We will also discuss the possibility that Arthur was a real person. Several other bards, in addition to Taliesin, wrote about him. One such bard, Aneirin, from the seventh century, writes in reference to one of the warlords at the Battle of Catraeth, that he "fed black ravens on the ramparts of a fortress, though he was no Arthur". Gives me chills!'

Sarah clearly feels very passionately about the subject. I've heard plenty of Welsh people say that King Arthur was theirs first, but most say it with an air of defeat, not with determination to get him back. Mind you, I'm sure the Cornish would disagree. Sarah does a lot of work on 'reclaiming' these tales for Wales, as it were.

Last year she and her husband were in the village of Nefyn in north Wales, where Gerald of Wales, in the twelfth century, claimed to have found some of Merlin's writings. Then, in the thirteenth century, on his forty-fifth birthday, following his conquest of Wales, King Edward I held a tournament there in the spirit of King Arthur. He even had a round table built and gave names from the Arthurian legend to his barons while he played the role of King Arthur. He also went to Llyn Cwm Dulyn, where legend said Arthur's sword Excalibur (or *Caledfwlch*, in Welsh) was found.

'We were looking at the field where Edward held this tournament when a woman walked by and asked what we were doing,' Sarah tells me. 'We told her we were looking at Edward's field, which is known locally as "Cae Edward" to this day. She immediately became irate and said, "We don't want to have anything to do with him around here!" so I asked her *"Da chi'n siarad Cymraeg?"* (Do you speak Welsh?) which she did, and thankfully we were able to rail against Edward in Welsh for five minutes, which seemed to calm her down. Eight hundred years later and she's still mad about this. So although people have forgotten or may not know about a lot of these old legends, there is still a strong energy and passion present about events that have happened in the past.'

Sarah then asked me if I speak Welsh, and we continued the rest of our conversation in my native tongue – though I'll tell you about it in English here. She said that most of her readers don't speak Welsh, but that she's finding new readers with a Welsh background every year, many of them drawn to her series, *The Welsh Guard Mysteries*, which are set in Caernarfon Castle.

I learned a lot speaking with Sarah, and as is becoming standard practice with my interviewees, I invited her for a pint if she's ever in Wales again. 'Okay thanks, will do.'

Reflecting on her words, I consider my earlier dilemma concerning King Arthur's Cave. I was so preoccupied with the border between England and Wales that I wasn't sure going there would 'count' if focusing on Welsh folklore. Now I'm thinking the Cornish would say it doesn't matter which side of the border the cave is, because King Arthur is theirs, in any case. And yet, a lot of the lore we attribute to him derives from the imagination of a Frenchman, which makes me consider his popularity outside Britain and how people who might not have ever been to this country hold his tales dear.

While the possibility of Arthur being based on a real person is truly fascinating, all this makes me think of some of Joseph Campbell's theories and I ask myself: should we be treating these tales as someone's biography at all? If myths and legends are representations of any given individual's hopes and fears, does it matter what King Arthur's nationality was, or who came up with him, rather? Would finding out who he really was do anything to discredit his importance to all these different nationalities?

Perhaps, instead, we should consider what he represents. The flawed leader from the earlier myths suggests, to me, that a person can do great things but is still a human being after all, and the squeaky-clean Superman from the later tales – perhaps that is the person we are all striving to become …

12

Where the folk
did all the Welsh gods go?

I'm sitting in a semi-circle of chairs in a church hall. Of course I am. The other five handpicked unique individuals selected to take part in this course for people with health anxiety are taking advantage of the free tea and biscuits as we wait for the trainers, or mentors, whatever they are, to come back from their break.

Gemma is telling us all about her wedding plans: 'Both my partner and I grew up attending Welsh primary schools so the Welsh traditional tales were a big part of our childhood. I'm now a teacher myself and I use some of these traditional stories with my class.'

I'm listening … 'We've covered stories like Blodeuwedd and the story of Branwen and Bendigeidfran. We have also taught other Welsh legends such as Cantre'r Gwaelod. The children have loved hearing and retelling these Welsh stories. It's important for us to celebrate our Welsh heritage and that's why we chose traditional Welsh tales to be included in our wedding day. We used this as inspiration for our wedding and named the tables after characters from the *Mabinogion*. Each table will also be accompanied by a little information card explaining to our guests who each character is.'

I, of course, find this all very interesting, and I don't normally find wedding plans very interesting at all. It also reminds me that I haven't talked about the *Mabinogi* yet. Well, not the four main branches, anyway.

Our teacher-trainer puts down his takeaway coffee cup (he never touches the free stuff given to us for some reason) and resumes the session: 'Alright guys, settle down. Thanks for being back on time. Now, before the break we talked about our vicious flowers and how we can pick away at those petals. For the second half, I would like to talk about mindfulness. You each have a bottle of essential oil in front of you. Without opening your eyes or revealing what the scent is, please, take a moment to really take in their essence and tell me, what can you smell?

'Mine kind of smells like Vicks.'

'Mine smells a bit like those lemon and honey Strepsils you can get.'

'Can anyone smell anything that isn't associated with medical products?'

A prolonged silence, then our mentor-teacher says, with a sigh: 'That's alright, you can open your eyes.'

The tales of the *Mabinogi* derive from the Matter of Britain, a collection of medieval literature and oral legends associated with Brittany and the UK which featured many legendary figures, including King Arthur. They were written in Middle Welsh between the twelfth and thirteenth centuries, but the stories derived from old oral tales that had already been passed down by generations of storytellers before then. There are two main manuscripts, the *White Book of Rhydderch*, dated *c.*1350 and the *Red Book of Hergest*, dated between 1382 and *c.*1410.

They cover eleven stories in total, the order of which differs with each translation. Each tale is so different that some earlier scholars argued that they are not a 'collection' at all. You've got drama, philosophy, romance, tragedy, fantasy, comedy and political spoof all in, well, two books.

The tales reverted to their oral roots following their first publication and it was not until 1795, 1821 and 1829 that they appeared in print again as English translations by William Owen Pughe. It was Lady Charlotte Guest, between 1838 and 1845, who first published the entire collection in a single book (bilingually, in both English and Welsh) and those soppy Victorians lapped it right up. The book was quickly translated into French, then German, and a newfound interest in Celtic literature swept across the globe.

Now, you may have noticed that, so far, I refer to these tales as the *Mabinogi* and yet, whenever I mention Lady Charlotte Guest, I call them the *Mabinogion*. The correct term has been widely debated for many years.

From the eighteenth century right up to the 1970s, most scholars thought of them simply as pre-Christian tales from Celtic mythology. However, in recent times, they are believed to be far more complicated than that, more of a combination of those Celtic tales and Anglo-French narratives, teeming with political undertones. Basically, old Celtic tales re-written to suit the social, political and religious environment of the time. We love reinventing the *Mabinogi* in today's popular culture, but I never knew that even the very first edition was a 'modernised' version.[1]

In order to learn more about the origins of the *Mabinogi*, Peter Stevenson has arranged for me to speak with his friend David Moore, a historian and an archivist at the National Library of Wales in Aberystwyth who also writes a blog on the *Mabinogi*.

'So let's talk about the *White Book of Rhydderch* and the *Red Book of Hergest*. That's when the *Mabinogi* were first put into text, am I right?'

'Right.' David nods, then hesitates. 'Well, as far as we know. We don't know much about what earlier versions there might have been. But these earliest surviving manuscript versions date back to the thirteenth and fourteenth centuries – they're the earliest we know of.'

'And which one do you keep at the library?'

'That would be the *White Book of Rhydderch*. The *Red Book of Hergest* is kept at the Bodleian Library at Oxford.'

'Are the public allowed access to the *White Book of Rhydderch* to see it for themselves?'

'Yes,' he says, then hesitates again. 'Well … we have digital versions online that anyone can access, but actually seeing the actual manuscript? Virtually no one is allowed to see that, for conservation reasons. Even top professors would need to have a pretty good reason to see it, like if there was something they could learn only by looking at the manuscript itself and there was no other way around it.'

I've got mixed feelings about this. On the one hand, it's a travesty that such an important manuscript is kept hidden away from … hold up – I just remembered the time we went to a museum in sixth form, and Gwyn, when the curator's back was turned, pretended to pocket a valuable artefact that they had brought out of the archives for us all to see – nah, it's definitely a good thing that they do this. 'So how many times in your career, would you say, that someone's actually been allowed to see it?'

'Well, there would only have been the conservationists when they digitised it to be put onto the website. They would have taken it apart then put it back together again after taking photos. Obviously some of the digitisation staff would have handled the manuscript as well. They are the only people I know of who have handled the manuscript during my time there.'

I'm keen to know more about where these manuscripts came from in the first place. David says that the *White Book of Rhydderch* was originally written in south-west Wales and that both would have been kept at various monasteries and stately homes for centuries. In the seventeenth century, the *White Book* was owned by the antiquarian Robert Vaughan, who kept it at his house at Hengwrt, near Dolgellau, and the *Red Book* is associated with a house on the border between Radnorshire and Herefordshire. But they would have been moved around a lot between places like this for quite some time.

'What about the origins of the name "*Mabinogi*" then, what's your understanding of that?'

'Well, at the end of three of the four "Branches" that are considered to form the main bulk of the *Mabinogi*, it says, "… and so ends this branch of the *Mabinogi*". But at the end of the other one, it says "the *Mabinogion*". Now, this is actually very important. Most Welsh people refer to them as the *Mabinogion*, but many Welsh speakers will argue that *Mabinogi* is, in fact, the correct term. Most think of "*Mabinogion*" as the coined term of Lady Charlotte Guest.'

'But "*Mabinogion*" is actually in the original texts?'

'It is. Then over the years, most people went for the term "*Mabinogion*". But there is a theory that the word refers to youthful deeds, maybe of the hero Pryderi. Another interpretation is that it means "stories for young boys", so who knows.'

Hmm. I think I'll stick with '*Mabinogi*'. David tells me his theories about the narrative structure of the *Mabinogi*. As he read them, it became clear to him that the stories were originally meant to be performed, not read. They are very repetitive, there's a heavy use of dialogue and there are segments that come across almost as a stand-up routine.

'Is this something you think people miss out on when they read the English version?'

'Absolutely. You do get some sense of it, but you also get something very different.'

I've got to be honest, I've never read the Welsh version nor heard an oral telling of one of the tales, and after my conversation with David, I can't help but feel that I've cheated myself out of something very special.

While the majority of the tales don't follow a single narrative as such, there are four that do, kind of. These are called the Four Branches of the *Mabinogi*. Essentially, although each tale focuses on different characters in different locations, the four 'branches' span the lifetime of Pryderi, from his birth in the first branch to his death in the fourth. He doesn't feature heavily in the second or fourth branches, but he is certainly the main force behind the narrative of the first.

Sometimes called 'The Story of Pwyll, Prince of Dyfed', it tells of Pryderi's somewhat troubled childhood and the circumstances leading to his birth. His father, Pwyll, rules over the west, Pembrokeshire way. One day, he decides to take his dogs hunting at Glyn Cuch (Cwmcych) but becomes separated from the pack. Instead, he stumbles upon another pack of hounds; white ones with pointy red ears. They are hunting down a stag, which Pwyll claims for his own and uses to feed his hunting dogs after driving away the mysterious hounds.

A man on horseback approaches and accuses him of stealing his kill. Turns out, he's only King Arawn, ruler of Annwn. Those spooky hounds, the Cŵn Annwn, were his own. In order to repay him, Pwyll agrees to kill Arawn's troublesome neighbour in the Otherworld, Hafgan, who can only be killed if he is hit with a single blow. The two men switch bodies (as you do) and agree to meet a year to the day, when Pwyll was to carry out the deed. And so they switched lives for a while, with Pwyll sleeping with his back to Arawn's beautiful wife so as not to be tempted by her, which must have really messed with her head.

When the day came, an injured Hafgan begged him to put him out of his misery, but Arawn had warned Pwyll not to do so, for if he wasn't killed in the first blow, then he would never die. Pwyll took control of Hafgan's kingdom and men and returned to Arawn with the news. An impressed Arawn switched back their bodies and resumed his leadership. He thought he could celebrate with a night of sweet, sweet lovemaking, but his enraged wife wanted to know what happened for the last twelve months and an argument ensued. He tells her the truth and the pair seem equally impressed with Pwyll's loyalty and respect.

Meanwhile, Pwyll finds that Arawn has ruled his own kingdom well in his absence. From then on, the two become quite good friends and Arawn sets him up with a date. He tells his new BFF that if he would sit on top of a certain hill, something wonderful would happen. Pwyll took his word and went to sit at Gorserdd Arberth, where he saw the most beautiful maiden he had ever seen, sporting a golden dress and riding over the ancestral mound on a white horse. But she's too fast, and he loses her.

He goes there again the next day, even sending his men after her, but again, she gets away. On the third attempt, he calls after her as he rides away, and she stops and turns to him. She introduces herself as Rhiannon and tells him that she is to be married against her will in a year's time to a man named Gwawl, at her father Hyfaidd Hen's insistence.

But the two are besotted, so Pwyll puts a plan together. A year later, he makes a deal with Gwawl that would give Gwawl permission to sleep with Rhiannon, who wasn't too impressed. However, Pwyll tricks Gwawl into stepping inside a sack for a little game of 'Badger in the Bag', upon which Pwyll and his mates trap him inside and beat the living daylights out of him. Then Pwyll and Rhiannon spend the night together instead.

They enjoy three wonderful years of marriage, with Rhiannon giving birth to a son, whom they name Pryderi. One night, she goes to bed and leaves young Pryderi in the care of the servants, who doze off on the job. When they wake up, they find that the boy is gone. Panicking, fearing for their lives, they smear a sleeping Rhiannon in puppy blood and frame her for murder. As punishment, Rhiannon is made to carry guests at their court on her back, like a horse, whilst explaining her crime to them.

Meanwhile, Teyrnon Twrf Liant rules over Gwent Is Coed. He owns a horse who gives birth to a foal each year, but each year, the foal vanishes. And so, one day, he decides to guard the horse as it gives birth. A monster with a 'giant claw' attacks the stables and Teyrnon injures it. Fleeing, it drops a human child as it vanishes into the woods.

Teyrnon and his wife raise the child as their own, naming him Gwri Wallt Euryn, or Gwri of the Golden Hair. He grows into a fine young man, looking more and more like his father with each passing year. When Teyrnon and his wife hear the news of Pwyll and Rhiannon's missing son, however, they realise who the boy really is and return him to his parents, freeing Rhiannon from her sentence. The story ends with a good-ol' knees-up at Pwyll's court.[2]

You may have heard of Rhiannon before – the Welsh goddess was Stevie Nicks's muse for her song 'Rhiannon', released in 1975. Some say that she was inspired after reading the 1972 novel *Triad: A Novel of the Supernatural* by Mary Bartlet Leader, which tells of a character named Branwen who is possessed by a witch named Rhiannon. Nicks often introduced the song on stage by saying 'This is a song about an old Welsh witch.' So although she was inspired by Rhiannon, she got the wrong end of the stick. Only after writing the song did she learn that Rhiannon was in fact a Welsh goddess known to have been beautiful, clever, politically strategic and well known for her generosity.

She is thought to have derived from an earlier Celtic deity, her name stemming from the Brittonic name *Rīgantonā*, which comes from the word *rīgan*, meaning 'queen'. Many compare her to the Gaulish horse goddess Epona, often depicted riding a horse. Nicks was further astonished that her lyrics mirrored the Rhiannon of Welsh legend. She began researching the *Mabinogi*, which gave rise to several other songs, including 'Stay Away', 'Maker of Birds' and 'Angel'.[3]

Rhiannon also features heavily in the Third Branch of the *Mabinogi*, but her trio of faithful, mystical birds, Adar Rhiannon (the Birds of Rhiannon) also make an appearance in the Second Branch, as well as in the Triads of Britain and in the story of 'How Culhwch Won Olwen'. Those mysterious birds were said to have had the power to wake the dead and lull the living to sleep.

In any case, I quickly discovered that I had opened Pandora's Box by looking into locations associated with the *Mabinogi*. There are lots of locations featured in these tales, all over Wales and the world, in fact. Most of the First Branch is based in the old kingdom of Dyfed, down Pembrokeshire way. However, there is one place nearby that I could go to: Nant Teyrnon, the spot where Teyrnon Twrf Liant fought off the monster with the 'giant claw' and found the missing Pryderi.

The *cantref* (division of land) of Is Coed was an important kingdom at the time and included the fortress of Caerleon as well as Caerwent, capital of the Silures tribe. The Teyrnon Valley itself is found near Cwmbran and it's where you can find Llantarnam Abbey.[4]

It's a beautiful place, I'm sure, but I'll be honest, my mind is elsewhere today, because tonight, for the first time in ages, I'm going out! We're limited to groups of six, mind, and there shall be no dancing and it's table-service only, which I'm perfectly fine with. It's my friend's birthday and I'm meeting some of our mutual pals for a pre-drink at The Claude before catching up with the others on Womanby Street for the main event.

When I get there, I learn that one of the group has cancelled and that a girl called Sophie is coming instead. 'You'll like her, I think.'

Time passes and we sit apart for a while, then one of the boys gets up to go to the toilet and we are left facing each other with no one in between. It feels weird being out again after God knows how long. My head is a bit spacey, and each interaction is almost dream-like.

'Hi!' she says with a friendly smile.

She has the best curls I have ever seen. 'Alright?'

'You don't sound like you're from around here … what brought you to Cardiff?' she asks.

'Came for uni, stayed for the bigger gene pool … I'm from up north, from Snowdonia.'

'I came here for my undergraduate degree back in 2009, studied French and Spanish at Cardiff Uni, and … well, I never really left!'

Sophie refers to herself as 'honorary Welsh' now, having fallen in love with the people and the culture. As a musician, she also loves the music scene in Cardiff. 'You'll have to come see me play one day!'

'I will.'

My friend comes back from the toilet and we jump back into the group discussion. Sophie doesn't join us on the night out and we pass her by in the taxi on the way to town. I'm left wondering if I'll ever bump into her again. Ah, what am I on about? I'll just track her down on Facebook tomorrow.

The next morning, I wake up with a terrible hangover. Groaning,

I reach out for my phone and spend the best part of the morning mindlessly scrolling, pausing now and then to screenshot funny memes. Then I go to check my email and my hangover magically vanishes. I sit upright in bed, heart racing as I read the words over and over again. 'No way!'

I'm going to be published! With the blog having gained momentum, I emailed a few publishers a while back in the hope of turning *Where the Folk* into a book, and someone's actually said 'yes'! But they want me to cover all of Wales... I need to crack on with my research, I need to go further afield, I need more interviews, more ... more ... oh, my head ... the hangover's back. Maybe I'll sleep this off for a couple of days first (I need more than a day as of late), but then I had better start packing – I have an adventure to go on!

Crossing the Threshold:
The Western Coasts

13

Where the folk
did everyone go?

Digging around in the depths of my drawers one evening, I chance upon a single piece of paper, sitting all crumpled up and alone between a pile of bank statements and some old receipts. Why do I keep these things? Picking it up, I realise that it's the list of contacts I made when attending a life and travel writing course at Tŷ Newydd way back in 2013.

Run by Literature Wales, Tŷ Newydd is the National Writing Centre of Wales. It's an old manor house in the countryside up at Llanystumdwy. There, budding authors can spend time strolling the grounds for inspiration. Then, in the evening, they drink red wine in the lounge and read out their stories and poems to their groups. My girlfriend at the time's stepmother, Helen, had paid for it as a Christmas present.

In any case, I had taken everyone's email addresses when I left, then hadn't looked at them for some eight years. I decide to send an email out and, in no time at all, my old friend Angela Brushett gets back to me. Back in 2013, Angela sorted me out with an internship with the *Herald Sun* in Melbourne. I was about to go travelling anyway and she knew the chief of staff there – next thing you know, a young Welshman with a mullet that no one knew anything about casually strolls into the office of Australia's biggest-selling newspaper one morning and takes over the vox pop.

It'll be nice to speak with her again. Mind you, she takes some coaxing: Angela suspects that I might be a fraudster and asks that I send her photos of my ID as well as some information that only she and I would know before we arrange any Zoom calls.

We spend the first few minutes of our chat catching up, with Angela telling me all about her dodgy knee and complaining about the state of the NHS, then the conversation shifts to folklore: 'So you studied Arthurian legends in uni, did you?'

'Oh yes, yes. Of course, I had known the legends of Arthur as a child, but that was the Arthur everyone knows. I had no idea of his Welsh roots until then. I grew up in colonial Africa, which of course was very different to over here. Now, Wales, for me at the time, was a strange land whose people spoke a language that I did not understand. It was a land of superstition that still held the beauty of the past.'

'And being English yourself, do you see any differences in attitudes between the English and the Welsh when it comes to folktales?'

'Oh, yes, absolutely, yes. Now, I used to teach in an all-girl grammar school in Caernarfon. This was in the 1960s. One thing I noticed is how those girls truly owned their language, how they owned their stories, owned their culture. They're very proud of their heritage up there.'

The conversation turns to Welsh choirs and Angela's old university days for a while, then she exclaims, 'Oh! This might be a good one for your folklore-thingy – a lot of old Welsh tales are told through song – now remember, until very recently in historical terms, most people weren't able to read, so this is how these stories were kept alive. They are meant to be heard.'

'And how important is it to keep these legends alive, do you think?'

'Very important. They represent our past, our personas, everything! It's how it still works in a lot of places in Africa today. Children need to learn about life and this is done through songs, through nursery rhymes. Melodies are memorable, so folktales still serve a purpose in today's world. You know, Mandela wrote a book on African folklore when he was in prison, it's worth a look.'

Speaking with Angela was not only nostalgic but also reminded me of two things: that folktales aren't some endangered species in need of human intervention, they are still very much a big part of our lives. Also, that these stories are always changing, always adapting to a new society.

Several months have passed since I received that fateful email about the book. It is now springtime 2022 and lockdown restrictions have eased to the extent that everything feels almost normal again. Indeed, in stark contrast to the last couple of years, life suddenly feels very hectic – my resolution this time around is actually to go out less.

Sophie and I did meet up afterwards, you see, and we became official pretty swiftly after our first date. Sophie's a socialite and time has absolutely flown by ever since. I feel like I'm in university again, only this time the hangovers are terminal.

Sophie will join me on the first leg. The plan is to begin my journey on the western coasts, using a rented cottage as a base, then stopping at a couple of campsites when we move on. Sadly, Sophie can't be with me for the second leg of the trip due to work commitments, so I shall have to complete my journey up north, my home turf, on my own.

'Did you lock the door?' she asks.

'Oh, why would you ask me that? You know I've got to check now!'

Dad always drummed it into me to check over the car before long journeys, so I was sure to check the tyre pressure and the water, oil and screen-wash levels this morning while Sophie put together a little packed lunch for us. She's a foodie and a feeder – happy days! 'Did you tell Gwyn everything he needs to know about Loki?'

Loki. My sweet, demonic black cat. I had assured Gwyn that he was a *hogyn da* and had left it at that, completely neglecting to remind him to keep him away from water and not to feed him after midnight. 'I did. He'll be fine, babes.'

'Alright.' She gets into the car and shuts the door.

'Pick a CD – we've got a long journey ahead of us!'

Now, a 'long journey' is relative and for most Welsh people, or Brits in general, you take a sandwich or some sweets with you for anything that takes over an hour. It takes us just under two hours to get to our first stop, being the town of Narberth. That's the good thing about Wales – you don't have to travel very far to get places. You can't.

We're here for the Third Branch of the *Mabinogi*. I know, I know – I've jumped ahead a little here – but you shouldn't get too confused. The Second Branch takes place after the First, of course, with young Pryderi appearing in it briefly, fighting alongside his best mate Manawydan in a war against the Irish, but the main story focuses on other characters and his presence is nothing more than a cameo.

In the Third Branch, being the story of '*Manawydan fab Llŷr*', the story shifts back to Pryderi and his family. In it, we return to Dyfed, where Sophie and I now stand, for a direct sequel to the Second Branch. It begins with Pryderi and Manawydan having just got back from the war.

Pryderi's mate Manawydan, now the rightful king of Britain following the death of his brother Bendigeidfran, the giant king who led the Welsh into battle in the Second Branch, honours his brother's final request by burying his head at the spot where the Tower of London now stands, facing France so as to ward off foreign invaders. With no family of his own left, Manawydan comes to Dyfed to stay with Pryderi, Pryderi's mum Rhiannon, and Pryderi's wife Cigfa.

Rhiannon is now a widow and it isn't long before she and Manawydan get a bit frisky together, but Pryderi's surprisingly cool with his best friend marrying his mum. Soon after, Pryderi heads over to Kent to pay homage to the usurper Caswallon, who defended Britain against Julius Caesar. Not long after that, a strange mist descends over Dyfed and every human and domestic animal vanishes, apart from our four main characters, that is.

Struggling to survive in this new, desolate landscape, Pryderi and Manawydan decide to go to England to look for work (one of the places mentioned is Hereford), but they keep having to pack up and move whenever the local men eventually get jealous of their extraordinary handicraft (saddlemaking, shieldmaking, shoemaking; whatever craft they pick up, they are always the best at it). After being driven out of three towns for this reason, the pair return to Dyfed.

They decide to hunt to survive instead. One day, they come across a white boar. Chasing after it, they stumble upon a fortress that they had never seen before. Manawydan is wary, but Pryderi ignores his friend's advice and enters the castle, where he finds a beautiful golden bowl. As soon as he touches it, he loses the ability to speak and his feet freeze to the ground. Manawydan, waiting outside, figures something is wrong and races home to inform the girls.

Rhiannon is not impressed that her husband didn't enter the fortress to look for her son and decides to go look for him herself. Once there, she suffers the same fate as Pryderi and then they, along with the mysterious castle, vanish into thin air.

Cigfa weeps for her husband, but Manawydan is also quick to, ah … comfort her, shall we say. The two flee to England, but again return to Dyfed when people get jealous of their craftsmanship. They decide to grow crops of wheat over three fields, but they keep getting destroyed by plagues of mice. One night, Manawydan waits for the mice to appear and manages to catch one, which he decides to keep so as to hang from the neck. I know, I know.

Over the next three days, a scholar, a priest and a bishop all pay him a visit, each one pleading with him to spare the mouse's life. Poor thing is on death row! He declines each time, but keeps the mouse alive. On the third day, it is revealed that all three visitors were the same man all along and that the mouse was in fact the guy's pregnant wife. His name is Llwyd ap Cil Coed and he is the one behind all the strange goings-on in Dyfed. It was all payback for the fate suffered by his friend Gwawl at the hands of Pryderi's father, Pwyll, in the First Branch. Remember 'Badger in the Bag'?

Manawydan spares her life in exchange for Pryderi and Rhiannon's safe return, and the powerful spell cast over Dyfed is lifted and life goes back to normal again.[1]

I dare say that 'Manawydan fab Llŷr' is the lesser known of the four branches of the *Mabinogi*. Along with the story of 'Culhwch and Olwen', the other three branches definitely get more screen time.

I've been to Narberth before, when I stayed in a holiday cottage for the week with my family. I remember there being a town square up on the hill, not unlike Llantrisant. 'So have you come across many Welsh legends since living over here, then?' I ask Sophie as we make our way down the high street towards the castle.

'Not so much. The first time I really heard of any of them was when I was living with a first-language Welsh speaker who told me all about the *Mabinogi*. A hundred per cent, more should be done to promote them. Maybe they should teach them in the curriculum?'

You can find several art galleries in Narberth (or Arberth, in Welsh), as well as numerous independent shops, pubs and cafes. Mind you, it's quiet here today because it's a Sunday, but it's a popular tourist destination and a great base for exploring the surrounding area.

Dominating the high street is Narberth Town Hall, where the leaders of the infamous Rebecca Riots, which took place between 1839 and 1843, were held prisoner. That was when farmers in west and mid Wales attacked tollgates in response to high taxation, often dressed as women. You can still visit the cell today.[2]

The town was founded around an old Welsh court but was later invaded by the Normans. Could the old Welsh court have been the one occupied by Pryderi and his family, perhaps? Climbing up a grassy mound beyond the town hall, we are suddenly confronted with Narberth Castle, now but a ruin.

Indeed, Narberth Castle isn't one of those castles that dominates an entire town and you can easily miss it altogether unless you are looking for it. Oliver Cromwell held it during the English Civil War then it fell out of use thereafter, becoming the victim of looting and neglect, like so many castles after that fateful war. When it reopened to the public in 2005, the story of 'Culhwch and Olwen' was adapted into a children's play and was performed here as a celebration.[3]

The castle is actually mentioned in the First Branch of the *Mabinogi*; it's the castle in which Rhiannon must carry guests upon her back after Pwyll blames her for Pryderi's disappearance. However, more interestingly, for me, at least, just outside town sits Camp Hill, the site of an old Iron Age hillfort. That hillfort is rumoured to have been the location of Gorsedd Arberth, the hill atop of which Pwyll first met Rhiannon after she managed to slip his grasp over a period of three days. It is also where Manawydan rescued Pryderi and his mum in the Third Branch. Well, there are those who speculate that it could actually have been one of a handful of other possible sites, but Camp Hill is considered the most probable.

It is often considered a sacred site, a tear in the rift between our world and Annwn, as it were, and frequently catches people's imagination. It featured in the 1995 four-issue comic book series *Indiana Jones and the Spear of Destiny*, which involved Indy getting a flat tyre in rural Wales and taking a nap up on the hill, where he sees the vision of a mysterious blonde woman (Rhiannon).[4]

After grabbing a bite to eat in one of the local pubs, we head back to the car in search of this mysterious hillfort. Now, Indiana Jones and the Nazis might have been able to find it, but we drive around the hillsides surrounding Narberth for ages to no avail. I have read other people's blogs on the place and a few people seem to be equally as confused as to where it is. In any case, it's on private land, apparently. Maybe I need to get a drone.

Oh, well. Losing daylight, we head to the big Tesco in Haverfordwest to buy some supplies – which end up mainly consisting of large quantities of wine, beer and gin – and then we make our way to Ambleston, hoping it will be easier to find than the elusive Gorsedd Arberth.

14

Where the folk
can I find a beautiful princess and the ghost of a killer ape?

'Oh, it's lovely!'

'Not looking forward to climbing down that thing when I'm drunk, mind.' I point to the ladder heading up to the bedroom.

It is indeed a lovely cottage. It is also perfectly located for exploring Pembrokeshire, being smack-bang in the middle of everything. Ambleston (Welsh: Treamlod) lies seven miles north of Haverfordwest and can be found somewhere inside a maze of tall hedges and narrow country lanes where the Google Maps driver dare not venture. The name means 'Amlot's farm', Amlot being a Norman-French name.[1] Indeed, those French invaders left their mark big time in this part of Wales.

An old road called the Landsker Line can be found to the north of Ambleston, which takes you to St Davids. The Landsker Line also marks the northern frontier of 'Little England beyond Wales'.

When I say 'Little England beyond Wales', I am referring to an area that spans from south Pembrokeshire to south-west Carmarthenshire that has been a predominantly English-speaking region for many centuries, despite being miles away from the English border. The place earned its nickname way back in the sixteenth century, when the English antiquarian William Camden called it *Anglia Transwalliana*.[2] The place is called this because it has seen more Saxon, Irish, Norse, Norman and Flemish settlements than anywhere else in Wales, and each occupant made damn sure to distinguish themselves from the rest of us peasants.

However, it would seem that it is becoming something of a despised nickname, for some, at least. Earlier this year, an ice-cream maker named Upton Farm, based at Pembroke Dock, got into trouble for putting 'Made for you in Little England beyond Wales' on their packaging, which sparked a public outcry. The company has since agreed to replace it with 'messaging that more clearly celebrates our Welshness'.[3]

'Bet you feel right at home over here, eh Soph?'

'Shut up!'

After unpacking our things, we crack open a beer and sit down with all our acquired leaflets. There is a lot to see and do in Pembrokeshire and I soon realise that there are other places we could go that might be more interesting than what I've got lined up. Then two words in particular grab my attention: 'killer' and 'ape'.

'Oh wow, we have got to go here!'

'Where's that?'

Carew Castle. It has been the site of many paranormal investigations over the years and is believed to be haunted by several ghosts, including that of a Celtic warrior, a mischievous young kitchen boy and a beautiful princess. It is also home to the ghost of a Barbary ape who, in life, killed his owner one dark, stormy night …

The story goes that Sir Rowland Rees, tenant of the castle in the seventeenth century and by all accounts a total bastard, brought the injured ape to Wales from the Barbary Coast, having rescued it from a shipwrecked Spanish galleon. Over time, he trained it to obey his every command using a series of whistles.

One day, Sir Rowland's son ran off with the daughter of a local merchant named Horwitz. Sir Rowland wasn't very happy about it and that night, with thunder clapping outside, the ape grew restless, sensing Sir Rowland's vile mood. Then Horwitz came knocking at the door. An argument ensued and Rowland, in his rage, released the ape from its chains and set him on Horwitz.

Horwitz somehow managed to fight the ape off and escape, albeit badly injured. As the castle's servants attended to his wounds, he cursed Sir Rowland, wishing evil upon him. As he did so, they heard terrible screams coming from upstairs. The servants, too scared of their vile boss, dared not go up to check on him. Either that or they all sat there with their fingers crossed!

In the morning, they entered the deathly silent room and found Sir Rowland's body, lying in a pool of his own blood. The ape was nowhere to be seen. In the years that followed, however, numerous people have reported hearing howling noises and angry shrieks coming from the tower, always on stormy nights. Or it might have just been the wind.

That beautiful princess I mentioned is Princess Nest. Much like the Barbary ape, numerous residents of Carew have come across this 'White Lady of Carew Castle' over the years. But unlike the Barbary ape and more akin to the Green Lady of Caerphilly Castle, Nest is said to be a friendly ghost.

In life, she was the daughter of Rhys ap Tewdwr, the king of Deheubarth. At the time, she was considered to be the most beautiful woman in all of Wales and a great host. At the end of the eleventh century, she spent some time with Henry I down in London and the two fell in love and had a son. To avoid the embarrassment of having to tell his court, however, Henry sent her packing to Carew Castle, where she was to marry the constable, a Norman knight by the name of Gerald de Windsor. Naturally, she wasn't very happy about it, so Henry sweetened the deal by allowing her to take her servant with her, being her best mate from childhood, the Welsh-speaking Branwen.

As it turned out, Gerald wasn't all that bad, to be fair. A regular Prince Charming, he was admired by all who knew him and was a bit reluctant about it all himself, for he was still mourning the death of his mistress. They got married and, as the years went by, they grew to love each other and had at least five children.

But Nest had a few secret admirers herself, one of whom was her cousin Owain, whom she had met once at a banquet. Owain wasn't going to hang around; he laid siege to Carew Castle one night and took her for his own. Gerald and the kids escaped through the sewers. Mind you, reports suggest that she hardly put up a fight.

Regardless, she was held 'prisoner' at Cilgerran Castle for six years and had at least two children with Owain. Then, one day, Prince Charming came back for her. In a dramatic showdown, Gerald killed

Owain and took Nest back to Carew. Unfortunately for him, he himself died just a year later.

However, someone like Nest doesn't sit on the shelf for long. In the end, she married Stephen, castellan of Cardigan Castle, and gave birth to a son just a year later. But this is no happy-ever-after; Nest died shortly after giving birth and her spirit returned to Carew Castle, her true home, much like the Green Lady of Caerphilly returned to hers.[4]

'What do you make of Princess Nest, then?'

'She kept herself busy, didn't she? I won't pass judgement though – I didn't know the girl!'

I simply couldn't give this place a miss, so the following morning, we head down to Carew to see the place for ourselves. When we get there, we learn that the castle looks out over a tidal estuary. The structure you see there today would not have been the same one Princess Nest would have called home, mind. It was originally the site of an Iron Age fort, then her old fella Gerald built a stone keep here in 1100. It was their son, William de Carew, who later built the outer stone walls and the great hall.

The place changed hands a few times after that. Falling on hard times following the Black Death, the de Carews mortgaged the castle out to Rhys ap Thomas, a made man after he decided to side with Henry Tudor at the Battle of Bosworth. He pimped the place up with luxurious apartments and some fancy decor, only for it to fall back into the hands of the de Carew family in 1607.

Then, even though most of Pembrokeshire supported the Parliamentarians when the Civil War came, the castle was refortified and put into proper military use by the Royalists. After that, as we have seen with other castles, it was purposefully rendered useless, with the south wall being pulled down.

It then fell back into the hands of the de Carew family until 1686. Eventually – this is all getting pretty familiar now – the place was abandoned, looted and left to rot. It wasn't until 1984 that Cadw stepped in (Cadw, a Welsh word meaning 'to keep' or 'to protect', is the Welsh Government's historic environment service) and, with the help of the Pembrokeshire National Park Authority, turned it into the museum and tourist attraction that it is today.[5]

We enjoy a tea and a scone at the cafe on our way in, then take the obligatory route through the gift shop to buy our tickets. We head through a small garden and take photos of ourselves sitting on a giant deckchair before heading to the castle grounds. Along the way, I spot an unusual-looking wooden sculpture of a very friendly looking giant.

'What's this?' I lead Sophie over to the first of many information boards. 'The story of Skomar Oddy ... who?'

I consult Google. According to legend, at one point, the whole world was green and fresh and Wales was inhabited by giants and other magnificent beasts. One day, two sea monsters had a falling out and a fight broke out. They ended up rolling about in shallow water, churning up mud that splattered all over the homes of the villagers.

It also stirred up the local Merpeople. Then the villagers stumbled upon a small creature trapped in the roots of a tree. He said that only Skomar Oddy would know what to do. And so, the local headman led a band of monsters and oddballs on a series of adventures in search of this elusive giant. Eventually, an elf led them to the cave where Skomar Oddy lived. He was the biggest living thing they had ever laid eyes on, big enough to pick up one of the duelling sea creatures with one hand.

They woke him up by singing 'Skomar Oddy! Skomar Oddy! Big head and big body! Help us, help us! Help us, help us! Get the mud back in the sea.'

Skomar Oddy awoke and agreed to help them. All the weird and wonderful creatures clung onto his body with their tentacles and whatnot and off they went to sort out the two sea monsters. Weeks of travel took Skomar Oddy just six strides; they were there in no time. He released all the creatures that were trapped in the mud then turned his attention to the sea monsters. The mere sight of him sent the pair fleeing back into the depths, never to be seen again. And so, Skomar Oddy returned to his cave where he still sleeps today, waking every one hundred years for a bite to eat.[6]

Unicorns, elves ... it's unlike any Welsh legend I've ever heard. I'm intrigued, but can't find much on the origins of the tale online. Then I remember when I spoke with Peter Stevenson about the folktales of Pembrokeshire a few months back, he told me that practically all our stories are tied in to the landscape and the people, and every area in

Wales is different. People move about and they take their stories with them and they grow roots in a new landscape.

The stories from Pembrokeshire, he reckoned, are particularly interesting and quite unique: 'I think it's because you have a coming together of peoples in the south-west; you have the "mountain people" in the north of the county, traditionally Welsh-speaking, then down south you've something completely different ... there was a huge mix of people migrating between Ireland and Pembrokeshire.'

We head into the castle, stopping for one more silly photo opportunity on the way in (mounting a wooden horse, I hand Sophie my phone and give her my best regal look). 'Honestly, you're such a child!'

From there, we make our way through the many rooms, stumbling upon the tower that is said to be haunted by the ghost of the Barbary ape. Opposite that is a tower that is off-limits to humans, for it serves as a hotel for protected bats. I read out the information board: 'Carew Castle South West Tower welcomes all bats. Facilities on offer; tall, old, stone tower; Four-Star Restaurant Menu, moths, midges, beetles; nursery, darkness provided ...'[7]

'That's hilarious!'

Once done exploring the castle itself, we decide to take a walk around the estuary. Along the way, we pop into Carew Tidal Mill, the only restored tidal mill in all of Wales. The mill's origins aren't known, but a functioning mill operated here as early as 1542, at least. The causeway was built sometime around 1630. The building you see here today was built in the nineteenth century. The place has also been referred to as the 'French Mill' due to its architectural design.[8] Thanks to being on an estuary, the tide would have provided significantly more power than your average river mill. It is not a functioning mill any more, but you can explore the inside and see all the big machinery that was used.

And when it's all done and dusted, we make our way back to our lovely cottage. 'Best to rest up tonight, we've got a few burial mounds to see tomorrow.'

'Well, aren't I a lucky girl.'

15

Where the folk
can I find militant dancing fairies and a retired giant-beaver-monster-thingy?

Did you know that Wales has its own Loch Ness monster? Well, sort of. Ours isn't some innocent plesiosaur that got stuck in a lake; our Nessie is a great, big, crocodilian-beaver-like-thing with a soft spot for mass destruction, pretty young women and scrapping with heroic knights, including King Arthur himself. Oh, and he shoots poison darts and can turn invisible. No, this isn't 'The Beast of Craggy Island' (one for *Father Ted* fans) – this is the story of Yr Afanc …

… or one of them, at least. For you see, this bizarre lake monster has terrorised many places in Wales over the years. You've got Llyn Llion, where he is said to have caused a flood so bad that it killed everyone in Britain save for two people, Dwyfan and Dwyfach, ancestors of every Brit thereafter. Then there's Llyn Barfog, where King Arthur ultimately slew him, and Llyn Syfaddon, where he lived in a cave near the 'Palace of the Sons of the King of the Tortures'.[1] The list goes on.

The Afanc's (sometimes spelt Addanc) appearance varies greatly in these tales, from a beaver–crocodile hybrid to a humanoid dwarf. The reason why I referenced 'The Beast of Craggy Island' is because it almost feels as though people weren't sure where to go with the Afanc and he became more and more extravagant with each description. Regardless, he has always been a big player in Welsh folklore and mythology and is associated with the origins of many Welsh place-names.

Needless to say, the Afanc's a pretty big deal here in Wales. Or was, at least. Some say that his final resting place is at Bedd-yr-Afanc (the Afanc's Grave), here in Pembrokeshire. That is where Sophie and I are currently headed, if we can find it.

The story goes that the Afanc once terrorised the countryside around the village of Brynberian. A meeting was held by the wisest people in the area, who came up with a very cunning plan. It would seem that our infamous Welsh supervillain was fond of digging, for they asked the monster to dig a massive hole for them, to which he agreed. However, when he reached about a hundred yards down, the villagers dropped a bunch of stones on him.

They of course intended to crush him, but the next morning they found him there alive and well, still digging away. He told them there had been a heavy downpour the night before which had caused him some minor inconvenience. As the wise folk scrambled to come up with another plan, the Afanc dug on, and on and on, until, eventually, he died of exhaustion. He was consequently buried on the hillside.[2]

As always, there are many variations of this story, but the general consensus is that he caused terror in the countryside and was tricked into digging a hole, one way or another. One version tells of how he lived in a pool beneath Brynberian Bridge.

'Where?'

'Brynberian Bridge … that's the name of this village, right? Brynberian?'

'Yeah, but … Bryn-ber-ian Bridge … doesn't ring a bell, and I should know! Let me have a look?'

I hand my phone over to the postman. I've been driving up and down the streets and back lanes of this tiny village for half an hour now and have yet to come across any bridges. He squints at the screen then shakes his head and hands it back to me. 'Sorry, mate.'

'No worries, *diolch*.'

I half-run back to the car, empty handed.

'Any luck?'

'Nah. Oh well, let's just head to the grave itself … could do with a pee first, mind … I'm bursting!'

Just outside the village, I pull in by the side of the road.

'Russell!'

Uh-oh. She used my full name. 'It's alright; I'll hide behind the wall, look – down there.'

Switching off the engine, I get out and navigate my way through the overgrown bushes to a secluded spot down by the side of the road. There is a small stream running beneath the – I stop dead in my tracks and look at my phone again. 'This is it!'

'What?' Sophie calls from the car.

'This is it! This is the bridge. We were driving over it the whole time.'

Needless to say, it isn't much to look at. But we're here for the Afanc's grave, in any case. The site is actually the only Bronze Age gallery grave in Wales and it dates back to around 1500 BC. Today, like with most European gallery graves, only two parallel rows of stone remain.[3]

Pulling up at the side of the road a few miles from Brynberian Bridge, I lead Sophie up a small dirt track and up to a locked gate. Looking down at my phone, I tell her that this must be the place, but it looks like private land.

'Is there anyone we could ask?'

'Hm. I'll go knock on someone's door …' I step outside again.

A pile of Amazon packages. No one home. Then, across the road, I spot a man hauling stuff from his car. Doing my usual half-run across the road, I holler over to him: 'Alright, how's it going?'

'Hi …'

'I'm looking for Bedd-yr-Afanc. Any idea if I'm allowed to go walk through that field up there?'

'Oh, yeah. Yeah, it's open to the public. Just head up that lane there, through the first gate, past the horses, then keep going – you won't be able to see it from the gate – you've got to cross through some boggy bits to get there.'

Everyone I have asked for directions from today has been familiar with Bedd-yr-Afanc, but this is the first person who's actually been able to tell me where it is.

'Thanks for that, much appreciated. What's your name, by the way?'

'Jeff … so are you … visiting all the burial mounds, or something?'

I tell him all about the book, then he says, 'You know, I think it's great to celebrate their existence 'n everything, but I do hate it when archaeologists and what-have-you go up to these places and desecrate them. I mean, these places were sacred to our ancestors, you know? Like that place in Australia, Ayer's Rock.'

'Uluru. Yes, the Aborigines hate people climbing it.'

'Exactly. I just think we should show these places the same respect, you know?'

An interesting statement. Neglecting to ask whether he spells him name 'Jeff' or 'Geoff', I thank him for the directions then half-run back to the car. 'This is the place. You coming?'

Sophie gets to play with some white horses on the way up, then we navigate the swampy bogland in search of a small mound with two rows of …

'Is that it?' Sophie sounds disappointed.

It is. A rare sight, but not that exciting unless you're a druid or an archaeologist.

'What do you make of all that, then? Should these places be protected from excavation?' I ask her.

'I agree with Jeff (or Geoff), I think they should be left as sacred sites. Leave them in peace – it's a burial mound! I mean, how soon is too soon to dig up a grave, right?'

Pembrokeshire is absolutely teeming with ancient burial mounds, stone circles and megaliths. I mean, we do love our stone circles here in Wales and we are still erecting new ones each year for the National Eisteddfod. Mind you, the 2005 Eisteddfod at Faenol was the first to use temporary fibreglass stone, so who knows, this tradition might be coming to an end as we enter a new era of Plastic Circles.[4] But you can't move for stone circles and burial mounds here at Pembrokeshire, at least.

Bedd-yr-Afanc is found in the Preseli Hills, where it is believed that the Bluestones used for the earliest parts of Stonehenge came from. Everyone knows Stonehenge – it is the biggest and most impressive of all the stone circles on the British Isles. Preseli Bluestone International Ltd found the Preseli Bluestones again (seeing as our ancestors didn't leave a record of where they were) on 3 May 2000.

The technological achievements of our ancestors have often

been attributed to aliens and other supernatural beings and the transportation of the Preseli Bluestones to Stonehenge is no exception. Legend goes that Merlin's the one who moved the stones over to England, also using them for the construction of Camelot and King Arthur's Round Table.[5] There is also a stone circle in the Preseli Hills named Bedd Arthur (Arthur's Grave), another site claiming to be the legendary king's final resting place.

But we've already covered King Arthur, so how about a band of militant fairies who force people to dance for eternity, instead? Pentre Ifan is the name of an old manor in Nevern, but found on the site and sharing the name is the biggest and best-preserved Neolithic dolmen in Wales. It translates to 'Evan's Village'.

'Another burial mound?'

'Just one more, I promise.'

Built around 3500 BC, Pentre Ifan was originally thought to have served as a communal burial mound. However, no bones have ever been found there.[6] A study by Cummings and Richards in 2014 offers another explanation and points out several things that hint at it being a dolmen. This means that the place was purely a place for our ancestors to show off their status and building skills, which explains the lack of bones.[7]

Today, it consists of three standing stones that hold up a sixteen-foot-long capstone, estimated to weigh about sixteen tonnes. Honestly, to see this thing balancing on the tips of three other rocks is quite awe-inspiring. There are three other stones present to complete what is left of the dolmen, forming a doorway.[8]

The site is now managed by Cadw, who state on their information board that many people have reported seeing *Tylwyth Teg* near the dolmen over the years, with many accounts describing them as 'short soldiers wearing military caps'.[9]

Most of these stories originate from the 1700s, but some people even claim that the dolmen itself was built by these militant fairies. They were considered a friendly bunch and lived out in the woods near the site, helping build the dolmen for us using magic. They would often make an appearance if you were to leave out gifts for them, particularly bread, butter and honey, which they couldn't get enough of.

However, as friendly as these fairies were, it was advised that you didn't hang out with them whenever they came out to play, for they would eventually begin to sing and dance and this would put people into a trance whereby they would not be able to stop dancing. Those unfortunate souls would prance off with the fairies, never to be seen again.[10]

This reminds me of the story of Iolo ap Huw, otherwise known as Ned Pugh, from Llanymynech. He made a drunken bet with the local choir that if he were to play his fiddle from the top of Llanymynech Hill on Sunday morning, then the congregation would still be able to hear him playing over them. They accepted his bet, but advised him to avoid the old cave on the Sabbath.

The next morning, Ned went up the hill to play his fiddle but failed to stay far away enough from the cave. A voice enticed him inside and he was never seen again. However, it is said that if you stand outside that cave on 29 February, then you will be able to hear poor Ned still fiddling away, for he is cursed to spend an eternity playing his fiddle in Annwn.[11]

Ned Pugh isn't the only Welsh musician to suffer this fate, with tales of people being forced to dance or sing or to play an instrument for all eternity popping up all over the place. So what's all that about?

It could be that these stories stem from our ancestors' fear of being stuck in some never-ending dancing frenzy, once a genuine threat to Europeans. I know this sounds a bit unbelievable, but there's some real history behind it. Well, there are those who say that these accounts are either fake or were staged at the time, but there are numerous reports from the fourteenth and seventeenth centuries of entire crowds of people entering such trances, in a social phenomenon known as 'dancing mania'. It has also been called the dancing plague, choreomania, Saint John's dance, tarantism and Saint Vitus's Dance.[12]

Children and adults from all over Europe would dance and dance until they either collapsed in exhaustion or from spraining their ankles. The phenomenon would even, on occasion, involve thousands of people at once. The first major 'outbreak' occurred in Aachen in 1374, then the strange phenomenon spread across the whole of Europe.[13]

I know, I know – it sounds too ridiculous to be true, but these events were well documented. They would often start without any music being played at all. Musicians would sometimes join in and actually play music to see if that would get them to stop, but it only encouraged them to dance more. Some crowds danced for months on end, even. Exorcists were brought in to deal with it, to no avail, and some people were even isolated from the rest of society in case the madness spread, just as people isolate the infected in any pandemic.

There have been many proposed theories as to why this happened, but the general consensus is that it was some kind of mass psychogenic illness or hysteria. Indeed, they often correlated with times of hardship such as war or famine; perhaps it was the human brain trying to deal with widespread trauma. Others argue that it could even be due to some hallucinogenic bacteria that might have been infecting their crops, sending everyone on one hell of a trip.[14] Regardless of why, these bizarre events really did take place, so it would make sense that people would turn to the supernatural in search of both an explanation and a solution.

But I think we'll be alright – we forgot to bring any bread, butter or honey with us, so there shouldn't be any *Tylwyth Teg* at Pentre Ifan today, at least.

16

Where the folk
is the only patron saint
in the village?

If you were to go up to someone in the UK in the Noughties and tell them, in a Welsh accent, that you were the only gay in the village, then asked them for a Bacardi and Coke, many people would get the reference. Thanks to the BBC's comedy sketch show *Little Britain*, millions of people suddenly became aware of an unassuming village of about 500 people in Ceredigion. People flocked to Llanddewi Brefi to snap a photo of the village's road sign, myself included. But some people took it upon themselves to steal the sign, with several disappearing in 2005.[1]

Llanddewi Brefi became a household name because it was the home of the show's fictional character Daffyd Thomas, but the village's name pays homage to Saint David. It is there that the patron saint of Wales performed his greatest miracle.

Saints seem to always be popping up in this book, so it seems fitting that I should talk about ol' Dewi Sant. He lived in the sixth century and was the bishop of Mynyw, which we now know as St Davids. His symbol was that of a leek, something that has since become synonymous with Wales.

In 1630, the Welsh wore leeks on their hats in order to distinguish themselves from the enemy on a battle that took place on Saint David's Day.[2] Today, people take inflatable leeks to rugby matches. In a way, the Welsh are still taking leeks into battle.

Born and raised in Wales, David was the son of Saint Non and grandson of Ceredig ap Cunedda, king of Ceredigion. Both his date of birth and the date on which he died are unclear, but the latter is often said to have been on 1 March, which we now celebrate as Saint David's Day, often by wearing daffodils.[3]

It isn't so clear as to why daffodils have become synonymous with Wales. They were brought over here by the Romans, who used them for medicinal purposes after they found that they thrived in Welsh soil. Some theorists suggest that at one point, people confused the Welsh word for daffodils, *cennin Pedr*, with the word for leeks, *cennin*. David Lloyd George, a former prime minister, popularised the association by regularly wearing a daffodil to flaunt his Welshness.[4]

It is said that Saint David made a living as a teacher and a preacher, setting up churches all over Wales. But for most people, he is famous for the time the ground beneath him rose up into a hill as he was preaching to a crowd one day at the Synod of Brefi, after which a white dove landed on his shoulder. That's what supposedly happened at Llandewi Brefi, by the way.

As archbishop of Wales, he ran a pretty tight ship, with monks having to pull their own ploughs without the use of any animals, made to only drink water and to eat only bread seasoned with salt and herbs, and banned from having any personal possessions whatsoever.[5] He was buried at St Davids Cathedral here in Pembrokeshire, where we now stand.

What makes Saint David different from most other Welsh saints, crucially, is that he was officially recognised as one by the Roman Catholic Church. People are now calling for Saint David's Day to be made into an official bank holiday, and Cyngor Gwynedd, the county council for Gwynedd, recently became the first to give their staff a day off for it.[6]

'Do you think it should it be a bank holiday?'

'Absolutely,' Sophie replies. 'And Saint George's Day, 'n all!'

'Have you ever seen any Saint David's Day celebrations, then?'

'I saw a Saint David's Day parade in Cardiff once, they had the traditional Welsh lady dresses on and there were lots of daffodils.'

Saint David has also played a big part in Welsh folklore throughout the years and was often associated with corpse candles. There are accounts of them popping up all over Wales and have been explained by Saint David praying for Welsh people to have some sort of warning before they lost a loved one. The size and colour of the candle would indicate if the person about to die would be a man, woman or child. It would light up outside the house of the doomed individual and float the route to the spot of their imminent burial.[7]

It is because of all this that we have come here, to the smallest city in the UK. Mind you, you wouldn't think it's a city if you ever came – it looks and feels more like a village, really. It's the cathedral that gives it its city status, received in the twelfth century. The status was withdrawn in 1886 but eventually given back by Queen Elizabeth II in 1994. The Welsh name for the place is Tyddewi, which means 'Dewi's House'.

We passed numerous pubs and art galleries on our way in, but we are currently inside the cathedral itself, admiring all the religious decor with our hands behind our backs, desperately trying to make it seem as though we know what we are looking at.

'Is that him?' It's hard to distinguish the faces on these old stone crypts. I'm looking for Gerald of Wales, the Norman archdeacon of Brecon and part-time historian who had a profound influence on Welsh folklore, although many question both the motives behind and the accuracy of his accounts.

He wrote of a talking marble footbridge that once crossed the Alun rivulet here at St Davids. The Llechllafar ('the talking stone') was so-called because people once heard it talking to a corpse as it was being carried over into the church. The effort it made to speak caused it to break apart and no corpse was ever carried over it again. The original stone was replaced in the sixteenth century and its whereabouts are currently unknown.

Interestingly, there's another legend associated with that bridge: it is said that Merlin once prophesied that an English king who had conquered Ireland would die on it. The doomed king would also be injured by a red-handed man. Now, apparently, King Henry II visited Llechllafar after returning from Ireland and crossed the bridge before laughing and declaring Merlin a liar. However, local bystanders pointed out that he had not yet conquered Ireland and thus was not the king from the prophecy. Henry never did manage to conquer the Emerald Isle.[8]

After walking around the outside of the Bishop's Palace, being too tight to pay the entry fee, we head back to the car and drive a couple of miles outside the city (saying that feels so wrong!) to the Chapel of St Non, where Saint David was born.

Now, much like David himself, there's a lot of speculation surrounding his mum, Non. It is said she was a nun at Tŷ Gwyn, over at Whitesands Bay, who was raped by Sanctus, king of Ceredigion, the product of which was Saint David. After conceiving, Non survived only on bread and water and never slept with another man for the rest of her days.

While she was pregnant, a preacher found himself unable to preach in her presence, which was taken as a sign that the child would become a great preacher one day. A local leader heard about this and set out to kill Non before she had the chance to give birth. However, on the night she fell into labour, a great storm made it impossible for anyone to travel outdoors.

A great beam of light shone down on the spot where Non gave birth that night and it is said that the pain was so bad that she left finger-marks on a rock that, out of sympathy for her, split in half. A church was built on the spot where Saint David was born, the split rock being concealed in its altar.

Not exactly an elegant arrival. But, hold up, didn't I say earlier on that his dad was called Ceredig? Like most of the tales I've come across, the story of Saint David's birth and origins also has its variations. Others say that his father was a local chieftain named Xantus, Sandde or Sant. The latter means 'saint'; quite fitting that a nun and a man named Saint would produce a prophet, which offers us the hope that Saint David's conception was consensual.[9]

The ruins of Chapel of St Non are found at the aptly named St Non's Bay. Nearby you can find her holy well, at which we stop to throw in a penny (that's a miracle in its own, we never carry cash these days) and make a wish. The well is said to have healing properties, perfect for a hypochondriac such as myself.

After making our wishes, we decide to cleanse our atheist souls by going for a pint. Finding a beer garden, we lay our acquired leaflets out on the table and look for our next adventure. That's when I spot a photo of a neat-looking chapel built into some cliffs, with stormy seas raging below it.

'Class! We have to go!' I declare.

'Another church? It's like the burial mounds all over again!'

17

Where the folk
can I find a
pirate-fighting monk?

'Come on, let me take a screenshot of yours.'

'No, sorry.' Sophie shakes her head defiantly.

'Aw, come on, they won't let me in otherwise.'

'I'm sorry, but no.'

'Argh! You're all just a bunch of sheep, you are!'

We're out in Tenby and an unvaccinated woman is trying to convince Sophie to let her use her COVID pass. It's the first year of the vaccination roll-out and the world is divided between those who have been vaccinated and those who haven't. Tensions are high, with some of the unvaccinated lot angry at society's eagerness to listen to the government, and the vaccinated crowd angry with them both for not taking one for the team and for holding what they deem as disease-spreading rallies to get their message across. It is unclear as of yet just how limited a life without a pass is going to be, but some pubs won't let you in without one, at least.

But Sophie and I, despite being 'stripped of our rights', enjoy a debauchery-fuelled night in one of Wales's most popular stag and hen destinations. Having said goodbye to our cosy little cottage in Ambleston, the next day, we struggle through our breakfast at the Bates Motel then hit the road again, heading west towards St Govan's.

Note that the following is a cautionary tale about how you should always look up the history and lore of a place before visiting or you might end up missing out, even if some things were staring you right in the face.

To get to St Govan's you must pass through Castlemartin Firing Range, an MOD-owned army tank range. During training, the roads and lanes leading to the small chapel on the cliffs are shut. You can check the firing times online before going to avoid a wasted journey, but the roads are usually open on weekends.

When we arrive, we are greeted by the most magnificent view: miles of steep, mighty cliffs, waves crashing against them in dramatic fashion and, behind us, a canvas of rolling green hills. You must walk through a bit of the military training ground to get to the chapel, passing trenches and bunkers along the way. You can also join the Wales Coast Path from here.

There it is – St Govan's Head, looking far more dramatic than any photograph can give it justice. We climb down a set of steep, narrow steps then head inside. After looking around we step back outside near the water's edge and see a strange-looking rock formation that we can't make heads nor tails of. Naturally, we use it as a chair and take in everything else, instead.

After that, we huff, puff and curse as we climb back up those bloody steps and make our way back to Griff, completely oblivious to the marvels we had just seen. We are so hungover that we just want to get the tent set up and head to the beach, to be honest.

The legend of St Govan's (Welsh: Sant Gofan) told on the information board in the car park leaves a lot of stuff out. One version of the story says that Govan was an Irish monk who came to Wales in search of the friends and family of the abbot who had trained him back in the day. That abbot was none other than our boy, Saint David.

En route, Govan was attacked by pirates, with different versions of the story claiming they were Irish and others claiming they were from nearby Lundy Island. Govan was doomed, with the pirates hot on his trail. Then, miraculously, the cliffs themselves opened up, providing a space just big enough for him to squeeze into. He abandoned his boat and hid until the pirates gave up their search and went along their way. It is said that his ribs left an imprint in the rock and that you can still see them running along the rock face today. Yeah, that we missed, perhaps due to our fuzzy hungover heads.

To show his gratitude, he vowed to stay there and protect the locals of nearby Bosherston from pirates by raising the alarm should they ever come back. He spent the remainder of his days living as a hermit in a small cave in the cliffs, surviving by catching fish and drinking from two nearby springs, both of which were said to have magical properties. One was a Wishing Well, the other, a Healing one, found where the medieval chapel (which is made of local limestone) now stands. Both wells have since dried up, however.

The chapel was built in the fourteenth century; way after Govan's time, who reportedly died in AD 568, but the site may have been of monastic importance way before then, perhaps as far back as the fifth century. It is said that the pirate-fighting monk is buried beneath the altar. They also say that his handprints can be seen on the ground there. Something else we missed.

Other rumours abound that when the chapel was built, the place had some magical healing properties due to the remnants of the old well that lay underneath it. It could apparently help sort out eye problems, skin conditions and stiff joints, though I'd be surprised if anyone's knees didn't ache after climbing those stairs.

Those are said to be a bit 'magical' themselves, by the way; it is said that no mortal man nor woman can count them. As in, if you counted the number of steps on the way down, the figure would always be different on the way back up. You guessed it, we didn't know that at the time, either. All I know for certain is that the chapel did nothing for my awful skin or poor eyesight.

But Govan's tale doesn't end there, for you see, the pirates did, indeed, come back. Although, for the sequel to make any sense, then Govan would have to have been alive for several hundred years. The story goes that he kept a silver bell in the tower of the chapel, but this was actually built centuries after Govan's time. The bell had the most perfect tone when pealed, apparently.

Govan put up a good fight when the pirates returned (even though he should have been dead for centuries by this point), but they nicked the bell regardless and went out to sea with it. However, a group of angels swooped down from the heavens and snatched it off them, taking it back to Govan. Then, as a precaution from more marauding pirates, they encased it in stone, thus forming the Bell Rock, being the strange-looking formation we had sat on to admire the view. An altar was later carved into the rock for travelling pilgrims to come and pray. It is said that whenever Govan as much as gently tapped the Bell Rock with his finger, it would give out a massive chime.[1]

Another interesting thing about St Govan's that we didn't know at the time is that there is a huge cave system deep within the cliffs called Ogof Gofan, which they reckon was used by people thousands of years ago, back when the sea lay several miles further out than it does today.[2]

Now, some people claim that Govan wasn't an Irish monk at all and was, in fact, Gawain, one of the Knights of the Round Table. Gawain, also known as Gwalchmei, was King Arthur's nephew and featured in many Arthurian legends, including 'How Culhwch won Olwen'. He has been referred to as one of the greatest knights of his time and one of Arthur's best mates.[3]

It is said that this sparkly eyed dreamboat took early retirement and chose to live a solitary life in a cave in the cliffs. However, as you know, he was eventually brought out of retirement Steven Seagal-style to fight the pirates.

The divine intervention that I spoke of makes it a Christian tale, which some say supports the claim that he was, in fact, an Irish monk. Then again, King Arthur et al. have long been associated with the Christian faith and religious symbolism, so the debate lives on. Whatever his origins, the moral of the story remains the same: Google places before you go.

'Have you ever missed out on something before, after going somewhere without researching the place first, then?' I ask. 'Is it good to do your research? Or is it better to go in blind and be "surprised", you think?'

'See, I really enjoy researching a place before going. I did this for whenever I had extended periods of travel abroad and would treat travelling in Wales no differently. I'd be pretty annoyed if I went up north, say, and missed out on the best views.'

We had it in our heads to camp near a beach, but each and every seaside campsite in south Wales is fully booked, what with the hordes having been set free from lockdown. But we manage to book a night at the Freshwater West & Gupton Farm campsite, owned by the National

Trust, right at the edge of the Castlemartin Peninsula, near Pembroke.

We make our way past Pembroke, then Maiden Wells and Castlemartin, before finally arriving at a small cluster of farm buildings with a handful of tents set up nearby. Due to the pandemic, there's no staff here to greet us. Instead, we check ourselves in and pick up a brown envelope full of leaflets on local attractions and a handy little map they had prepared for us. Out on the field, from where we can just about see the ocean over the hedges, there are enough people for everyone to feel 'alone' but without the niggling fear of being murdered – perfect! The only downside is that the main view is that of a huge power station.

From the field, you can go down a long walking trail which takes you down to the beach, which itself is huge and very popular with surfers. After pitching our tent, we head down to the dunes. The fence poles along the way are covered in clusters of snails, a phenomenon that never fails to offer a great photo op. Once there, we drink some berry-flavoured Belgian beer and watch the surfers bobbing and swaying like seals in the water as the sun sets on the horizon. See, this is what Pembrokeshire is all about.

In the night, we notice a strange hissing sound that we initially think is the sound of crashing waves. Turns out, there's a puncture in the air mattress. I shift my body so that my back covers the hole, delaying the inevitable. When we wake up in the morning, we're lying flat on the ground in agony, blood rushing to our heads from pointing in the wrong direction on the sloping field.

'Bloody hell,' I groan, rubbing my lower back. 'I could do with that magic well right about now.'

Mattress binned and tent packed up, we continue our journey up the coast.

18

Where the folk
can I find a talking seal
and an angry Welsh lady?

There's a reason why, in 1954, John Huston chose to film some of *Moby Dick* here in Fishguard. The English name for the place derives from the Old Norse word *Fiskigarðr*, which means 'fish catching enclosure' (the Welsh version, Abergwaun, refers to the mouth of the River Gwaun). As we descend the winding road that takes us down to Lower Fishguard, the oldest part of town, it is also clear to see why the film adaptation of Dylan Thomas's *Under Milk Wood* was filmed here; the place fits the author's description of the fictional town of Llareggub (now read that backwards) almost perfectly.

Lower Fishguard sits at the bottom of a valley, where the Afon Gwaun meets the sea. 'Main Town' sits on top of the hill on the other side of the river; this is where you'll find the parish church, the high street and everything else you'd expect to find in a small town.

The place is rich in maritime history. Trust me, if you like pirates, fishing and pubs adorned with oil paintings of naval ships, you'll love it here. A privateer known as the Black Prince raided and bombarded the old port in 1779 when the town refused to pay his £1,000 ransom. As a result, Fishguard Fort was built to protect them from further raids.[1]

But we didn't come to Fishguard as literary fans nor for pirates or giant sperm whales. We came because Fishguard, in 1797, was the site of what is often referred to as 'the last invasion of Britain', an event that had a profound impact on the town's culture and sense of identity. But this real event has become something of a legend in itself, complete with its own leading lady …

116

The story I originally heard was that a bunch of local women put on their traditional outfits and stood on the beach to confront an invading French army. When the French saw a bunch of red coats and black hats they retreated, thinking they were British soldiers. Well, that's the simplest version I can give you (and isn't even correct, but it's the version people told me before I came here), but as always, there is far more to it than that.

In fact, the French did come ashore and they ran amok in the Welsh countryside for a couple of days. British soldiers and local volunteers joined forces in a bid to stop them in what became known as the 'Battle of Fishguard'. However, a bunch of angry Welsh ladies were also involved, led by a woman named Jemima Nicholas, who is still widely adored here in Fishguard to this day.

Jemima Fawr (Jemima the Great) lived from 1750 to 1832 and was the wife of a cobbler. When 1,400 Frenchmen turned up in 1797, it is said that she armed herself with a pitchfork and led a group of women to help the resistance. They managed to round up twelve soldiers who had been drinking in a local pub, locking them up overnight at St Mary's church. The French promptly surrendered, signing a peace treaty at the Royal Oak pub, and Jemima was awarded a lifetime pension for her efforts.

She died in 1832 at the age of 82 and was buried at St Mary's church, where a plaque was raised in her honour in 1897, which you can still see today. The town holds a tradition of having a Jemima Nicholas re-enactor who attends events and ceremonies and such dressed as her. Having also been included in the list of 100 Influential Welsh Women, it's safe to say that Jemima is more than just a local heroine.[2]

She also features in the Last Invasion Tapestry, a response to the Bayeux Tapestry, which is quite the sight to behold. At a hundred feet long (just like the Bayeux Tapestry), it's bloody massive. It was commissioned by the Fishguard Arts Society in 1997 and can be found up in the gallery at Fishguard Town Hall. There's also a hilarious 'face-in-the-hole' photo opportunity up there, by the way. But her story is often mistold and, as the tapestry shows you, the story of the Battle of Fishguard is far more intricate than what most would recite.

The French assault was led by Revolutionary France during the War of the First Coalition. It didn't last very long, taking place between 22 and 24 February. It remains the most recent landing on British soil by an enemy force.

The French's original plan fell to pieces due to bad weather and unruly soldiers, so they landed in Wales with a plan to march to Bristol disguised as a Russian fleet. They came ashore under the cover of darkness at around two in the morning, unloading boxes of ammunition and explosives. However, most of the force consisted of 'irregulars', that is to say, deserters and prisoners of war who had been forced to fight in the first place. Unsurprisingly, most of them took the opportunity to leg it.

The British navy managed to capture two French vessels and, after a few skirmishes on land, Colonel William Tate, the invading force's Irish-American commander, was forced to surrender unconditionally. His troops, officially named the Seconde Légion des Francs, were nicknamed the Légion Noire (meaning 'The Black Legion') due to their tendency to wear the uniforms of captured British troops dyed black (or a very dark brown, at least).[3]

So if Jemima Nicholas was a real person and this was a real event that really did take place, then why is it included in this book on folktales? I'll let Peter Stevenson take the fall for this one: 'There were other folktales similar to the Last Invasion. There was a story from Devon in the 1500s when the French tried to invade and guess what? The women dressed in uniforms and scared them off! And that was two hundred years before Fishguard.'

He then went on to warn me not to mention this when visiting Fishguard myself, saying: 'People ask me what the art of storytelling is – the art of storytelling is listening!'

Great advice, but the fact that the official account of the event provides so much detail regarding what happened was bugging me. As such, I decided to get in touch with the museum staff at Fishguard Town Hall. After several weeks of back-and-forth emailing, they referred me to a local man named Edward Perkins. Edward has taken upon himself to go through the events of the Battle of Fishguard with a fine-tooth comb.

I originally gave him a bell to arrange an interview but, after telling me all about the PowerPoint presentation that he's made on the subject, he jumped straight into it.

'So the original plan was to sack Bristol then march north to invade England, because they believed this would cause an uprising in the British countryside and people would join the revolution. But they completely misjudged this. I mean, there were hardly any French people living in the English countryside at all. Don't get me wrong, there were those who wanted democratic change, but not many who would be willing to put a knife in the king's back. Their other target was Ireland. Now, they sent 15,000 troops to Galway but none of them landed. A strong gale came and they decided to turn around. I think if they would have landed, British history would have been very different.'

Colonel William Tate was Irish-born but had moved to the Americas. After the war, he got into trouble down in Louisiana and fled to France. How he ended up leading this attack however is anyone's guess – Edward points out that he couldn't even speak French.

'But the main issue I have with Jemima's story is the location, her and the girls' positioning,' he says. 'They were supposed to have walked to the south-west of Fishguard. The furthest that the French troops got was to the farm where I now live, it's called Garn Gelli. Now, from the top end of Garn Gelli, you can actually see where Jemima and the girls were meant to be, but you would need a telescope to pick out what colour coats they would have been wearing. I mean, I stood there myself and had a look – there's no way you could have spotted them in the distance and been like "Look! British troops!" Personally, I think the whole thing with them wearing red coats, the Welsh lady outfit, all that was added in years later.'

It's clear to see that Edward has considered the events of that day from all possible angles.

'I looked at the whole thing logically, and when you do that, you deduce that Jemima and the girls wouldn't have been out wearing their coats on the Wednesday, because they wouldn't have known what the hell was going on. On Thursday, there would have been general panic, no one to organise them other than themselves. If they did go up on the Thursday, as I just said, nobody would have seen them. When you look at the maps and pinpoint where the French were, most of them wouldn't have been able to see Fishguard, let alone Jemima and the girls. And by the Friday, the French had already surrendered, in any case, so if they were there that day, they would have just been there to have a look at what was going on, I'd say.'

I'm keen to learn more about the similar event that took place in Devon. I ask him if he thinks that event really happened, and whether using civilians to trick invaders was ever a military tactic.

'It's possible, but here in Fishguard, it's been confirmed on record that no one organised for the women to parade up on the cliffside. It was never done as a military tactic here on that day. Those reports also say that there were no ladies in red whatsoever, that it's all total rubbish. So there's a degree of legend to it, but I don't mind that – it's good for the tourists. I do tours out on boats here in Fishguard, it's great fun!'

I enjoyed listening to Edward's unpicking of the events of that fateful day, but I've got to be honest with you, I feel like I'm robbing a place of its magic a little. But I do find it fascinating how folklore can slip its way into an actual event and distort history for so many, and how it can also give rise to real-life heroes who are celebrated on a national level.

'So Sophie, Jemima scaring off the French … would you call it a feminist tale?'

'Yep! Ladies taking control and telling the Frogs to *allez vous faire foutre!*'

There's another interesting tale said to have taken place near Fishguard. It concerns a lazy fisherman who would much rather have a nap than fix the holes that local seals made in his net in their attempts to steal his catch. One morning, some tourists turned up and asked if he would be willing to ferry them back to Goodwick, which falls under the Fishguard constabulary, from Newport Sands. He agreed, for a price, of course, figuring it was an easier job than fishing. Moreover, he could have a nap at lunchtime before dropping them off at the agreed time of two o'clock.

However, when he awoke from his nap, he took one look at the positioning of the sun and figured that he'd never make it back to Newport Sands in time. Wondering what to do, he heard a voice calling from the water: 'What's the problem?'

Looking down, he saw a seal staring back at him. 'Yhm ... I didn't know seals could talk!'

'You don't know much,' said the seal. 'Throw me a rope.'

Tying one end of the rope to the boat, he threw the other end into the water. The seal grabbed it with its mouth and towed the boat back to Newport Sands, then picked up the tourists and managed to drop them off at Goodwick in time for tea. They were chuffed and left him a big tip. After that, the fisherman never once complained about the holes in his net.[4]

I'm not really sure what the moral of this one is, nor am I certain of the tale's origins, but it's intrigued me enough to make me take a detour to Newport Sands as we head out of Fishguard. Newport itself, the one here in Pembrokeshire, I mean, is another former fishing town. These days, people mostly come here to see Newport Sands, the aptly named Traeth Mawr ('Big Beach'), one-and-a-half miles of golden sand dunes, separated from the town by the River Nevern estuary.

Parking up, we take off our shoes and go for a stroll, stopping to write our names in the sand before heading back to the car. Standard. But I can't get the strange story of the talking seal out of my head and it gets me wondering how big a role sea creatures play in Welsh folklore. Turns out, tales of marine monsters, mermaids and selkies are abundant along the Welsh coast, particularly here in the west.

One that stands out to me for being particularly gritty took place at nearby Aberbach and tells of how a farmer found a mermaid one day and took her back to his place, filled up a bathtub with saltwater and kept her as a sex slave. For punishment, she cursed the men of that farmhouse to be forever infertile.

The farmer eventually grew old and rented the place with a young farmhand. 'I'm a lucky man,' he told him one night after telling him all about the curse.

'Why's that?'

'Because at least I never got into trouble with my wife for flirting with a mermaid!'[5]

But mermaids don't explain the talking seal. Rather, this story might have stemmed from the legend of the selkies, who have seal-like skin when in water but look just like regular humans when on dry land.

There are stories of encounters with selkies all over the British Isles (and beyond – there is a famous statue of a selkie at Kalsoy on the Faroe Islands and they also feature heavily in Scandinavian folklore), but they were originally a Scottish myth, with the name 'selkie' having derived from the Scottish word *selch*, which means 'seal'. Most stories involving selkies feature a female selkie being tricked or lured into a life on dry land by a greedy human man, similar to the Lady of the Lake tales.[6]

Most tales of mermaids and talking sea creatures tend to share a common ethos that usually involves maintaining respect and balance between the human world and the underwater world. This is common the world over, proving that these tales often carry important, universal messages. Perhaps the message here is to give back to the ocean, not to take all the fish for ourselves.

Who knows? In any case, I'm hooked (pardon the pun). Time to dive deeper (and that one!) into the realm of offshore Welsh folktales …

19

Where the folk
is the 'Welsh Atlantis'?

Stories of sunken cities and lost civilisations are present in numerous cultures from around the world. They've been around for thousands of years and have even influenced religions. It comes as no surprise, then, that the Welsh also have a couple of Atlantis stories to tell. There is apparently a sunken kingdom named Llys Helig up in the Conwy estuary ruled by Helig ap Glanawg, but perhaps the most well-known 'Welsh Atlantis' is the lost kingdom of Cantre'r Gwaelod, supposedly found somewhere here, along Cardigan Bay.

For hundreds of years, people have reported seeing the ruins of ancient buildings emerging from beneath the waves during great storms. Some have even gone as far as to say that they heard the chime of a bell during low tides. Tales of the 'Lowland Hundred' have been retold and reimagined for centuries, but most versions paint a portrait of a wealthy and densely populated region made up of around sixteen individual townships that stretched out some twenty miles from where the land now reaches.

Cantre'r Gwaelod (also called Cantref Gwaelod) was under constant threat from rising sea levels at the best of times, but the sea also played a crucial role in its success. The inhabitants built large dykes and steep embankments which they would occasionally open (using a series of gates known as 'sluices') so as to water their crops. The land was so fertile that to buy an acre there would cost four times as much as an acre on the mainland.

The story that is told today (which emerged in the seventeenth century) goes that the kingdom was ruled by Gwyddno Garanhir, who held court at Cantre'r Gwaelod's capital, Caer Wyddno. Gwyddno appointed one of the many princes of the land, Seithenyn, to be in charge of the sluices. Unfortunately, Seithenyn was notoriously lazy and a bit of a party animal. One night, he fell asleep and forgot to lock the gates. The kingdom and all those who dwelled there was lost to the sea.[1]

As always, the story varies depending on the narrator, with some versions portraying Seithenyn as a sexual fiend who forgot to lock the gates because he was thinking with a different organ other than his brain, but both he and Gwyddno Garanhir are mentioned in the *Black Book of Carmarthen* (Welsh: *Llyfr Du Caerfyrddin*) in the thirteenth century. In this 'original' version, it was a maiden by the name of Mererid who drowned the place after she forgot to put the lid back on a well. Another version says how she failed to lock the gates because she was being raped by Seithenyn.

The *Mabinogi* also refer to a drowned kingdom out in the Irish Sea, as do some Arthurian, Irish and Cornish tales. But I wonder if there's any proof out there that Cantre'r Gwaelod was, indeed, a real place.

The BBC recently reported on a finding that just might offer some form of evidence that it did exist: a medieval map uncovered by Simon Haslett of Swansea University and David Willis, Jesus Professor of Celtic at the University of Oxford. The map depicts two islands off the coast of Cardigan Bay, one near Aberystwyth and Aberdyfi and the other near Barmouth. Put together, they would be about half the size of Anglesey. The islands are clear to see on the Gough Map, being a thirteenth-century (the earliest) complete map of the British Isles.[2]

But what about actual, solid evidence? Surely, with the technology we have today, if Cantre'r Gwaelod was a real place, we would know about it, right?

Well, there is solid evidence that proves that the land once reached further out than it does today. There is a drowned ancient forest at Newgale and another at Ynyslas, though you need to go after a storm if you want to see the oak, pine, birch, willow and hazel stumps in all their glory. These forests are estimated to be around 4,000 and 5,000 years old. The skull and antlers of a red deer were also found there, as well as evidence to suggest that the land was a swampy environment covered in reeds.

What happened was that 8,000 years ago, the ice caps from the Ice Age finally melted and the sea rose to a similar level to what it is today, though our cliffs have been eroding and giving way ever since, so there is no doubt that our ancestors would have had to retreat towards drier land at some point. That being said, no official records were kept (that we know of) that confirm the names of any cities or cantrefs lost to the sea – we have only bold tales of drunken gatekeepers to go on.

What is interesting, however, is that they have found the remains of timber walkways in these ancient forests, along with human footprints preserved in the peat, a Mesolithic tool, the skeleton of an auroch (an ancestor of modern domesticated cattle) and stones that show evidence of having been burnt. There's no denying, therefore, that our ancestors were out there.[3]

I spoke with Peter Stevenson about all this.

'In the Second Branch, Bendigeidfran walks across the sea to Ireland, crossing two rivers, until the Irish see the masts of his ships. Archaeologists working in Cardigan Bay are now finding that around twelve thousand years ago when the glaciers began melting, the Irish Sea was a mixture of forests, swampland and river valleys. This sounds like a long time for us, but to an archaeologist, it seems like yesterday!'

'Which increases the chances that Cantre'r Gwaelod was a real place?' I suggested, somewhat hopefully.

'That's right.'

He told me that there was once dry land in Cardigan Bay, so Cantre'r Gwaelod probably existed and, over time, the story became mixed up with dreams, memories and fantasies and we made archetypal heroines and villains of the people who once lived there.

'Then there's the story of Plant Rhys Ddwfn, the children of Rhys the Deep,' he said. 'Rhys built a utopia out there, a whole other world, in the same area as Cantre'r Gwaelod. For those of us on the mainland, the idea of there being a hidden utopia out there must have been very appealing, as it is now … an inspiration to create a better world. Tryweryn has become a post-modern "submerged civilisation" story, a new creation myth that links in with the politics of water.'

As we make our way up Cardigan Bay towards Aberystwyth, we look out at the Irish Sea and let our imaginations run wild. Alas, we can't go deep-sea diving today, for there's a glamping pod with a hot tub waiting for us at Devil's Bridge with our names on it …

20

Where the folk
has the most extortionate
toll charge ever?

I've been here before, or at least came close. It was when a friend and I went to a nearby village to pick up a certain tiny black kitten. His litter was found dumped on the side of the road at a time when most of the population was stuck indoors going mental thus pet prices had skyrocketed, but luckily for me, Loki and his siblings were picked up by some good Samaritans. It cost me more in petrol to get here than it did for Loki himself. I remember it was a two-hour drive back to Cardiff (this was during a window of time when it was allowed) and, just ten minutes in, he got carsick. Pulling up in a lay-by, I got out to clean up the mess and that's when I spotted the sign for Devil's Bridge.

It is said that around the eleventh century, the Devil went on a tour of Wales, seeing as he had never been before and had heard that the scenery was amazing. Whilst exploring Ceredigion, dressed as a monk, he came across Megan Llandunach, an elderly local woman. She seemed upset, so he asked her what was up.

Megan spotted his hooves and immediately saw through his disguise. Not much of a disguise, really, was it? Despite this, she told him that her cow had wandered into the river and that she couldn't get it back.

He responded: 'What you need my dear, is a bridge, and I am just the man to build you one! Why don't you go home, and in the morning there will be a bridge waiting for you … all I ask in return is for the soul of the first living thing to cross the bridge …'

'Deal!' she said. '*Nos da!*'

However, Megan regretted it later and didn't sleep a wink all night, but by morning she had a cunning plan ... taking her faithful dog with her, she headed back to the river, where stood the best bridge she had ever laid eyes on.

'I told you I could do it!' the Devil gloated, appearing out of nowhere. 'Now it's your turn to keep your end of the bargain ...'

He had spent the entire night gathering stones from all over Wales and Ireland, stopping only once, when he was preached at by the vicar of Llanarth. Megan walked up to the bridge, stopped and threw a large loaf of bread over to the other side. Bewildered, the Devil watched and frowned as her poor, innocent dog ran after it, ultimately becoming the first living thing to cross the bridge.

Fuming, the Devil threw a hissy fit and vanished, taking the dog's soul with him. He was never seen around these parts again, despite the amazing scenery.[1] I, however, vowed to return one day so as to cover the story of Devil's Bridge for this book. Now here I am, with Loki's adoptive mother ...

We took the scenic way up, through the Elan Valley. Cwm Elan is found to the west of Rhayader, in Powys. Covering an area of seventy square miles, it is often referred to as the 'Welsh Lake District'.[2] We stopped for a break in the picnic area next to The Arch, built in 1810 by Thomas Johnes (owner of the nearby Hafod Estate, who we shall get to in a minute) to mark the Golden Jubilee of King George III. It is situated about a mile and a half from Devil's Bridge, on the A4574, and marks the point where the road across the Cambrians to Rhayader becomes a mountain road. The road once ran straight under the arch, but it has since been moved so as to protect it from an ever-growing flow of traffic.[3]

Parking up near the train station at Devil's Bridge itself, we realise that we have a couple of hours to kill before we can check in to our glamping site. As such, we decide to head straight to the bridge, passing a quaint little chocolate shop and a tiny post office along the way. Turning the corner, we are faced with the magnificent view of a heavily forested valley. An old, grand hotel dominates the village, with visitors wearing raincoats and ponchos (good idea if going on holiday in Wales) sat drinking outside, admiring the view. And just around the corner, crossing over the Afon Mynach, lies the infamous bridge itself.

It's special in that it is compiled of three separate bridges, each built on top of the other. At the bottom, you've got the original medieval bridge, the one rumoured to have been built by the Devil, and then you have a stone bridge on top of that, built in 1753. The most recent bridge, the one we now stand on, is an iron bridge built in 1901. The resulting structure was Grade II listed on 21 January 1964. It stands over Mynach Falls, a point where the Afon Mynach joins Afon Rheidol, dropping ninety metres (300 feet) in five steps into a steep and narrow ravine.[4] Paying the £2 fee at the booth, we head down a steep set of stone steps towards The Punchbowl, standing in line with a long queue of shuffling tourists.

The Welsh name for Devil's Bridge is Pontarfynach, which means 'the bridge over the Mynach'. *Mynach* is the Welsh word for 'monk'. Some believe that Afon Mynach got its name because it ran through land owned by a nearby monastery and that the original bridge, the one allegedly built by the Devil, was actually built by the monks of Strata Florida. This was to help them get to their abbey in Pontrhydfendigaid. The name 'Devil's Bridge' did not appear in official records until 1734. So why the sudden shift from the holy to the satanic? Why, money, of course.

Pontarfynach became Devil's Bridge for the sole purpose of attracting visitors. This will come as no surprise if you were paying attention; the Devil came to Wales for the amazing scenery and built a bridge that was truly a marvel to behold – it sounds like a Victorian tourist brochure! The name first appeared around the time Thomas Johnes, owner of the Hafod Estate and builder of The Arch in the Elan Valley, wanted to show off his new hunting lodge but nobody was interested. Needless to say, they came in droves following the name change, and his hunting lodge grew to become the Hafod Hotel and coach houses, now the main focal point of the village, excluding the bridge.

Thomas Johnes had allegedly visited Switzerland before building his lodge, the chalet-type architecture he saw there influencing his design. Coincidentally (or maybe not so much), the story of Megan outsmarting the Devil is very similar to a Swiss tale, in which the Devil builds a bridge so as to reach a lost goat.[5]

In fact, there are numerous stories from all over Europe that follow a similar narrative. Here in the UK, there's also a Devil's Bridge at Kirkby in England, where he comes across another woman and her cow. Then there's Devil's Bridge in Yorkshire, where the Evil One helps out a local shoemaker; Kilgrim (now Kilgram) Bridge, where he takes the soul of a shepherd's dog named Grim; and the bridge at Kentchurch in Herefordshire, where he faces off against Jack o' Kent.

A legendary character often thought to have been based on a real person (or persons), Jack o' Kent roamed the Welsh Marches and was well known around Herefordshire and Monmouthshire. He was known for playing dangerous games with the Devil, whom he often outwitted.[6]

After taking a few photos and still having an hour to spare, we head back to the Hafod Hotel for a pint. The place is teeming with tourists and we are advised to book a table for our return visit later this evening. 'So Sophie; people using folktales to make money or to encourage tourism ... good thing, or bad?'

'I think it's a good thing, to be honest. It encourages people to get interested in history and learn more about local culture; I'm all for it!'

With that done and the pod all ready for us, we head back to Griff, eager to get into the hot tub and pop open a bottle of bubbly. But the excitement is bittersweet, for we know that tonight is our final night together. Well, for a week, at least. I'll drop Sophie off at Aberystwyth train station in the morning then continue my journey on my own, heading north to my home county of Gwynedd.

But it isn't long after settling in that our quiet evening is interrupted by a phone call. 'Who could that be now?' I huff.

Dad. Wonder what he wants ...

Freedom to Live:
The Rugged North

21

Where the folk
did the flower-faced
girl go?

'Hello,' I say with a smile. 'Sorry to disturb you. We're looking for Llech Ronw ...'

'Oh, sure. It's back the way you came.'

'Hello, sorry to disturb you ...'

'... you take a left down there ...'

'*Lle* what?'

'No idea, sorry.'

I've come to the tiny village of Bont Newydd, on the outskirts of Blaenau Ffestiniog. This is the first stop on my 'Magical Mystery Tour' of the Fourth Branch of the Mabi–

'What did she say? Was I right?'

Oh yeah, Dad's with me.

'This must be the place, look. Go knock and ask them,' he says.

'Bloody hell, we've knocked every door in the village, do we really need to?'

'Well, you're the one who keeps getting the directions wrong, I was right the first time. Go ahead.'

Sighing, I approach the small farmhouse at the top of the hill and knock the front door. It's too early in the morning for this. A white-haired old lady answers and goes 'Here for the slate?'

'Yeah, I am, yeah.'

She points to the small gate leading into the field directly opposite the house – 'Through there' – then she raises her finger ever so slightly, pointing towards the furthest corner of the field. 'Then over there.'

'Thanks.'

'It's a good thing you asked, saw a young couple walking in the opposite direction the other week. I did try shouting at them from up here, but they just waved at me and wandered off. Haven't seen them since. Oh well.' She shrugs.

Whether it was the thought of me being alone in the perilous campsites and glamping pods of deepest, darkest Wales, or the sheer horror of knowing how much that might have cost me, Dad had insisted on joining me on my adventure. 'And you can use our place as a base, too, to save some money. So where shall I meet you?'

I asked him to meet me here so that I could begin the northern stretch of my adventure with a bang by visiting locations from the Fourth Branch of the *Mabinogi*. '*Math fab Mathonwy*' is a huge tale featuring many characters and takes place all over Wales, although most of it is based up north. The Fourth Branch should come with a content warning, as it is packed with upsetting events such as rape, incest, murder and abuse. Indeed, it would give *Game of Thrones* a run for its money.

It concerns the family of Math, the magician king of Gwynedd, and tells of their brush with Pryderi. Math believed that his feet must be continually held by a virgin whenever he was at war and it was this bizarre ritual of his that kick-starts the whole thing. His nephew Gilfaethwy was infatuated with Goewin, you see, his latest 'virginal royal maiden foot-holder'. Gwydion, Gilfaethwy's older brother, decided to help him out.

Gwydion is a well-known character in Welsh mythology. Often referred to as a 'hero', this Welsh sorcerer was also a devious rapist who enjoyed inciting wars and getting involved in other people's affairs. Featured in *The Book of Taliesin* is a medieval Welsh poem called '*Cad Goddeu*', which means 'Battle of the Trees'. It features many of the characters mentioned above and involves Gwydion raising an army of *Lord-of-the-Rings*-type walking trees to help him face off against Arawn, king of Annwn.

In any case, Gwydion came up with quite a cunning plan for helping his little brother. Using magic, he tricked Pryderi into giving him his beloved pigs, which were a gift given to his father in the First Branch of the *Mabinogi* by Arawn. I'll go into more detail on all this later, but his trickery ultimately resulted in Pryderi declaring war and Math heading down south to sort it all out, which left Goewin unattended. Once she was alone, the two brothers raped her.

So the plan was a success; however, Gwydion and Gilfaethwy didn't escape Math's wrath. He punished his nephews in the most obscene way possible: he turned them into animal pairs (beginning with deer, then boars, then wolves) and forced them to mate together. This went on for three whole years, until Gwydion eventually offered his sister Arianrhod to be his uncle's new virginal foot holder. Math also married Goewin following these dreadful events.

But Math decided to test Arianrhod's virginity first and got her to step over his magic wand. This caused her to immediately give birth to a son, Dylan ail Don (or 'Dylan the Second Wave'), who, when baptised, fell into the sea and became at one with the ocean, changing in form (some say into a sea creature, others the form of the ocean itself).

Dylan has a very interesting backstory himself, with some interpreting him as the Welsh God of the Sea. The sound of the sea rushing up Afon Conwy was once referred to as 'Dylan's death-groan'. He also features in the Black Book of Carmarthen. Dylan was accidentally killed by his uncle Gofannon in the end and his grave is said to be found near the location of Dylan's Rock, just offshore from St Beuno's Church at Clynnog Fawr.[1] Gofannon was another deity worshipped by the Celts. He was one of the ones who gave Culhwch a hand in his quest to impress Olwen's dad.[2]

In any case, a strange lump of life also fell out of Arianrhod that day. Gwydion spotted it and incubated it in a chest in his bedroom. When the strange lump grew up to become a boy, he presented him to Arianrhod, who rejected him. She was so disgusted with him, in fact, that she put a curse on him which meant that he would never have a name of his own, that he would never have any warriors unless she gave them to him and that he would never marry a human woman.

Being the good Samaritan that he was, Uncle Gwydion came to the rescue. He used his shapeshifting abilities to trick his sister into naming the boy Lleu Llaw Gyffes (meaning 'Bright, Skilful Hand')

and into thinking that they were under attack by a foreign army, so that she handed them some arms. All that was left was to find young Lleu a missus. For this, Gwydion turned to his own uncle for help.

Using flowers from oak, broom and meadowsweet, along with a little bit of magic, they created a gorgeous wife for him whom they named Blodeuwedd, which means 'Flower-Face'. But Lleu wasn't Blodeuwedd's true love; her true love was a man named Gronw Pebr. Gronw and Blodeuwedd ended up having an affair and the pair came up with a plot to murder Lleu.

The trouble was, Lleu was protected by magic and was therefore very hard to kill. They needed to know how to defeat him and Blodeuwedd got it out of him in bed one night, saying that she needed to know so as to be able to protect him from his 'enemies'.

It wasn't going to be easy. Turns out, he couldn't be killed during day or night, indoors nor outdoors, whilst riding nor walking, not naked nor clothed, nor by any weapon that had been lawfully crafted. The only way to kill him was at dusk, wrapped in a net with one foot on a cauldron and the other on a goat and the only weapon that would kill him was a spear forged over the course of a year only when everyone else was at mass.

Now, most people would have given up right then and there, but the two lovers prevailed and they somehow managed to trick the gullible Lleu into getting himself into that most ridiculous situation. But even after all that, he transformed into an eagle, left his human body behind and flew away. Gronw and Blodeuwedd legged it and Gwydion set out on a quest to find Lleu. After tracking him down, Gwydion sings a magical poem to tempt him down from a tree, then uses his wand to turn him back into a human. Lleu was in a bad shape after his ordeal, so Gwydion tasked the best physicians in Gwynedd to nurse him back to health. After that, the two set off together to find Gronw Pebr.

Gronw apologised and offered to compensate him, but Lleu insisted that he have a pop at him with a spear at least, which seemed only fair. Gronw hid behind a stone, but the spear pierced it and killed him. Gwydion then turned his attention to Blodeuwedd and transformed her into an owl as punishment. She flew off into the night, never to be seen again.[3]

Like I said, a long and complicated tale. The elaborate scene set up in order to kill Lleu I find particularly weird, along with the gullibility of the man. But it's a well-known tale from the *Mabinogi*, and Blodeuwedd, in particular, has featured heavily in Welsh popular culture ever since.

So where did this story take place, then? Too many places for me to cover, but I have got time to visit a handful of them, so here we are at Llech Ronw, said to be the stone which Lleu's spear pierced when he killed Gronw Pebr.

'Get that plastic bag out of the way so I can get a picture, will you?'

'Gronw's Slate' is essentially a standing piece of slate with a hole in it, found along the banks of Afon Bryn Saeth, which leads to the much larger Afon Cynfal at the foot of the hill. The village owes its name to the bridge crossing that river.

A man named Frank Ward found the stone along the banks of Afon Cynfal in 1934 and left it there. He reckoned it must have washed downstream from nearby Ceunant Coch, because a local woman was said to have seen it there before. Then, years later, a stone similar to the one described, possibly the same one, was spotted along Afon Bryn Saeth, where we now stand. Bryn Saeth, by the way, translates to 'Hill of the Arrow'.

It seems that the events of the Fourth Branch of the *Mabinogi* have had a huge influence over place-names in this area. As well as Llech Ronw and Bryn Saeth, there is also a farmstead down the road called Llech Goronwy (Goronwy's Stone/Slate).[4]

So could this really be the slate from the tale? Could it be proof that these extraordinary events really did take place? Doubtful, but it is odd how this thing keeps popping up in different places. Just don't freak out if you ever spot it down by Afon Dyfi, the river once considered to be the border between north and south Wales, for the one found there is just a replica of this one, made by local stone mason Edward Rowlands for the filming of *The Owl Service*, a Granada Television series from the sixties – a sexy modern re-telling of the tale, I believe.[5]

So what could it be, then? Hag stones (which go by many other names) are formed when water erodes through stone, creating a natural hole. Spiritualists have held them dear for centuries, believing them to have magical protective qualities. However, these are usually smaller stones, small enough to be worn. The important detail here is that they were formed naturally through erosion and that Llech Ronw was found along the banks of a river, so there's a good chance it was created by natural means.

But we shouldn't rule out the possibility that the hole is man-made. That is to say, that it's either a hoax or something that was never meant to be made a big deal of in the first place. One theory is that it was simply a stone gatepost. Indeed, stone gateposts with holes in them are found all over the countryside.

'So what do you make of it?' I ask Dad as we make our way back to Griff.

'Personally, I think it was a slate pillar with a hole in it, part of an old gatepost, which was moved here to promote the story, and the area, most importantly.'

'A publicity stunt, then? Do you think places like this should be preserved better?'

'I think so, yeah.'

Whether it be true or not, it certainly wouldn't be the first place to do something like this. It seems unlikely that it was pierced by the spear of a shape-shifting sorcerer, that's for sure.

Time to head to the next stop on our Magical Mystery Tour. Tomen y Mur is a Roman fort dating back to the first century AD. It is found along the slopes of an isolated hill north-east of Llyn Trawsfynydd, not far from here. These days, Trawsfynydd is mainly known for its nuclear power plant. The A470 runs between the Roman fort and the plant, a road I have driven countless times, yet I had no idea this place even existed until I started writing this book. Sarn Helen, the Roman road named after the wife of Emperor Magnus Maximus (Welsh: Macsen Wledig) from 'The Dream of Macsen Wledig', also runs nearby. More on them later.

The site was built by the Roman governor Gnaeus Julies Agricola in AD 78 and was abandoned around AD 140. It stood as a ghost town for many years, the land perhaps used by local farmers, until the Normans built a motte there in the eleventh century. Today, the site is owned and managed by the Eryri National Park Authority.

The name Tomen y Mur means 'Mound of the Wall', probably being a nod to the old Norman motte. As such, the place couldn't have got its name until the eleventh century. There are no records of the name given to the place by the Roman occupiers.

What remains here today are traces of a flat parade ground, a bath house, a Roman *mansio* (pub), a few roads, some burial mounds, the site of what was possibly a temple and a small military amphitheatre.

At Harlech Castle, said to be the site of the giant king Bendigeidfran's court from the Second Branch of the *Mabinogi*, you will find a number of inscribed stones believed to have originated from Tomen y Mur. Each one is dedicated to the Roman Centuria who built each of the fortress walls here and gives details on the length of each structure. Some of these 'Centurial Stones' are also on display in the museum at the Roman fort of Segontium in Caernarfon. Note that the north-western fortress wall here at Tomen y Mur is merely a reconstruction.[6]

We came here today because Mur-y-Castell, as the place is known in the Fourth Branch of the *Mabinogi*, was recognised as the legendary palace of Ardudwy at the time, way before Roman occupation. Ardudwy features heavily in the *Mabinogi*. In the Fourth Branch, Lleu built his palace in the area after he was given control of both Eifionydd and Ardudwy by Math.

Alas, we currently have no evidence of such a palace ever existing, so again, who knows if we're at the right place. But it was worth the trip, regardless; the views here are amazing, despite the radioactive centrepiece.

'That's where we're off to next,' I say, pointing towards the woodland surrounding the power plant.

'Come on then, let's make the most of daylight.'

'Ever gone jungle trekking before then?' I ask, raising a brow.

'Eh? Why do you ask?'

22

Where the folk can I find a genuine Celtic rainforest?

The next stop on our 'Magical Mystery Tour' is the village of Maentwrog, which lies just up the road from Tomen y Mur. This part of our tour focuses on the death of Pryderi. Gwydion and Gilfaethwy popped down south incognito when they came up with their little scheme to rape their uncle's virginal 'royal foot-holder', taking with them a band of bards and minstrels. Seemingly impressed by the entertainment, Pryderi offered them a gift for the effort, to which Gwydion asked him for his herd of pigs, even offering to buy them off him instead.

Pryderi reluctantly agreed, but made him promise never to sell them to anyone else. However, the previous morning, Gwydion had gone into the woods and picked twenty-four mushrooms, transforming them into twelve steeds and twelve hunting hounds. He then decorated them in gold before presenting them to Pryderi.

What follows is a long journey in which Gwydion and Gilfaethwy herd the pigs back up north, stopping at various places along the way. This section gave rise to many Welsh place-names, most notably Mochdre up in Conwy, which means 'Pigtown' or 'Town of the Pigs'. Meanwhile, Pryderi went to fetch his new dogs and horses to go for a hunt, only to find a bunch of mushrooms waiting for him instead. It suddenly dawns on him who the leader of the travelling minstrels was and he rallies up the troops.

The war reaches its climax when Pryderi and Gwydion meet at Y Felenrhyd, at a spot chosen by Gwydion called the 'Yellow Ford', being a long stretch of sand along the Dwyryd estuary that appears at low tides. He chose this spot for a reason, for the places where the land meets the sea and the sea meets the sky are magical hotspots, apparently, so his spells were powerful enough to kill Pryderi, himself but a mortal man, but a fierce warrior nonetheless, who fought bravely until the end.[1]

Pryderi fell in the woods outside Maentwrog, Y Felenrhyd, a place classed as an actual rainforest, would you believe it. But first, we're stopping off at the churchyard in Maentwrog, for here lies a boulder with a peculiar past …

Maentwrog lies in the Vale of Ffestiniog, between Blaenau Ffestiniog and Harlech. Sarn Helen runs through here, as well. It is said that Pryderi was laid to rest at this spot, Maen Tyfiawg. However, years later, people would claim that the standing rock was thrown there by a saint (though some say a giant) named Twrog when he faced off against the Devil himself (though others say a she-devil), who lived here with his/her worshippers, who were the original settlers.

Twrog was a missionary (this much is true; he came to Wales in the sixth century) and came to rid the place of its evil and set up a good, law-abiding Christian community in its place. We learned at St Govan's just how badass some of these saints could be; Twrog was one of those badass saints. He squared up to the Devil, spending half a day engaged in a wrestling match with him. Or her, whatever.

Retreating to the Moelwyn Mountains, Twrog sat and prayed and an angel appeared. She showed him a clearing in the woods where unearthly fruits (though some say mushrooms) grew. Upon eating one of those fruits/mushrooms, Twrog gained superhuman strength and abilities. Perhaps this is why some people mistakenly refer to him as a 'giant'.

From up on the hill, he spotted the Devil down in the valley and hurled a boulder at him/her/them. It landed between their legs, embedding itself in the ground. The Devil realised it must have been some divine intervention and turned into his/her true form, growing wings and horns and flying off into the distance, never to be seen in the area again. Twrog then built his church there, setting up his little Christian community. I'm not sure what happened to all the Satanists, whether they fled or converted, but I assume that everyone lived happily ever after.[2]

'Here we are, down this turning, look.' Dad points frantically. 'Alright, alright!'

I have driven past Maentwrog countless times but had no idea I was driving past such an important monolith. The churchyard truly is a very pretty spot. We make our way around on foot, admiring the surrounding flora. 'These trees are pretty cool, what are they?' I ask.

'These are yew trees, which can live for over a thousand years. Growing them was encouraged, to prevent livestock from grazing in the cemetery. They were also great for making bows, apparently.'

The stone stands just outside the back of the church. Some say that if you rub against it, then you are destined to one day return to Maentwrog. It is also said that you can see the mark of Twrog's hand on the stone, if you look closely enough.[3]

It's time to move on to our next destination, Coed Felenrhyd. Along with Llennyrch and a few other woods nearby, Coed Felenrhyd are what's left of a huge woodland that once stretched all the way from Scotland down to Portugal. It's officially classed as a rainforest and was barely touched by humans for centuries. That's right – we're heading to a genuine Celtic rainforest!

Referred to in the *Mabinogi* as 'Melenrhyd' or 'Y Felen Rhyd', Coed Felenrhyd, together with Llennyrch, cover an area of 765 acres and stretch from Llyn Trawsfynydd with its nuclear power plant in the east to where the Prysor and Dwyryd rivers meet in the west. Living along the many streams and craggy gullies of these woods are a number of rare lichens (including forty-two rare UK species), mosses (some twenty-five rare UK species) and liverworts. They thrive in the forest's uniquely humid air, which is what makes this place so special. It is among the best places to see rare lichen in all of Wales and you can find barnacle lichen and acid-bark specialists here, the likes of which you would normally only find in the jungle.

Like I said, these woods, boggy marshes and pockets of grassland went largely untouched for years, with the nearby Snowdonia Hall-House built sometime in the 1500s. The house was occupied right up until 2009, when the last owners died. A number of other farmsteads were also built around this time, all plotted on small areas of open grassland, and you can still see remnants of them here today.

Perhaps the most frequented and well known of these, however, is Tŷ Newydd.

In 1739, the Industrial Revolution brought the timber trade to the area, then the slate quarries opened in 1760. By 1763, most of the timber was gone. Then the First World War brought with it an increase in the demand for timber once again, so efforts were made to replant large areas of oak for future forestation. Then, in the 1960s, other large areas were cleared completely and replanted with non-native conifers. These foreign trees blocked much of the sunlight from the forest floor, changing the ecosystem in those areas completely.

At the same time, a lot of the woodland was cleared to make room for grazing sheep. You would think this would only do further damage, but the grazing sheep actually helped bring some sunlight to the forest floor, saving some of the rare lichens and bryophytes. Alas, it would seem that this 'ancient forest' isn't really that ancient, after all. Although, some of the original trees do still exist.[4]

We stop along the banks of a fast-flowing river to eat the little picnic Mam prepared for us. There's always heaps of cake to get through whenever I come home. We choose this spot because we believe it to be the pulpit of a famous preacher named Huw Llwyd, but as I would later find out, we are very much mistaken; we should have headed to Afon Cynfal when we visited Llech Ronw earlier on. Still, it makes for some boyish fun as we clamber over the boulders to get to the other side.

At the height of his fame, Huw Llwyd would exorcise those believed to be possessed by demons at his pulpit at Y Felenrhyd, where crowds of people would come to witness the spectacles. The demons would apparently come out of their victims' bodies as black shadows and were caught in the current and cast down Rhaeadr Ddu (the 'Black Waterfall'). Huw Llwyd's daughters apparently threw his book of spells into a river following his death, which was subsequently grabbed and taken by a demonic hand or claw.[5] We stop at Rhaeadr Ddu on the way back, after momentarily losing each other in the woods: 'I told you not to wear that camo jacket!' I exclaim, flustered.

We then join a narrow country lane that takes us down towards the Maentwrog hydroelectric power station. Just off the road, in the woods, we see tents and shelters made of large branches, with fire pits and clothes lines dotted all around the place. It would seem that some people have taken to living in the jungle.

'Hm ... can't blame them!' Dad says. 'Right, where to next?'

'Harlech,' I reply, though my aching legs are already longing to go home. 'For the Second Branch.'

'The Second? It's like bloody *Star Wars*, this! Why aren't you doing them in order?'

'I– it's how it landed geographically, is all. Besides, it doesn't really matter, it's not a continuing narrative or anything. Not really.'

'Hmm ...'

23

Where the folk can I listen to talking starlings and a Welsh banger?

'So why hasn't he got any arms or legs, then? Vandals?'

'"Vandals"!' I scoff. 'It's meant to be … artsy.'

'What do you mean?'

'You know, it symbolises something. You're supposed to, like … interpret it.'

'Hmm.'

We stand there for a moment, squinting in the sunlight as we gaze up at Ivor Robert-Jones's bronze statue of Bendigeidfran. The legendary giant king is depicted riding a horse, upon which is mounted the body of his deceased nephew, Gwern.

'… I think it's supposed to represent the loss of something you love, or something that's important to you. "Like losing a limb", kind of thing.'

'Look – there's a plaque over there!' Dad walks over to where he was pointing at.

'… only thing is, in the story, Gwern was only a baby, or a young boy, at least, and he was thrown into a fire … and Bendigeidfran never rode home on a horse, he was beheaded.'

'The dimensions are all wrong, anyway!' Dad declares. 'I thought he was supposed to be a giant – how the hell could he be riding a horse?'

'Hmm … wonder why it's called the "Two Kings" as well – Bendigeidfran was a king, sure, but I don't think Gwern was – future king of Ireland, maybe …'

The Irish offered to make Gwern king of Ireland the same time they built Bendigeidfran a palace in order to make peace when they were losing the war, you see. But you shouldn't look to Wikipedia for such information; Gwern's page states that Efnysien cast him into the fire 'seemingly without motive', when in actual fact he did so after discovering that what the palace offered to his brother was nothing more than a Trojan horse.

Dad returns to my side and looks up at the statue for a moment, then turns and heads back towards the car park. 'Come on, then.'

The Second Branch of the *Mabinogi*, often referred to as 'Branwen, daughter of Llŷr', is one of the most beloved and well-known Welsh tales. According to whichever version you read, the main focus is either on Branwen or her brother, Bendigeidfran (also known as Brân, meaning 'crow' or 'raven', the Blessed), but the narrative structure always stays the same and goes something like this.

Matholwch, king of Ireland, sails to Harlech to ask Bendigeidfran, king of the 'Island of the Mighty' (Britain), to ask him for the hand of his sister Branwen in marriage. This, in turn, would form an alliance between the two kingdoms. It makes sense, so Bendigeidfran duly accepts the proposal and holds a feast to celebrate. However, he forgets to invite his half-brother Efnysien (whose name means 'trouble' or 'strife') or to consult him on the proposal in the first place, for that matter.

Efnysien takes this personally and decides to mutilate Matholwch's horses, cutting the celebrations short (pardon the pun). Naturally, Matholwch is furious. To compensate him, Bendigeidfran gifts him with *Y Pair Dadeni* (the 'Cauldron of Rebirth'), a magical cauldron that has the ability to bring the dead back to life.

Accepting the apology, Matholwch takes Branwen back to Ireland to rule by his side and she gives birth to a son, Gwern. But the honeymoon period doesn't last long. Efnysien's actions are still niggling at the Irish and they take it out on poor Branwen. She is put to work in the kitchens, where she is beaten daily by the head chef and is made to sleep alone in squalor.

This goes on for a while, but little do the Irish know that Branwen uses her spare time to tame a starling, teaching it to speak. Don't scoff – a trained starling can be just as chatty as a parrot. After tying a letter to the base of the bird's wing, she sends the starling across the Irish Sea back to Harlech to ask Bendigeidfran for help, who immediately musters together an army. Among the ranks are Taliesin, the aforementioned Pryderi and Manawydan, the main character of the Third Branch, along with warriors from all 154 cantrefs (medieval Welsh land divisions) of Britain.

Being a giant, Bendigeidfran walks across the Irish Sea with ease and, when the Irish see him and his army approaching, they initially mistake him for an island. It is important to mention at this point that it wasn't until after the glaciers melted following the last Ice Age (around 7500 BC) that Britain and Ireland became two separate landmasses. The existence of so many legends involving characters walking between the two places has led many to believe that, at some point, there existed two channels instead of the one body of water that we all recognise today, making it easier to travel from one country to the other.[1]

A terrible war ensues and the Irish retreat, seeking refuge beyond a river. But Bendigeidfran forms a bridge using his own body for his army to cross, proclaiming 'He who is a leader, let him be a bridge', which remains in use as a Welsh proverb to this day: *A fo ben, bid bont.*

Interestingly, the Irish name for Dublin, Baile Átha Cliath, translates to 'Town of the Hurdled Ford'. In the tale, hurdles were placed across Bendigeidfran's back to make it easier for his men to walk across (not the Olympic kind you're thinking of – that would have made it far more difficult, albeit entertaining).[2]

Cornered, the Irish offer to make peace by building Bendigeidfran a house big enough for him to live in. Accepting the offer, the Welsh lay down their arms and join the Irish for a good-ol' knees-up. But Efnysien is suspicious and goes to inspect the house. There, he finds a hundred bags of 'flour' hanging from the ceiling. Prodding the bags, he discovers that they actually contain armed men, lying in wait for an intoxicated Bendigeidfran. A furious Efnysien crushes the head of each warrior then re-joins the party.

He asks if he can hold baby Gwern for a bit, only to cast him into the fire in front of everyone there and it all kicks off again. With the Welsh losing, Efnysien discovers that the Irish are using the magic cauldron to revive their dead and so decides to sacrifice his own life by hiding among the corpses. With a living soul cast inside, the magic cauldron is destroyed.

Only seven individuals survive this battle; among them are Manawydan (Pryderi's mate in the Third Branch, who ends up marrying Rhiannon), Taliesin, Pryderi and Branwen, who kills herself out of grief shortly after. A mortally wounded Bendigeidfran (poisoned spear) tells the survivors to cut off his head and to take it back to Britain. Doing so would make the Brits forget all about the horrors that they witnessed during the war against the Irish. For the next seven years, his still-talking head entertains them all at his court back at Harlech.

After that, he is moved to Gwales (Grassholm Island, off the coast of Pembrokeshire), where he is kept for a further eighty years, until a guy named Heilyn fab Gwyn opens the forbidden door that faces Cornwall, breaking the spell of forgetfulness. After this, he is taken to his final resting place at Gwynfryn ('White Hill'), considered to be where the Tower of London now stands, and is buried facing France so as to ward off any French invaders.

As for Ireland, the war leaves only five pregnant women left alive in the whole country, who give birth to five sons, who then repopulate the entire country using the only women available – their mothers. Through these individuals alone, the entire country is repopulated and divided into five districts – Connaught, Meath, Leinster, Munster and Ulster.[3]

'Harddlech' was the location of Bendigeidfran's castle, being the rock upon which Harlech Castle was built in 1283. At the time this tale was set, the rock sat right beside the Irish Sea, but water levels have since retreated and the sea now lies almost a mile away.

Heading through the gift shop, we are treated to a short film that sums up the history of the place then we cross the bridge over the moat and head inside. A World Heritage Site, construction began here in 1282 as part of Edward I's invasion of Wales and lasted until 1289. Eddy was a strong advocate of building impenetrable castles as a means of keeping control and with the help of French architect Master James of Saint George, he built an 'Iron Ring' of castles around Wales.

What they found with such castles was that you didn't need much manpower to defend them. They were also useful tools for psychological warfare; as the courts (*llysau*) of Welsh princes fell, Eddy and James would carefully deconstruct them then re-erect them within the walls of their own castles, often using them as barns or pantries and such out of spite.

Harlech Castle's defences were first put to the test between 1294 and 1295, when Madog ap Llywelyn led a failed Welsh uprising against the English. His forces tried taking Harlech, which was manned by a garrison of around thirty-six men (with a blacksmith, a carpenter, a stonemason and the constable included in this number). The Welsh thought they could starve them out at the very least, but they were unaware of Eddy's 'secret weapon', being a water gate round the back where the English could sneak supplies in from the sea. Needless to say, Madog's efforts proved fruitless.

And so, the English ruled over Harlech from their castle on the hill for over a hundred years thereafter, until a certain Welsh rebel disturbed the peace once more: the man, the legend, Owain Glyndŵr, who, as a result of an argument between him and his neighbour, Reginald de Grey, Lord of Ruthin, instigated another revolt. In 1404, he was crowned Prince of Wales, holding parliament at Machynlleth.

Despite all this, with the use of better equipment and sheer numbers, the English turned the tide of the war in 1407. In 1408, following the orders of future king Henry V, English forces undertook a siege of Harlech Castle, bombarding it with cannons and destroying the southern and eastern parts of the outer walls. This didn't quite do the trick, but Henry gave the job to a man called John Talbot while he went off to try to take back Aberystwyth Castle instead and Harlech fell to the English a year later, with many of the Welsh having died of exhaustion.

Glyndŵr himself managed to escape, disguising himself as an old man and running to the hills with a band of loyal supporters. Like Robert Carlyle in *28 Weeks Later*, he left his family behind to face the music and they were incarcerated in the Tower of London. By 1409, the English had taken back most of Wales. Glyndŵr spent the rest of his days hiding in the woods, ambushing English forces. The last recorded sighting of him was in 1412, when he attacked English troops on a road in Brecon. Despite there being a handsome reward offered for his capture, he was never betrayed.

How he died and where he is buried remains a mystery. In fact, his disappearance transformed him into something of a mythical figure amongst the English and the Welsh. He became a folk hero, someone with unearthly powers who would one day return to liberate the Welsh from their oppressors, much like King Arthur. What really sent everyone over the edge was that during Glyndŵr's revolt, a meteorite passed so close to the Earth that it was visible even in the daytime. It looked a bit like the Christian cross and stuck around for several weeks (or up to three months, some say).

The castle was also the site of another historic battle that had a huge impact on Welsh culture and inspired one of the most popular songs of all time. The Wars of the Roses were caused by a feud between two rival factions of the House of Lancaster and the House of York. During this time, in 1460, Queen Margaret of Anjou fled to Harlech Castle after losing the Battle of Northampton. Led by Dafydd ap Ieuan, the Lancastrians held the castle from 1461 to 1468, under what became known as 'the seven-year siege', being the longest known siege in the history of the British Isles.

This siege inspired the song and military march 'Men of Harlech', otherwise known as The March of the Men of Harlech/Through Seven Years, though it has often been associated with the time Glyndŵr held the castle. I first heard it when I watched the film *Zulu* on some lazy afternoon between Christmas and New Year's Eve when I was a child.

Later, in 1642, the English Civil War between the Royalist supporters of Charles I and the Parliamentarians saw war returning to Harlech Castle once more. After that, like most castles, it became nothing more than a muse for budding artists until its eventual restoration as a museum and tourist attraction.[4]

I arranged to speak with local blue badge tour guide Siân Roberts about Harlech's history. Siân did a foundation degree to become a blue badge tourist guide for Wales. Those with the degree refer to themselves as 'Wales Official Tourist Guides Association' as they are the only guides officially recognised by the Welsh Government.

After telling me about the Mari Lwyd she once found in a skip, she jumps straight into it.

'The story starts with Bendigeidfran looking out from his rock at "Hardd Lech", which means "a fine rock" and that was the original name for Harlech. The rock upon which the castle stands is suspected of being this rock. They say that Edward I, who built the castle, was a big fan of these legends and often attributed himself to them, like he did with Macsen Wledig up at Caernarfon and all the Arthurian legends.'

She tells me that Harlech was a great place to build a castle, strategically. You had great views of both land and sea, from all directions. When asked whether she thinks Edward knew about the connection to the *Mabinogi*, she said that it's very likely that he did. Trouble is, Eddy kept very detailed reports on how he built his castles, but he never really got into the why.

'The stories of the *Mabinogi* were already well-established oral tales by the time they were written down in the thirteenth or fourteenth centuries,' she goes on. 'I've heard one archaeologist say that the Second Branch of the *Mabinogi* has nothing to do with Harlech because the castle wasn't built then. But to me, it's clear that it's linked to Harlech. People were here long before the castle was. I also enjoy telling it because of its relevance today – it's an anti-war story, something that will always be relevant.'

After taking in the view from each tower, legs wobbling like jelly, we head back towards the car park. And so ends my coverage of the Second Branch of the *Mabinogi*.

'So where to now?' Dad asks.

'Adra.'

'Home?'

'Home.'

24

Where the folk
do skeleton brides, disgraced kings and Nazi spies go to hide?

The following incestuous tragedy is a tale of love, tradition and a man's innate ability to overlook romantic details. It's the tale of *Rhys a Meinir*. It's a popular one, this one. I first heard it in school; I remember having to sum it in a four-pic comic strip. Mine went something like this:

1. Little boy and girl *cwtsh* up in the shade of an oak tree.
2. The girl, now an adult and wearing a bridal gown, runs off to hide inside the old oak.
3. The boy, now a full-grown man in a suit, searches the hills for his childhood sweetheart.
4. Crying on his knees, he looks up at the old oak tree, now ablaze and looking very biblical, with the skeletal remains of his bride-to-be, still wearing her wedding dress, looming over him.

The story in its entirety goes more like this: in the year 1750, in the secluded valley of Nant Gwrtheyrn on the Llŷn Peninsula (Welsh: Pen Llŷn), there lived a young boy and a young girl named Rhys and Meinir. They lived very near each other down in the village of Nant, spending many days playing in the hills of Yr Eifl. At the time, there were only three farms in the whole valley: Tŷ Uchaf, Tŷ Canol and Tŷ Hen. This has led some to speculate that the pair might have been cousins. Their favourite spot to play was beneath the shade of an old oak tree up in the hills.

Eventually, their friendship blossomed into love and they decided to marry. Meinir immediately went about setting a date and making plans for her dream wedding. The 'inviter' was a local man named Ifan y Cilie, who spread the word to the locals that Rhys and Meinir were to get married at nearby Clynnog Church that Saturday.

Some of those locals headed down to the Nant the day before the wedding to present the young couple with gifts. One gave a piece of cloth; another brought some yeast flour … all things that were considered handy to have around at the time. Back then, the people of Nant celebrated an old tradition called the 'Wedding Quest', in which the bride would play hide-and-seek on the morning of the wedding and the groom's friends had to go and find her.

And so, when the big day came, with everyone gathered at Clynnog Church, Meinir ran to the hills. Rhys's mates played their part and went after her, but couldn't find her anywhere. They returned to Rhys, who was waiting at the church with all the other guests.

Rhys decided to go look for her himself and set out on a solo search party that would last years and ultimately send him down the path of insanity. He spent the rest of his days roaming Yr Eifl in search of his childhood sweetheart, only to stumble upon her skeletal remains one night when a storm broke out. He sought cover underneath the old oak and lightning struck it, splitting it apart. Meinir had seemingly gotten stuck in her hiding spot all those years ago. Rhys instantly died of a broken heart.

The original tale ends there, but reports tell of strange goings-on at Nant Gwrtheyrn. There is a tree in the village commemorating the couple, but of the original tree, wherever it may be, it is alleged that no bird will ever land on its bark except for owls and cormorants. Visitors have also reported seeing the ghosts of Rhys and Meinir walking hand-in-hand along the beach late at night. They describe them as being 'a man with a beard and long hair and a woman with hollow sockets for her eyes'.[1]

It is for these reasons, plus the fact that *Rhys a Meinir* is such a popular tale, that I have decided to head to Nant Gwrtheyrn with my family to see the place for myself. Joining me on this outing are my mother, father and my younger brother, who has autism.

'Did you two learn about Rhys a Meinir in school like I did, then?' I ask my parents as we make our way to the famous village.

'I didn't, it was never taught to us,' Mam shakes her head.

'Yes it was!' Dad protests. 'I attended a school outing, a weekend at Glynllifon, which focused on some of the *Mabinogi* sites and stories.'

'Well, it was never taught to me, anyway.'

'Oh! Here it comes, now ...' Dad nods.

Dad has been warning us about the steep and perilous road down to the village ever since we left the house – the aptly named 'corkscrew road'. Driving past a car park at the base of Yr Eifl in my parents' blue people-carrier, we stop at the top of the hill and the craggy landscape suddenly gives way to a magnificent sea view. The village sits at the foot of the hill, in the shadow of Yr Eifl.

'What do you make of it, then?' I ask them.

'I like it. It's about how love can turn into tragedy,' Mam replies.

'You mean how some of the old customs could end in tragedy,' Dad declares.

'Hm.' Mam turns to look out the window.

When we eventually reach the village, we are presented with something of a ghost town: the cafe and visitor centre are shut and the rows of holiday cottages lie empty and cold. Taking our sweet time, we make our way towards the seafront, eyes peeled for the symbolic torn tree that commemorates the doomed lovers.

'You ever been to Nant Gwrtheyrn before?' I ask.

'I have, on a knees-up with work not long after the place re-opened after lockdown,' Mam replies.

Dad frowns and shakes his head. 'Don't think so, but I knew of the place.'

The village's heyday was between the years 1860 and 1920, when it was a booming mining town. At one point, over 2,000 men worked the granite here. Shops, offices and a chapel were also constructed at this time. But the quarries eventually shut and ran into ruin and by the 1970s Nant Gwrtheyrn was quite literally a ghost town, officially abandoned.

Then, a local GP by the name of Dr Carl Clowes, with the help of other locals, formed a registered charity called Ymddiriedolaeth Nant Gwrtheyrn (Nant Gwrtheyrn Trust), eventually saving up enough money to buy the village outright. They quickly set about renovating the crumbling old buildings, developing a centre and a retreat for Welsh learners. Nant Gwrtheyrn is still managed by Ymddiriedolaeth Nant Gwrtheyrn today.[2]

The valley's name pays homage to Brenin Gwrtheyrn, the fifth-century king of the Bretons, otherwise known as Vortigern. Gwrtheyrn was considered a 'disgraced king' because he had sought the help of Saxon mercenaries in a desperate attempt to hold onto power. Naturally, this made him very unpopular with the Welsh. He then added salt to the wound by falling in love with Alys Rhonwen, daughter of the Saxon leader Hengist.

He asked for her hand in marriage and Hengist organised a huge banquet attended by all those who mattered to the Saxons. But Hengist had a cunning plan: on his command, each Saxon stood up and stabbed the Briton sitting next to him in a wedding massacre worthy of *Game of Thrones*.

Gwrtheyrn fled to this secluded valley with his tail between his legs, where it is said he spent the remainder of his days. His actions were blamed for the Saxon invasion and he was forever known as the king who betrayed his own people.

What happened to him next is widely debated, with some saying that he lost his mind roaming the hills of Yr Eifl, much like Rhys did. Others say that when he fled to Nant Gwrtheyrn, God Himself (so terrible was his betrayal of working with the Saxons) shot fireballs at him down from Heaven. Some attribute this to the frequent lightning storms that occur in the valley, which play an important role in the story of *Rhys a Meinir*. As Gwrtheyrn and his men attempted to flee, he and his son, Gwrthefyr Fendigaid, were killed by a local leader named Garmon.[3] Indeed, from dragons (more on that later) to the Saxons to God, Gwrtheyrn faced off against a lot in his lifetime.

Shortly after his death, three monks arrived at the valley. The locals did not take kindly to the Christian trio, who were on a pilgrimage to Ynys Enlli (Bardsey Island) and they especially didn't take kindly to them suggesting they help them out by building a church in their village. Needless to say, the monks were forced to flee for their lives.

Livid, they cast three curses on the valley so that:

1. Nant Gwrtheyrn's ground would never be consecrated again; therefore, no one could be buried there.
2. Members of the same family would not be allowed to marry each other. (Strange how this one is considered a curse!)
3. Nant Gwrtheyrn would succeed and fail three times before forever falling into ruin.

It is said that soon after the monks left, a nasty storm hit the valley and all the men who were out fishing that day perished. Without any men about, the women eventually left. Nant Gwrtheyrn had fallen for the first time.[4] The story of *Rhys a Meinir* came after. At a time when only three houses existed in the village, were they the relatives whose marriage was forbidden? Then Nant Gwrtheyrn would fall again following the closure of the quarries. It now exists as a centre for teaching Welsh; is this Nant Gwrtheyrn's last shot at redemption? But people have been buried at Nant, so perhaps not every curse will come true, right?

The lore surrounding Nant Gwrtheyrn doesn't end there. A tale from the early nineteenth century tells of another interesting character called Elis Bach (English: Small Elis), who lived at Tŷ Canol. A very small man indeed, his legs were said to be just thirty centimetres long. At the time, a livestock market was held at Nant and farmers from far and wide would come to visit. As it happens, despite his size, Elis Bach was considered the faster runner in the village and was therefore tasked with rounding up the sheep and goats ready for market each day.

Then one day, two strangers came, flashing their money and paying way over the asking price for their numerous purchases. They were invited back to Elis Bach's home to try some of his mother's home cooking, but Elis was wary of the men and hid inside a cupboard to spy on them. That's when he overheard the strangers conspiring to steal the sheep. When he saw them scrambling up the corkscrew road to the top of the hill with a flock of sheep later that night, Elis set off after them with his faithful dog Meg.

He overtook the men and lay in wait at a bend in the road, jumping out when they came around the corner. The pair scarpered, heading towards Pistyll, leaving the sheep behind for Meg and Elis Bach to lead back down the track to Nant.[5]

Was there once a man of short stature living at Nant Gwrtheyrn who rounded up sheep for the market and chased off a pair of sheep rustlers? Possibly.

Another, more recent story from Nant is more likely to hold some truth to it – during the Second World War, a mysterious stranger named Margaret Gladys Fisher moved to a lonely cottage above Carreg-y-Llam, on the western side of Nant. But the locals reckoned Mrs Fisher behaved a bit oddly and rumours began to spread that she may be a German spy, sent to Nant to send signals to German U-boats down by the beach.

We may never know if this was merely gossip, however, for in the early hours of one Sunday morning in 1943, her wooden bungalow burned to the ground. No one could identify the charred remains. Her dogs had never barked to alert anyone of a fire, leading some to speculate that she poisoned them before escaping to Germany on a fishing boat. Whoever she was, her disappearance certainly is a mystery.[6]

Honestly, I've never known a village to have as many folktales and urban myths as Nant Gwrtheyrn. We nearly walk past the symbolic torn tree in the end. When we do find it, I take a quick photo and, with that, we head back to the car. Mam is having none of it, but Dad and I have decided to climb Yr Eifl. As such, Mam heads on home with my brother, leaving us behind.

Growing up in a small village just outside Caernarfon, I could see this trio of hills from my bedroom window. Some locals refer to them as the 'Three Sisters' (perhaps due to their breast-like appearance, though they would only make up a sister and a half, really) and the English, who must have misheard the locals saying 'Yr Eifl', call them 'The Rivals'.

'What do you call them?' I ask.

'I've always called them "The Rivals", but Mam calls them by the Welsh name, Yr Eifls.'

Eifls. With an 's'. There's some top-notch Wenglish for you, right there.

Climbing Yr Eifl is pretty straightforward, as far as finding your way around is concerned, but be warned that it certainly isn't easy on the knees. From the car park, you head up a clear, straight path up to Bwlch yr Eifl, the small pass that sits between the central and highest summit of Garn Ganol (the latter being the highest point on the peninsula, housing a trig point and an ancient cairn) and Garn Fôr, the northern-most summit, which overlooks the Irish Sea. Ascending the path, you get a great view of Nant Gwrtheyrn.

Once at the top, you can choose to go up either hill, but from there, you will need to pass over Garn Ganol in order to reach the third summit, Tre'r Ceiri. For this reason, we decide to start with Garn Fôr. Also known as Mynydd y Gwaith (Mountain of Work/Work Mountain), it is clear to see from any direction that Garn Fôr has been heavily scarred by industrialisation over the years. Towering over Bwlch yr Eifl is a microwave radio relay station.

I would describe it as a short-but-intense scramble to the top. If you're into graffiti, discarded lager cans and empty baggies, you can stop to explore the numerous abandoned mining shelters along the way. There is a path but it is very narrow at times and the hill gets so steep that it would be very easy to lose your balance and fall backwards if wearing a rucksack. I very nearly learned this the hard way.

Once at the top, Dad makes the obligatory phone call home to Mam, waving as though she would be able to see us from the front porch. Mind you, if she had a pair of binoculars, she probably could.

Once back at Bwlch yr Eifl, we have another steep climb up to the top of Garn Ganol. This proves to be a far more gruelling climb, it being the tallest of the three peaks. We stop several times to 'admire the view' (catch our breaths) then sit to have our sandwiches at the top, looking down at the third and final peak, Tre'r Ceiri.[7]

The foundations of the old Iron Age hillfort are clear to see, from the fortified wall to the circular stone houses within. Its name derives from the Welsh word *cewri*, plural of *cawr*, which means 'giants' (the 'Town of Giants'). Built around 200 BC, archaeological evidence (most of which dates from around AD 150–400) suggests that the place survived as a local settlement throughout Roman occupation, which means that the Romans probably left them to it, or perhaps at least traded with them. It is now considered to be one of the best-preserved examples of a prehistoric hillfort in all of Europe.

The huge walls remind me of something out of *Jason and the Argonauts*. They are largely intact, with some reaching up to four metres high (thirteen feet). Beyond them are the remains of about 150 circular stone houses, which would have been covered by turf rooftops. It is estimated that around 400 people once lived here.[8]

With all three peaks conquered, we head back to the car park where Mam has returned to pick us up. We're dying for a pint but are aware that we have to go to church first. As mentioned, Rhys and Meinir were all set to get married at Clynnog Fawr, often referred to simply as Clynnog, which means 'the place of the holly trees'. The village sits on the A499, between Caernarfon and Pwllheli. The church itself can be seen from the main road. It's dedicated to Saint Beuno (sometimes hilariously anglicised into 'Bono') and has a very interesting history.

It is said to have been the site of a Celtic monastery founded by Saint Beuno in the early seventh century that was burnt to the ground by Vikings in 978 and then again when the Normans arrived. It was an important pit stop for pilgrims on their way to Ynys Enlli who were travelling along the 'North Wales Pilgrims Way'.

There is an ancient wooden chest there called Cyff Beuno (Beuno's Chest), made from a single hollowed-out piece of ash, which was used for securing donations left by the pilgrims. You've also got Maen Beuno (Beuno's Stone), which is said to have Saint Beuno's fingerprints on it, and Ffynnon Beuno (St Beuno's Well), a Grade II listed structure found at the south-western end of the village.

It is said that Beuno had a 'wondrous vision' prior to his death and, for many years after, people would cure their children of various ailments by washing them in the water from the well then having them spend the night asleep on top of Beuno's grave. But that's not all: as well as having a magical well, Beuno was also said to have raised at least seven people from the dead! Among them were his niece Gwenffrewi (Winefride) and his cousin and disciple, Aelhaiarn.[9]

Now, I'm not sure whether I tripped over something or if my legs simply gave way, but as I navigate the headstones in the churchyard, I somehow manage to fall flat on my arse, sort-of saving my dignity with a swift side-roll … the pub is calling, I think.

'*Peint?*'

'*Peint!*'

25

Where the folk

did the ancient oak, the royal court and the floating island all go?

I recall pulling pints during my stint as a barman that were named after various characters from the *Mabinogi*. They were all brewed locally and one of the most popular of the craft breweries was Bragdy Lleu, based in Dyffryn Nantlle. Their website states that they are 'passionate about the culture, history and language of Dyffryn Nantlle – the land of the *Mabinogi*. Every beer we brew is named after characters from the world-famous Welsh folklore legends, with elements of those characters conveyed in the unique character of each beer.'

They have a golden ale called Blodeuwedd made from the various flowers used by Gwydion and his uncle Math to create the famous 'flower-faced girl'. Considering Lleu to be a 'unique, strong, appealing and memorable character', the amber ale dedicated to him has an interesting mix of flavours to convey this. There is also a red IPA dedicated to Bendigeidfran, the giant king from the Second Branch, then there's the darker, more traditional Welsh ale dedicated to Gwydion.[1]

Nice as those beers are, we won't be visiting the brewery today. Instead, we are heading to Dyffryn Nantlle to complete our 'Magical Mystery Tour' of the Fourth Branch of the *Mabinogi*, with Dad at the helm of the blue people-carrier. Dyffryn Nantlle (from the name Lleu) is renowned for its rich collection of folklore. The stories were made known to the rest of Wales after they were compiled together by John

Owen Huws throughout the 1970s and 1980s and then published over three volumes in 2008.[2]

'Do you know much about Blodeuwedd and that, then?' I ask.

Mam shakes her head. 'We weren't taught about local history or legends at all in the schools I went to, so my knowledge is very limited.'

'Yes we were! Bloody hell, were you ever in school?' Dad asks suspiciously.

'We went to different schools, Steve!' Mam snaps.

'Well, we learned about it in my school, plus what I learned on that trip to Glynllifon I told you about.'

'So would you associate place-names like Dyffryn Nantlle and Dinas Dinlle, say, with the *Mabinogi*?'

'I do.' Dad nods affirmatively. 'We're very lucky up here, to be living and working in such a rich corner of Wales with such close association with the *Mabinogi*. I'm keen on my history, as you know, so my knowledge of place-names is pretty good.'

'Mam?'

'No.'

It's a grey and miserable day and the wind is howling loudly all around us. Light drizzle somehow manages to completely drench us whenever we stop to get out the car. We are driving around the trunk of Elephant Mountain – at least, that's what we locals call it. Its official name is Mynydd Mawr, which means 'big mountain'. We call it Mynydd Eliffant because, well, it kind of looks like an elephant.

'I always think of home whenever I see the elephant.' Mam looks up through the sunroof.

'That's because you are home!' Dad deduces.

Mam ignores him. 'I've called it "the elephant" ever since I first went on holiday to my grandparents' house in the village, before we moved here.'

What is it with this family's obsession with elephants? In any case, as you wind around the trunk towards Drws-y-Coed (Door of the Trees), the elephant suddenly turns into one side of a huge glacial valley, part of an enormous half-pipe, if you will. For geologists, this is actually a very important place. In the nineteenth century, it was part of a fiery debate between the Diluvialists, who believed that every event in the Bible was true and that stuff like the Great Flood helped shape the land, and the Glacialists, supporters of the more scientific Glacial Theory. Charles Darwin visited the site in 1842 due to its significance.[3]

The original road was built by Edward I when he chose this spot to mine for the materials needed to build his Iron Ring of castles around Wales. One of the first recorded jousting events in Britain was held here around that time, with some scholars believing that the rules written up that day later became the basis of the statute that regulated the whole sport.

Further down the valley, you will find a large boulder with a memorial placed before it. That's the very boulder that crashed through the roof of the local chapel on 17 February 1892. The chapel itself was relocated to a safer location further down the road.

But the main attraction, for me, has to be Llyn-y-Dywarchen, being the lake of the legendary 'floating island'. Legend goes that the island was once a meeting place for a fairy and her human husband after she was forbidden from ever walking on mortal land. Another 'Lady of the Lake' story.

Rumour has it that the herdsman, who lived on a nearby farm (which was demolished in the 1970s to make room for a car park), was minding his livestock in Cwm Marchnad one day when he came across a stunning blonde bombshell. Turns out, she was one of the *Tylwyth Teg* who lived up at Llyn-y-Forwyn. One night, when the full moon had set behind Y Garn, her father agreed to their marriage on the condition that the herdsman never touched his daughter with iron (if you recall, iron is like kryptonite for the *Tylwyth Teg*, particularly the females of the species).

The pair were happily married for many years and they had children, whose descendants are said to live in Cwm Pennant. But one day, the fairy's horse drowned at Llyn-y-Gader, sinking into the marsh like that traumatic scene in the film *The NeverEnding Story*. The man then helped his wife mount his own horse, sliding her foot into the iron stirrup. D'oh! The horse became bewitched and went back to Llyn-y-Forwyn with a band of dancing fairies, taking the herdsman's wife back to Annwn.

Later, the man's fairy mother-in-law created a magic island upon which her daughter could stand so as to be able to see and talk to him. And so, the lovers met like this for years thereafter, until the herdsman passed away and the fairy wife returned to Annwn once and for all. And just in case you don't believe me, it is said that after the herdsman died, a brown trout popped its head out of the lake and swore that it was all true. Allegedly.

But the idea of a floating island may not be as 'out there' as you might think: Gerald of Wales, Thomas Pennant (who claimed that cattle would often wander onto the island only to end up marooned out on the lake) and Edmond Halley, astronomer, all reported seeing it with their own eyes. Experts say that a part of the bank, itself held together by roots of various shrubbery, could at one point have broken off from the mainland. Anchored to the bank, this lump of earth could then have ended up floating in the water. But sadly, there's nothing to be seen here today.[4]

As we head further into the valley, it becomes more densely populated. The Nantlle Railway used to run through here, existing for the most part as a horse-drawn service for transporting slate from the quarries, but it was also a functioning passenger line. It became the last horse-drawn British Railways service, closing in 1963 only because the branch line that it connected to closed first.[5]

Heavy industry left its mark on the Nantlle Valley in a big way and it doesn't become more evident than when we arrive at our next stop. They say that this was the location of the oak tree upon which Gwydion found his missing nephew Lleu, who was stuck in the form of an eagle as the result of a failed assassination attempt at the hands of Blodeuwedd and Gronw Pebr. Due to industrialisation, however, the place has since been submerged by two man-made lakes. The oak tree, if it did exist, certainly doesn't any more.

The spot where I currently stand, which looks back up the valley from which we came down, is considered to be one of the best views in all of Eryri, but there's something bugging me. Three empty lakes, a car park … I consider how industrialisation has removed all remnants of the places linked to the folklore of Dyffryn Nantlle and can't help but wonder how many other places in Wales have fallen to the same fate.

Oh well, time to bring our 'Magical Mystery Tour' to an end. We head now to a place known to and often frequented by most, if not all, of the people of my hometown: Dinas Dinlle. I could see the long, sandy – well, pebbly, beach from my bedroom window growing up, and I have many fond memories of the place, from learning how to ride a bike to when I would go there to drink with my mates in my teenage years. I'm sure I'll keep returning for many years to come, as long as the place isn't completely engulfed by the sea, that is, for industrialisation isn't the only threat to places linked to Welsh folktales.

Dinas Dinlle is a huge stretch of coastline that offers views of the Llŷn Peninsula, the Irish Sea and the mouth of the Menai Strait. Here you will also find Caernarfon Airport, an old Second World War airbase which now offers flying lessons and pleasure flights, but you won't be jetting off anywhere from there any time soon, mind. This stretch of coastline is also a Site of Special Scientific Interest.

They have a real issue with erosion here at the moment, as Mam would testify: 'I remember being driven by my parents along the seafront road, which has since been completely eaten by the sea.' Efforts have been made to slow down the process, but from what I can see here today, the sea is very much kicking our arses.

But we're not here for the beach today – we've come to climb up Boncan Dinas, the old Iron Age hillfort that makes Dinas Dinlle so recognisable. Much of the site has been lost to sea and there is only one semi-circular rampart remaining. Coins and pottery found at the site in 2019 suggests that the place was occupied by the Romans in the second or third centuries CE. There might have been a Roman lighthouse here at one point and it's also the home of one of the biggest stone roundhouses ever found in Wales. It is also rumoured to have been the home of Lleu Llaw Gyffes and his dysfunctional family. Some say Dinas Dinlle is actually named after him: Din 'Lleu'.[6]

A man named Lewis Turner reached out to me through Facebook a few months ago concerning his interest in Boncan Dinas and the theory that characters from the *Mabinogi* are personifications of old Celtic deities. We chatted over Zoom, and he told me how Welsh mythology helped shape his pagan beliefs.

'I was lost and trying to make sense of everything, so I did my own research and came across all these tales about Welsh gods and deities and such and I just felt that it all made sense, in a way … during uni I actually gave lectures and talks to members of the community on various aspects of paganism, which I really enjoyed.'

'You mentioned that you came across some Welsh gods during your time studying in Wales. Is there a particular god that stands out to you, and if so, why?'

'Well, I'm an avid reader and I love gaining new knowledge, so any deities associated with teachings or learning, really … Taliesin, Ceridwen … they're certainly the ones I'm drawn to the most. But I'm also interested in gods that are very human, ones that are relatable. That's what I like about the Welsh gods; they have feelings, aspirations, traumas, they trick each other, they cheat … I love the humanity of them all.'

Lewis believes that we still have a lot to gain from hearing their stories: '… I really do think that the preservation of these stories, and their importance to not only a country's history and culture but for its future, is absolutely vital. We can't know where we're going if we don't know where we've been! Also, people know all the big stories, but they need to know more of them.'

Just offshore, if conditions are right when the tide goes out, you may also be able to catch a glimpse of Caer Arianrhod, a reef rumoured to be the remains of a stone structure built for Arianrhod, Lleu's mum. Mind you, others say that the reef is actually linked to a different story, when a town called Trearanrhag and its people were drowned for their sins and only three women survived.

Others claim that Caer Arianrhod was the original Welsh name for the Milky Way and that perhaps you could once see it from here. Sticking with the space theme, some say that the northern star constellation Corona Borealis is even named after Caer Arianrhod, as her name translates to 'silver wheel', perhaps a hint to her previous association as the goddess of the moon.[7]

'What are your thoughts on Caer Arianrhod, then?' I ask Dad.

'My understanding is that the site is made up of an old rock outcrop and was probably deposited by the retreat of the glaciers which ran down from the direction of Dyffryn Nantlle. The moraine clay has since been washed away, leaving the rocks exposed, especially at low tide.'

Sadly, Boncan Dinas will soon be lost to the sea. Archaeologists (led by the Gwynedd Archaeological Trust, itself funded by Cadw and the National Trust, who own the land, and the CHERISH project) are currently rushing to complete their excavations before the site is lost forever. It is estimated that a recently discovered roundhouse will fall to the sea in as little as fifty years' time.[8]

Another one bites the dust. I wonder how many of these places future generations will actually be able to visit themselves. And, on that sombre note, so ends my coverage of the Fourth Branch of the *Mabinogi*.

26

Where the folk
can I find space rock and
a martyred mongoose?

Like most people who live away from home and have gone back to stay with their family, it isn't long before I revert to being a moody teenager. As such, I have made plans to meet up with Danny and Alun, two mates from school. Danny is an artist and has kindly been providing me with illustrations for the blog. As Sophie would testify, 'He's a good egg!' Alun and I were best men at his wedding a few months back.

The plan is to head to Dinas Emrys, the site where the red and white dragons of lore battled it out. I'm waiting for them down the road at Beddgelert, a village that has a very special place in my heart. A week before my thirteenth birthday, Mam got me a job as a pot-washer in a cafe here so I could 'buy as many PS1 games as I wanted'. The chimney-sweeping jobs were all taken. In the end, Begel, as the locals call the place, witnessed the entirety of my teenage years, as well as my uni days. 'We saw the worst of you,' as my old boss Lyn once said.

The last time I was here was New Year's Eve before lockdown – Beddgelert does the best New Years, what with everyone dancing out on the bridge, a DJ all set up in the street, all the pubs rammed with their fires crackling, a crazy parade on with a different theme each year, local youths jumping into the river at midnight ... I remember, once, they had a full-size Tardis standing in the river that they set alight at midnight – it was like something out of *The Wicker Man*.

The village thrives thanks to the selection of pubs, cafes, shops, guesthouses and restaurants that align its pretty, picture-perfect streets. Think of the village in *Hot Fuzz* and you'll get the gist. It has won numerous floral competitions in the past – expect hanging baskets, ramblers and parking nightmares. Well, expect all that in the summertime, but come here in the winter and the place is a ghost town, with most of the businesses shut and all the holiday homes lying empty and bare. Such seasonal employment makes the village a hotspot for local teens from neighbouring villages who are looking for work between educational terms.

Alfred Bestall, who wrote and illustrated some of the *Rupert the Bear* stories, lived in the village for over forty years, having bought his little cottage at the foot of Mynydd Sygun in 1956. By all accounts, he was a quiet and lovely man. Many of his illustrations were inspired by the scenery here and you can really see the gorse-covered hills of Beddgelert in them as soon as you learn this.[1]

The surrounding countryside has also provided backdrops to numerous films over the years, including *The Inn of the Sixth Happiness* and *Tomb Raider 2: Lara Croft and the Cradle of Life*. These days, the village features more on local news on account of all the big lorries that keep getting stuck on the bridge after being led here by GPS.

One night, when I was working behind the bar at one of the pubs for some extra dough, the locals told me about a meteorite that crashed here on 21 September 1949. It came through the roof of the Prince Llywelyn Hotel early in the morning and made local headlines. Then Durham University put an ad up in the papers offering a reward to anyone who brought them a fragment of the space rock. Eager to make the most of the situation, or more likely so that he could fix his roof, Mr Tillotson, the hotel owner, sold them the piece of space rock. Well, half for them and the other half for the British Museum. Strangely, there have only ever been two such recorded meteorite falls in Wales and the other happened just fourteen miles away at Pontllyfni in 1931.[2]

But no one comes here for some space rock or for a scarf-wearing bear – people come to Beddgelert in droves to visit a certain dog's grave. A dog that never even existed.

The story goes that around the year 1200, Llewelyn the Great (or Llywelyn Fawr, for us Welsh), King of Gwynedd and eventually all of Wales, lived here with his newborn son. Llywelyn loved hunting down wolves in the surrounding woodland with his pack of hounds. Gelert was his favourite. He was the strongest, fastest and most loyal dog a man could ever ask for.

Llywelyn went out hunting one day, but when he got back home he found the place a bloody mess and his son was nowhere to be found. Gelert was lying on top of the cradle, blood dripping from his mouth.

Devastated and blinded by rage, Llywelyn sank his sword deep into Gelert's heart, killing him. But when the poor sod yelped, he woke up Llywelyn's son, who started crying. Llywelyn lifted the cradle and found his son safe and sound. Talk about having a Man Look.

But it gets better: he next spotted the body of a great big wolf lying on the flagstones. It then dawned on him what had actually happened – Gelert had slain the wolf to protect his little boy. Gutted, he buried Gelert down by the river and it is said that he never smiled again.[3]

By now, it is no secret that a south Walian by the name of David Pritchard made all this up after moving to Beddgelert in 1793. Struggling as the new landlord of the Goat Hotel, he devised a plan to attract tourists to the area. He put forth the story about Llywelyn and his martyred hound and, by 1800, the story had gone viral, made popular by the poet William Spenser, who wrote *The Grave of the Greyhound* after he stayed at the Goat that year.[4]

David Pritchard changed the fate of the village forever, but his story doesn't end there. It is said that he died before he had the chance to enjoy all the profit that he made or to write a will. As such, his restless spirit haunted the streets of Beddgelert for weeks following his death. The locals were so terrified that no one dared go outside in the night. Then, one night, a previous employee of Pritchard's by the name of Huw went to ask his old boss what he was hanging around for.

David Pritchard's ghost led Huw to his grave, where he told him that he was worried his wife would never find the money that he had stashed for her beneath a flagstone at the hotel. Pritchard's ghost told him that he could keep some of it for himself if he showed his grieving widow where it was. Huw kept to his word and the ghost of David Pritchard was never seen again. Mind you, some say that he, along with the ghost of Huw, still haunts the corridors of The Royal Goat Hotel today, smiling gleefully whenever someone spends their money there.[5]

A tale of a similar narrative to that of Gelert has already been told all over the world numerous times before, with the earliest example originating from India way back in the fifth century. That version, *The Brahmin's Wife and the Mongoose*, tells of a husband and wife, their son and their pet mongoose. One day, the wife asks her husband to watch the kid so that she can go fetch some water. However, the husband goes out to beg for food, instead. During that time, a cobra enters the house and goes to kill the boy. The mongoose bravely fights off the snake, killing it. Proudly, the mongoose goes to show the wife what he's done.

But when she sees the blood on his face, she assumes that he's killed her son and drops the jug of water on him, killing him instantly. Then, of course, she realises her mistake and puts the blame on her husband for being so 'greedy'.[6]

Drawing inspiration from this tale, Rudyard Kipling's *The Jungle Book* features a short story about a heroic Indian mongoose named Rikki-Tikki-Tavi who defends his family from a pair of cobras.[7] But, more importantly, the story's been reinvented countless times by different cultures from all over the world, with the animals and circumstances changing to suit each locale. Basically, this is exactly the same as what happened in Devil's Bridge. And the moral of these stories? Think before you react, perhaps? Don't be greedy? 'Assume' and one makes an ass out of you and me? They all apply and, best of all, fit into a short, simple narrative.

But the difference between Beddgelert and Devil's Bridge is that Beddgelert never changed its name as part of the big conspiracy to draw in tourists. The people put up a fake headstone, granted, but the place-name already referred to the grave of some Gelert or other in the first place – who was that, then? The village was called this for hundreds of years before David Pritchard moved in and is believed to refer to Saint Gelert, or Celert/Celer.

Saint Gelert was a seventh-century hermit who lived in a cave, now known as the Holy Well of St Celer, near Llandysul, from where he would heal weary pilgrims of their ailments. Eventually, a church called Capel Mair was built over the well, though its foundations are still there.[8] Some say that he was martyred here in Beddgelert, though plenty of people disagree.

And just to throw in one last spanner into the works, there was also a Venetian saint by the name of Gellért who became Hungary's first Christian martyr, so it seems that the name is synonymous with martyrdom wherever it goes.[9]

Today, people don't hide the fact that it was all made up, but they don't exactly broadcast it either, for without these folktales, places like Beddgelert and Devil's Bridge would surely struggle. Mind you, even when the magic is gone and people know the stories aren't true, they would still come. They're doing it right now.

I— oh wait, I think Danny and Alun are here …

27

Where the folk
did the Welsh get
their flag from?

On 28 February 2019, the Welsh flag was voted the 'Coolest Flag in the World' from a poll of over 140,000 people from across the globe. I mean, come on, it's a fire-breathing dragon, right? There are only two other countries that have a dragon on their flag, those being Bhutan and Malta,[1] but dragons, in some shape or form, feature in almost every culture and religion in the world. So why did Wales choose to make an idol of one of these mythical beasts and how has *Y Ddraig Goch* (the Red Dragon) embedded itself so deeply in Welsh culture and identity?

If you ask around, most Welsh people will tell you we got the flag from the time the red Welsh dragon fought off the white English one, something many Welsh children are told at school. That epic event supposedly took place here, at Dinas Emrys, but the tale is all too often mistold.

I am currently reciting the proper version to my poor friends as we make our way up through the woods from Craflwyn Hall, crossing rocky waterfalls as we make our way to the forgotten fortress on the hill, like some sort of modern-day Gandalf. Danny would later tell someone that he was 'trying to get Russ's thoughts on the wedding when all he wanted to do was talk about bloody dragons!'

'In any case, you've told us this one before, on your blog. It's the one with Gwrtheyrn, right?' Gwrtheyrn – 'the disgraced king'.

He's right. Glad someone read it. 'Well, what do you remember of it, then?'

Alun puts up his hands up and shakes his head. 'Don't ask me, mate.'

Danny sighs. 'From what I can remember, it took place in the fifth century or something. Vortigern, or Gwrtheyrn, whatever, decided to build a fortress here to hide from the Saxons, right?'

I think he's right – it was before he became a traitor.

'But building his fortress proved to be a bit of a nightmare. Every time they came near to completing construction, the thing would collapse in a pile of rubble. Again and again, the newly built walls crumbled and fell.

'You'd think Gwrtheyrn would have brought in a surveyor to find out what was going on, but he instead sought the help of local sorcerers and magicians. They told him that the obvious solution would be to find a child born unto a human mother and a father who was from the Otherworld, then kill said child and sprinkle the ground with its blood.'

'That poor sod was to be Myrddin Emrys from Carmarthen, aka Merlin. Young Merlin, keen to save his own skin, told Gwrtheyrn that the real issue concerned the two dragons that were locked in eternal battle in an underground lake beneath the hill. Gwrtheyrn was unusually hesitant for a man about to sacrifice a child, so he ordered his men to check it out. Lo and behold, they did indeed find there to be an underground lake beneath the fortress. Myrddin prophesised that, should the red dragon lose, then the Saxons would successfully invade Wales. Right?'

'Right.'

Alun smiles gleefully, somewhat taken aback that Danny remembers it all.

'But the excavation disturbed the dragons and the white one fled to the skies, never to be seen again. The red dragon chose to stay here and his name was celebrated by the Welsh ever since. Gwrtheyrn went on to successfully build his castle, which he named Dinas Emrys, after Myrddin. Mind you, when he eventually left the castle, it fell into the hands of Emrys Wledig, so the name more likely came from him. Yes?'

'That's right, spot on! What do you make of it all?'

Danny shrugs. 'It's an interesting myth. Probably inspired by true events. But true or not, I wear the flag with pride, from on my triathlon gear to my locker door going right through military training.'

'Did you know that the story was set here before you read the blog?'

'Nope, no idea.'

The old keep does date back to Gwrtheyrn's time and does show signs of having been re-built several times, but sceptics argue that it was destroyed either in battle or due to its poor foundations. As always, it's also a very familiar tale, if you look at myths and legends from around the world. In particular, it shares striking similarities with the legend of the construction of the Buddhist Samye Monastery in Tibet, for example, which features spirits and demons as opposed to dragons.[2]

We nearly walk straight past the fort when we reach the top of the hill, we were so engrossed in reciting drunken tales from the past. But what followed was a relatively sincere moment as we all stood on the foundations of the place where our nation's flag supposedly has its roots.

During my chat with David Moore, the archivist from the National Library of Wales, he told me that it was Geoffrey of Monmouth who popularised this story. But what most people don't realise is that the tale is, in fact, something of a sequel. The first part features in the *Mabinogi*, in the tale of 'Lludd and Llefelys' …

The story begins when Lludd inherits the crown from his father, Beli, and becomes King of the Britons. He considered his brother Llefelys to be one of the wisest men in the land and opted to help him marry a French princess, which would make him the king of France in the process. Lludd's reign got off to a good start, with the new king building *Caer Lludd*, which would eventually grow to become the city of London.

Not long into Lludd's reign, the British Isles were tormented by three plagues. The first came in the form of a bunch of invaders called the Coraniaid, a race who possessed the ability to eavesdrop on any conversation in the land, making plotting against them nearly impossible. The Britons learned to keep their mouths shut and their heads down in order to survive.

The second plague concerned some terrible screams heard in the night sky on May Day that caused pregnant women to miscarry and the leaves and flowers to drop off the flora. The third involved disappearing provisions; no matter how well Lludd guarded his stores, his food would vanish in the night. Not as scary as the other two, granted, but an inconvenience, nonetheless.

Lludd sought the help of his wise brother Llefelys, who sorted it all out for him by using a brass horn to deafen the Coraniaid and offering these solutions:

1. The creation of a potion made from crushed insects to kill the Coraniaid that was harmless to humans. Lludd arranged a meeting between the Britons and the Coraniaid and they threw the powder over everyone, thus defeating the invaders.
2. He proposed that the terrible screams were caused by two duelling dragons, namely a local red dragon and a foreign white one. They tricked the dragons by laying a trap for them down in Oxford that involved getting them drunk on mead and transforming them into pigs, then locking them in a stone chest and burying them beneath a hill in Eryri. In the sequel, I can only assume that the dragons had managed to break out of their stone chest beneath Dinas Emrys by the time Gwrtheyrn and his men began digging.
3. As for the missing food – well, that was to be blamed on a mischievous warlock, whom Lludd confronted. As an apology, the sorcerer vowed to be his loyal servant for the rest of his days.[3]

Lludd went by another name: Nudd Llaw Ereint, which would make him the father of Gwyn ap Nudd, king of Annwn and leader of the *Tylwyth Teg* (following Arawn's retirement).[4] Gwyn was also the leader of the 'Wild Hunt', a band of demonic horsemen who feature in folktales all over Europe. Seeing the Wild Hunt meant that something terrible was about to happen, such as a great famine, plague or war. Mind you, most European legends involving the Wild Hunt name Odin as the leader.[5]

Two tales, each concerning an invading force and a local dragon there to defend us from a foreign one. But the real reason why the Welsh adopted the red dragon as a national flag is far more … practical. It wasn't granted official flag status until as recently as 1959, but the red dragon has been associated with Wales for centuries. Some historians believe it was originally brought here during the Roman invasion.

The Romans often bore emblems of dragons, particularly their cavalry, though they themselves stole the idea from the Sarmatians, Alans, Parthians and Persians. Bear in mind that the Roman occupation of Britain began around AD 43–78 and lasted until around AD 383 – that's over 300 years. Now consider the reluctance of many contemporary Welsh people to call for independence from the United Kingdom; whether you call it being sensible or a bad case of Stockholm Syndrome, people get used to living under someone else's rule. When the Roman Empire collapsed and the Welsh were left to fend for themselves, they opted to favour Roman traditions and insignia over the ways of the invading armies that came after their departure. Mind you, a lot of them were direct descendants of Romans by then, in any case.

After that, Gwrtheyrn's tale was featured in *Historia Brittonum* in 830 and so began the association between Wales and the red dragon, though it is believed that the dragon was worn by the legendary King Arthur as well as other Celtic/Romano-British leaders, with evidence suggesting that it was the symbol of the Romano-British monarchy and high society. In China, which perhaps has the longest-established association with the scaly monsters, dragons also symbolise imperial rule and prosperity. Dragons also featured in Anglo-Saxon poetry and the red one, in particular, was widely associated with Cadwaladr, king of Gwynedd (655–82).

Indeed, here in Britain, the symbol was far from being exclusively associated with Wales; rather, it became a symbol of authority. In 1138, the Scottish adopted it as a royal standard; Richard I took a dragon standard with him on the Crusades; Henry III waved a red dragon at the Battle of Lewes, and Edward III at the Battle of Crécy. In 1400, Welsh rebel Owain Glyndŵr raised a similar banner when he rebelled against the English in Caernarfon – *Y Ddraig Aur* ('The Golden Dragon'). Just fifteen years later, his enemy Henry V used it to represent the English crown at the Battle of Agincourt.

It was in 1485 that the red dragon truly became synonymous with the Welsh, when Henry Tudor, claiming to have descended from the Welsh prince Cadwaladr, flew the red dragon during his usurpation of the crown of England. Arriving from France, Henry made full use of his Welsh heritage and gained their support in invading England.

After Henry defeated Richard III at the Battle of Bosworth, he carried the red dragon to St Paul's Cathedral, later adding the Tudor livery of white and green. The Tudors were not ashamed of their Welshness; it is said that Elizabeth I was raised as a Welsh speaker. Her dad, Henry VIII, however, was not so affectionate towards his heritage.[6]

In 1536, he signed the Act of Union, which officially declared Wales a part of England. Under these new laws, tougher restrictions were put on the use of the Welsh language, and we began to see a reduction in traditional Welsh names (the 'ap' you might have come across, based on patronymics) and the emergence of the common 'family name' surnames we all associate with the Welsh today: Jones, Evans, Davies, Williams (in the original Welsh alphabet, there were no 'j's nor 'v's).[7]

The Act of Union has been blamed by historians and nationalists alike for greatly damaging Welsh culture, but there is one thing we can be certain of: it is because of the Act of Union that the red dragon does not feature on the Union Jack. Actually, I should say Union Flag, for Charles II declared that it should only be called the Union Jack when raised at sea.

In 1350, Edward III adopted St George's Cross as the emblem of England. Saint George, mostly famous for being a dragon-slayer, was to be a symbol of good triumphing over evil, with the dragon representing the Devil. In 1606, James I combined the cross of St George with the Scottish cross of St Andrew when they formed the United Kingdom. But Wales was already a part of England – a former principality, not a nation – so the red dragon wasn't featured on this new flag, which wasn't called the Union Flag until 1707. Then, in 1801, George III formed a union with Ireland, so the cross of St Patrick was added.[8]

And that's why the Welsh have a dragon on their flag and why it isn't on the Union Flag, not because 'the red Welsh dragon beat the white English one'. Perhaps the real question is what *Y Ddraig Goch* means to us today; does it represent our reluctance to conform to others' ways, or our willingness to be governed by someone else …?

28

Where the folk can I find a relocated giant-beaver-monster-thingy?

Back at the car park, I manage to convince Danny to take me monster hunting. The target is the Afanc, the so-called 'Welsh Nessie'. All this proves too much for Alun, who heads for home and tells us he'll meet us at the pub. For this, we head to Llyn-yr-Afanc, near Betws-y-Coed. The lake (or pool, rather) is part of the Afon Conwy, which flows beneath nearby Pont-yr-Afanc (Afanc's Bridge, a Grade II listed building, over which goes the A470).

It is believed that the Afanc was relocated from this lake to Llyn Glaslyn on the fringes of Yr Wyddfa so as not to be a nuisance to the residents of the Conwy Valley, who were tired of him drowning their crops and eating anyone who was dumb enough to go swimming in the river.

Of course, approaching him would be suicide, but luckily they had heard a rumour that the Afanc had a certain soft spot. As such, they enlisted the help of a beautiful young maiden, who sat by the riverbank and sang a soft melody to the beast. Entranced, the Afanc swam ashore and fell asleep in her lap. The local men seized their moment and tied him up in iron chains, made by the best blacksmith in Wales. But the enraged Afanc jumped back into the pool and it took the strength of all the men plus two oxen to pull him back ashore.

It took so much effort, in fact, that it caused one of the oxen's eyes to pop out of its socket. Its tears were said to have formed Pwll Llygad yr Ych (Pool of the Ox's Eye), which sits on nearby Moel Siabod. They dragged the Afanc over the mountain then dumped him into Glaslyn (also known as Llyn Ffynnon Las), a place already shrouded in myth and legend (from the *Tylwyth Teg* to King Arthur's famous sword, Excalibur, which is said to be lying at the bottom).[1]

As well as wanting to see Llyn-yr-Afanc, I fancy checking out Pwll Llygad yr Ych, so we begin our hunt by climbing Moel Siabod. *Moel* is the Welsh word for 'bare/treeless hill', but the meaning of *siabod* has been widely debated.

We park up at Capel Curig, where you can find Plas-y-Brenin, the UK National Mountain Centre, currently run by Sport England, for some reason. From Plas-y-Brenin, we follow the track across Nant Gwryd over the ancient bridge of Pont-y-Bala and into the wooded Forestry Commission land. There's a great view of Llynnau Mymbyr along the way, being the two lakes found at Dyffryn Mymbyr, the valley that runs from Capel Curig to the Pen-y-Gwryd hotel. Before long, we arrive at some open access land that takes us up the entire northern side of the mountain.

It's a bright, sunny day and the climb to the top is long and gruelling. At 872 metres (or 2,861 feet), it's the highest peak of the Moelwynion mountain range. On a clear day, looking in a certain direction, you can see thirteen of the highest peaks in all of Wales without ever having to turn your head.[2]

Yr Wyddfa is to our right. To our left, we have a great overview of Pwll Llygad yr Ych, known on all the maps as Llyn-y-Foel, which means 'lake of the bare hill'. Water trickling down its south-eastern side eventually ends up in the Afon Conwy, where lies Llyn-yr-Afanc. I've heard that there is a rare species of brown trout to be found at Pwll Llygad yr Ych, the only place in the world where it is found, but I can't find a viable source to confirm this. I'd love to know if this is true – maybe I should take up fishing one day.

Navigating the steep rock falls to the bottom seemed too risky, considering our weary legs, so we decide to head back down the mountain instead, to the other end of Capel Curig. There, we pass by the village's famous postal stagecoach, standing across the road from the Tyn-y-Coed Inn. It's seen more new parts than Trigger's broom (one for *Only Fools and Horses* fans) and is far from being the original, but it's a great example of the kind of thing you'd find traversing the road from London to Holyhead in the nineteenth century. Roads like what is today the A5, which used to be the main artery through north Wales, were built for these.[3] Going to take my hat off in the shade beneath the canopy that protects the stagecoach, I notice that I'm not even wearing one – I must have left it up on Moel Siabod somewhere. '*Damia fo!*'

Once back at the car, we take the A5 towards Betws-y-Coed, passing the well-known Tŷ Hyll along the way. Tŷ Hyll ('Ugly House') is brimming with history and lore. No one is entirely sure who built it, but it is thought to have been a *tŷ unnos/un nôs*, or a 'one-night house'. It was tradition at the time that a house built on common land over the period of a single night that had a functional smoking chimney by dawn could be claimed by the builders as their own, free of charge. Some claim that it was built by bandits in the fifteenth century, who would prey upon vulnerable travellers taking the main road through Eryri, their 'ugly' or 'fearsome' appearance giving the place its reputation and name.

The first recorded resident (1900) was John Roberts, a local shepherd. Lilian and Ted Riley, who lived there the longest, welcomed many visitors into their home during their time there, showing off their pet cockatoo and reciting bold tales. Then in 1988, it was bought by the Snowdonia Society and the listed building was delicately renovated by a group of volunteers. In 2010, the society's headquarters moved, and in 2012, they turned Tŷ Hyll into a tearoom and honeybee exhibition.[4] I have vague memories from childhood of the exterior of the house being decorated with skulls and other eerie decor, but I'm starting to think I made all that up.

We head through Betws-y-Coed then drive a short distance down the A470 before arriving at Llyn-yr-Afanc, sometimes referred to as Pwll-yr-Afanc, meaning 'The Afanc's Pool'. We cross Pont-yr-Afanc (the 'Afanc's Bridge') and park up in a layby on the other side. We walk down a set of steps to the pebbly riverbank below, where the fair maiden was said to have sat and sang to the beast, and crack open a couple of warm beers that have been in the boot all day.

'Had you heard about Yr Afanc before then, Dan?'

'*Na.*'

'What do you make of it?'

'I reckon that, like many myths and tales, the creature was a way to make sense of the unknown. Perhaps inspired by beavers who flooded valleys by building dams. They always used to blame monsters or vengeful gods in those days.'

Indeed, it's hard to imagine there once being a giant-beaver-monster-thingy living here; the strip of river seems too narrow, too shallow – what is easy to imagine living here, however, is a family of actual beavers. Beavers were once widespread across the United Kingdom but were hunted to extinction some 400 years ago. *Afanc* is actually the Welsh word for 'beaver' – could it be that the story was inspired by real beavers who would flood the valley when building their dams?

Humankind's stance on pesky beavers has changed in recent years and we have grown increasingly aware of their ecological benefits. They are so helpful in maintaining healthy ecosystems, in fact, that they are referred to by Native Americans as the 'Earth's kidneys'. Coincidentally, just six months ago, the first beavers to live in Wales for 400 years were reintroduced to a nature reserve just outside Machynlleth. Mind you, many farmers and landowners aren't too happy about it, fearing that it'll only mean the return of damaging floods.[5]

I guess we'll soon find out, but I doubt that stories of giant-beaver-monster-thingys will be coming back with them as well. But we definitely won't find any here today, monstrous or average-sized. Downing our warm beers, we head for home.

29

Where the folk
is the highest story
in Wales?

On our way home, we pass the most famous mountain in Wales, Yr Wyddfa. 'How many times have you been up, mate?'

'I've been up most all the routes multiple times,' Danny replies. 'My favourite is the Watkin Path, it's got everything you need for a good mountain climb; a mixture of gentle inclines and steep scrambles, plus a river to cool down in on hot days.'

At 1,085 metres above sea level, the mountain formerly known as Mt Snowdon (to anyone who wasn't a Welsh speaker, that is) is the highest peak in Wales and would have been the highest in the British Isles if it weren't for those meddling Scots. It's classed as a national nature reserve due to the collection of rare flora and fauna that can be found there, such as *Lili'r Wyddfa* (the Snowdon Lily).

So not the tallest, but it is the busiest mountain in the UK. Around 600,000 people climb Yr Wyddfa each year and these numbers have only gone up since the pandemic, what with air travel being a bit of a pain in the arse these days and more people 'staycationing'.[1] Furthermore, when restrictions were tougher and people, myself included, started to go walking more, people flocked to Eryri in droves.

'How do the tourists treat the place? Do they litter and that?' I ask.

'There are inconsiderate tourists leaving rubbish, yes, but there are also plenty of considerate tourists who pick up the rubbish left by the former. This also goes for the locals, mind. As long as you don't play "hippity-hoppity" music while I'm trying to listen to nature and enjoy my walks, then I try not to judge.'

Photos of a long line of illegally parked cars snaking up the hillside towards Pen-y-Pass made headlines recently, but the fines were cheaper than what people paid to park for the day in their home cities, so there wasn't much incentive for them not to go, until they began towing the cars away, that is. I heard that the queue to the summit was at a standstill and litter rolled over the hillsides like tumbleweed.

'What are your thoughts on restricting access to some of the landmarks in Eryri, like the Infinity Pool, for instance?'

'See, now that's a tricky one,' Danny whines. 'We need to conserve the beauty of the mountains, but who are we to restrict anyone from seeing it for themselves?'

Most people take one of the six main paths to the summit, or hop on the Snowdon Mountain Railway from Llanberis. Once at the summit, you'll find a cafe called Hafod Eryri, which is open whenever the train is running. In 2011, some guy decided to drive his 4x4 up the tracks before abandoning it at the top. He was eventually charged in court for dangerous driving, but he didn't care – he said it was one of the fifty things on his bucket list that he wanted to do before he died.[2]

I've been up a few times, on different paths as well as on the train, so I think I'll sit this one out. But I do think I should at least tell you about the sheer abundance of folklore associated with Britain's busiest mountain. If you've ever been up there, I bet there's a lot of things you've walked past and thought nothing of.

In 2020, a petition that called for the National Park Authority to officially recognise the mountain as Yr Wyddfa as opposed to its English name was rejected by the Senedd after they found it to be the national park's responsibility, not the Welsh Government's. Then in April 2021, Gwynedd councillor John Pugh Roberts put forward a similar motion that Snowdonia be referred to as Eryri, but again the motion was rejected on the grounds that the national park already has a task force in place that focuses on the retention of Welsh place-names. Two years later, in 2023, the national park made it official.[3]

'Do you think it should be known as Yr Wyddfa instead of Snowdon, then?'

'Like many things, I'm on the fence and see it from the point of view of both sides. It would be nice to have the original Welsh name, but hearing some of my non-Welsh-speaking family, friends and colleagues try to pronounce Yr Wyddfa ...' He shakes his head. 'Honestly, the mountain would end up being called "Whyr Why-d-dva"!'

Wyddfa translates to 'tumulus' and refers to an old folktale involving King Arthur and a terrible giant named Rhitta (or Rhudda) Gawr, who is said to be buried at the top after dying by Arthur's sword. Rhitta's hobby was knitting himself a cloak made of the collected beards of men, you see, but when he tried claiming Arthur's beard, well, that was one beard too many.

Giants, or *cewri* in Welsh, were once considered to have been the original inhabitants of the British Isles and feature heavily in Welsh mythology, from the *Mabinogi* to the more localised tales. In his *Historia Regum Britanniae* ('*The History of the Kings of Britain*'), Geoffrey of Monmouth wrote that they were pushed to extinction by the arrival of man. But just like man, giants were a complicated race, with varying ambitions and emotions, with some even considered heroes of the people, such as Bendigeidfran from the Second Branch of the *Mabinogi*.

But Rhitta certainly wasn't a hero of the people. He held court in Eryri but invaded the lands of two kings, Nyniaw and Peibiaw, taking their beards and making himself a fashionable hat. The twenty-six kings of Britain joined forces and sent a great army to defeat the giant, but Rhitta kicked their arses and took their beards to make his infamous cloak.

Arthur was busy fighting the Red-Eyed Giant of Cernyw when all this was going on, but as soon as he had washed his hands of that matter, he came here to sort out Rhitta Gawr. In one version, Rhitta isn't slain but is forced to shave off his own beard as punishment, and wanders off a wiser and far less cocky giant. Either way, Arthur demands that a cairn be built, which became known as *Gwyddfa Rhudda*. Mind you, other versions say that Rhitta was killed by Idris, another Welsh giant who has his own mountain named after him: Cadair Idris. Regardless, as time passed, people forgot about the tale and the place became known simply as Yr Wyddfa.[4]

There are other places on and around Yr Wyddfa associated with King Arthur. Bwlch y Saethau, a ridge between Yr Wyddfa and Y Lliwedd, is said to have been the site where Arthur himself later died.

A cairn by the name of *Carnedd Arthur* was raised there and stood until around 1850, but has since vanished. The story goes that Arthur asked his mate Bedivere to throw his famous sword Excalibur into Llyn Glaslyn. Later, Arthur's body would be carried by boat across the same lake to Afallon (English: Avalon), a mythical island. His men then headed into a cave on the slopes of Y Lliwedd, where they are said to be lying in wait for Arthur's return.[5]

Glaslyn, in case you've forgotten, is also said to be the final resting place of the monstrous Afanc. But the myths and legends of Yr Wyddfa don't stop there: Merlin is rumoured to have concealed the Golden Throne of Britain somewhere in the cliffs north of Crib y Ddysgl after the Saxons invaded, and Llyn Coch in Cwm Clogwyn is said to be the home of a band of *Tylwyth Teg* and yet another Lady of the Lake.[6]

There is also a large stone found just below Clogwyn Du'r Arddu by the name of *Maen Du'r Arddu*. It is said that, if two people were to spend the night there, one would wake up a poet and the other completely insane.[7] So now, whenever anyone asks you where madmen and poets are made, which they likely will, you'll know.

'Russ?'

Hold up – all this sounds very familiar … there are several sites across Wales claiming to be able to produce either poets or madmen, too many to get into, in fact. Perhaps the most well-known place for this, however, is Cadair Idris, found at the southern end of Eryri. Like Yr Wyddfa, the place is brimming with folktales. It is said that some of the lakes surrounding it are bottomless, for one thing. The mountain's name stems from an old folktale involving the giant Idris, who was said to have used the mountain as a chair.

Other tales tell of how Gwyn ap Nudd used the mountain as a hunting ground. If you were to hear the distant howling of the Cŵn Annwn then you had better leg it, for these unearthly white hounds would herd your soul into Annwn.[8]

'Russ …'

Not that far from Cadair Idris is Llyn Tegid, also known as Bala Lake. Nearby there was said to have been the home of the legendary Ceridwen, another big name in Welsh mythology, who lived there with her husband, Tegid Foel. She is worshipped by modern pagans as the Celtic goddess of rebirth, transformation and inspiration.

She and her husband parented two children, the hideous Morfran and the beautiful Creirwy. Ceridwen was said to have owned a magical cauldron that possessed *awen*, being a Welsh, Cornish and Breton word that referred to the artistic inspiration that so many bards sought. In 'The Tale of Taliesin', in an effort to replace her hideous son Morfran with a more handsome and talented one, she gives chase to her servant Gwion Bach in a scene reminiscent of Disney's *The Sword in the Stone*, with the pair transforming into various animals before Gwion is eventually swallowed up. This results in Ceridwen falling pregnant and she gives birth to the real-life legendary bard, Taliesin.[9]

Taliesin was a sixth-century bard who wrote *The Book of Taliesin*. He is often referred to as Taliesin Ben Beirdd, or Taliesin, Chief of Bards. Chances are he wasn't conceived when his mother took the form of a chicken and gobbled up her servant, though. Some say that he was adopted as a child by Elffin, son of Gwyddno Garanhir, the ruler of Cantre'r Gwaelod. Indeed, Taliesin's origins are a mystery, but he played a huge role in Welsh mythology, even fighting alongside Bendigeidfran in the Second Branch of the *Mabinogi*.[10]

'Russ!'

'Huh?'

'You getting out?'

'Oh yeah, sorry.'

30

Where the folk
is the girl of my dreams, cont?

Macsen Wledig had a dream, a dream that eventually featured in the *Mabinogi*, becoming part of an entire nation's mythos. A dream that brought him here, to my hometown of Caernarfon.

Macsen Wledig, aka Magnus Maximus, was a Roman emperor who ruled Britannia and Gaul from the year 383 until his death in 388. Before that he was a distinguished general, serving in Africa in 373 before being sent to Britain in the year 380, when he faced off against the Picts and the Scots. He then usurped the imperial throne from Emperor Gratian, who was becoming unpopular here in Britain due to his soft spot for Christians. However, Macsen got greedy and tried invading Italy in 387, which led to his defeat at the hands of Theodosius I at the Battle of Poetovio the following year.

Macsen is considered to be the founding father of several medieval Welsh dynasties and was first referred to as an ancestor of a Welsh king on the Pillar of Eliseg in Denbighshire, which names Sevira as his daughter. Sevira was the wife of Gwrtheyrn, the disgraced king. Macsen also features in the Fifteen Tribes of Wales.[1] However, the story of his dream and how he met his wife Helen (or Elen, rather), which I am about to tell you, is considered a work of fiction, although there are some elements of truth to it.

The story goes that, one day, Macsen decided that he wanted to go hunting. According to the legend, he was a popular guy, considered to be very wise. As such, thirty-two kings joined him on this hunt. He took them to a valley just outside Rome and they hunted until midday, then Macsen fancied himself a little siesta. In classic imperial fashion, he got his men to raise their shields and form a protective barrier around him, then they gave him a golden shield to use as a pillow and off he went to sleep, leaving the poor sods to melt in the sun.

Cue the famous dream: Macsen dreamt that he was making his way up the valley, following the river towards its source. From there, he climbed over the highest mountain in the world, discovering on the other side the most beautiful region he had ever seen. He saw two rivers flowing down from the mountains and into the sea and began to make his way towards the mouth of one of those rivers, the biggest he had ever seen. I'm beginning to see a pattern here already ...

What he found there was a great city with a huge castle. Multi-coloured towers reached up into the sky and the docks held the biggest fleet of ships that he had ever laid eyes on. One of the ships was much larger and grander than the others. Crossing a bridge made of whalebones, he boarded the ship and set sail.

That's when he came upon the most beautiful island he had ever seen and decided that he should tour it. He explored the island from coast to coast, coming across valleys, steep, rocky mountains and rugged landscapes. He saw another island just off the shore and between him and that island was a country of vast mountains, forests and plains. From the highest mountain, a river flowed down to the sea and, at the mouth of that river, he saw a great castle.

Macsen travelled to this fortress, where he saw the most – oh, come on! He saw the most handsome guy he's ever laid eyes on. Prince Charming led him inside and he entered a great hall, where he saw two red-haired young boys playing chess. Probably the most ginger kids he'd ever seen, 'n all. Sitting in a nearby ivory chair was a bearded old man, carving out chess pieces.

It is worth mentioning at this point that chess wasn't actually invented until the sixth century, emerging from northern India. The *Mabinogi*, remember, were not written until the twelfth or thirteenth century.

And sitting there in front of him, on a chair made of gold, was a maiden so beautiful that to look at her was like trying to look at the sun when it's at its brightest. Really? We got this far and he's not going to say that she's the most beautiful girl he'd ever seen? She got up and threw her arms around him, so he took a seat next to her on the golden chair and began caressing her ... and of course, that's the exact moment Macsen woke up. Typical!

Macsen wasn't himself after his dream and couldn't eat nor sleep. It was as though his very soul had been taken from him and there was only one person who could give it back: the girl. His people were worried about him, so the wisest men of Rome were brought before him to find a solution. He told them about his dream and they said that they would send out three messengers to the three parts of the world for the next three years so that they may find the land that he dreamt of.

Alas, they returned empty-handed. Then the king of Rome suggested they followed the same path from Macsen's dream, following the river up north and over the mountains, then to the city by the sea and across to the island. Why they didn't do this the first time is anyone's guess. Another thirteen messengers were sent and came across a fleet of ships that would take them to Britain, where they eventually came across the castle from Macsen's dream – one supposedly found at Aber Sain – but don't forget that Caernarfon Castle did not exist at the time. Entering the castle, they found the family from Macsen's dream, as well as the beautiful maiden. They immediately fell to their knees and proclaimed, 'Empress of Rome, all hail!'

She was flattered, but told them that she would only accept if Macsen went and asked her himself. They sent word back to Rome and Macsen came running. This time around, he didn't suddenly wake up from a dream when it got to the good part.[2]

This girl's name was Elen (often anglicised as Helen), also known as Helen of the Hosts (from Elen Luyddog, a name given to her after she asked Macsen to build a few roads for her, which we shall get to in a moment), and she is recognised as Saint Helen of Caernarfon by the Welsh church (but not by Rome).

She is said to have been a daughter of a Romano-British ruler named Octavius, or Eudaf (or Eudwy) Hen, making her the sister of Conan Meriadoc, the Celtic leader who founded Brittany. She founded many churches here in Wales and there are over twenty holy wells dedicated to her, though some scholars argue that some of these are misinterpretations and are actually dedicated to Constantine the

Great's mum, Helen of Constantinople, otherwise known as Saint Helena. In any case, Elen was Macsen's wife in real life.[3]

Elen's name, as well as that of her offspring, which I'll get to in a moment, has been lurking in the background throughout my entire life. The woods of Coed Helen, nearby Coed Helen Holiday Park, a church at Penisa'r Waun (found just outside Caernarfon) ... wherever you look, Elen left an impression on Caernarfon.

In any case, the morning after their wedding, Elen laid down a few rules to their marriage: her father would rule the Island of Britain for her, along with any land found between the Irish Sea and the English Channel, and Macsen would have to build three castles for her at locations of her choosing. Those ended up being the Roman forts found at Caerleon, Carmarthen and Caernarfon.[4]

Growing up in Caernarfon, I would often take a shortcut through the fields of Segontium on my way home from school. My friends and I would walk along the fort's walls, carrying sticks and pretending they were swords. The A4085 cuts straight through the fort, splitting it in two. At one point, it was the biggest military and administrative body of the Roman Empire this side of the British Isles.

But here's the twist: Segontium was actually founded by Agricola after he defeated the local Ordovices in the year AD 77, a whole 300 years before Macsen came here. This would mean that Macsen did, indeed, travel to Segontium, but certainly didn't build the place. Moreover, the forts at Carmarthen and Caerleon were built in AD 75.[5]

And while we're on the subject, let's address the castle in which he found Elen and her family in the first place – with Caernarfon Castle not being built until hundreds of years later and Segontium supposedly built by Macsen after he had met Elen, what castle are they on about, then? Could it have been the court of Eudaf Hen, Elen's dad? There are so many things that already don't add up in this story and we're not even done yet ...

While these forts were being built, Macsen went hunting in Carmarthen and pitched a tent (no pun intended) on top of a mountain there; that mountain is called Cadair Macsen (Macsen's Chair). It is also said that, because he built the fort there with a small army (*byddin*) of men, he named the place Caervyrddin. However,

189

others would claim that the town got its name from Myrddin Emrys (Merlin), who was said to have been born in a cave just outside town. But that's not the main issue here: the real issue is that the Roman fort at Carmarthen was called Moridunum and the town itself was called Llanteulyddog until around the early Middle Ages.

When Macsen got back home, Elen still wasn't impressed. She demanded that he build her a series of roads leading through Britain (Elen did commission these in real life), leading from one fortress to the other. So off he went, and these are the old Roman roads that we still use here in the UK today.

Back to the story: Macsen stayed in Wales for a total of seven years before being called back to Rome to defend his throne. Off he went, burning down entire cities in France and Burgundy along the way. A whole year of fighting went by and Macsen's troops had made very little progress.

As such, Elen's two brothers, Cynan and Gadeon (likely to be the two ginger-haired chess players from his dream) came to his aid with a small band of warriors. Standing outside Rome, Cynan thought that they should take a different approach. Holding a ceasefire, the two emperors met for a drink. While this was happening, Cynan had his men scale the city walls with wooden ladders. The rival emperor didn't stand a chance as Macsen's men, led by Elen's brothers, seized the city, killing him and many others.

After this, the two brothers led a bloody assault on other European cities, roaming the countryside and pillaging anything that came in their way. But Gadeon eventually grew bored of it and came back to Wales, leaving his brother behind in Italy. The tale ends somewhat abruptly, with Cynan committing a most gruesome act: he cuts off the tongues of the local women so that they can't speak their native language and, because of this, the people of Armorica (an area of Europe that includes Brittany) would forever be called 'Britons'.

And that was 'The Dream of Macsen Wledig', emperor of Rome. That's the end of the story.[6] But Macsen didn't actually successfully invade Rome in real life – let's be honest, though, the ending wasn't the only exaggerated part of this epic piece of propaganda. Nevertheless, it has proven to be one of Wales's most beloved folktales.

Now, Llywelyn ap Gruffudd refused to pay our friend Edward I some tax in the thirteenth century, which brought forth the English invasion of Wales and the construction of Caernarfon Castle, which began on the site of an old Norman motte-and-bailey in 1283. It would become one of the largest and most imposing Edwardian castles in Wales, painted white so that it could be seen from miles around. It would also end up playing an integral part in Welsh politics and its relationship with the English monarchy.

As it turns out (or so the story goes), Edward was influenced by Macsen Wledig's tale when he built his castle here in Caernarfon. He interpreted the castle seen by Macsen in his dream as being Segontium and incorporated some Roman imperial architecture into his work when designing his magnus opus (the Eagle Tower comes to mind). When a body was discovered during the construction of the castle, he believed it to be that of Macsen and he ordered that it be buried in a local church.[7]

There have been many ghost sightings at Caernarfon Castle over the years, including that of a Roman soldier. There's also the 'Floating Lady', whose presence is said to tamper with electrical equipment. American tourist Kristi Ormand, from Dallas, apparently has some photographic and video evidence of another ghost at the castle; she reported 'feeling a presence' when she visited the place in 2001. When she looked back over her holiday pics, she saw what she reckoned was the figure of a short, crowned king wearing a cloak. Sceptics put it down to lens flare, though it only appeared in one photo and in the video. Could this have been our John Doe? Perhaps he was the original occupier of this elusive castle that Macsen was on about.[8]

Edward I would also use Caernarfon Castle as part of an elaborate scam that would give rise to the entire concept of an English Prince of Wales. He rushed his wife here to give birth to their son, Edward II (also known as Edward of Caernarfon). In doing so, he presented the Welsh with what they had previously said would be the only thing they would recognise as their ruler: someone who was born in Wales and didn't speak a word of English (for a baby can't speak any language whatsoever). Mind you, many have suggested that this is merely an urban myth. Prince Edward (later King Edward VIII) had his investiture as Prince of Wales here in 1911, as did King Charles when he became Prince of Wales in 1969.[9]

But despite Caernarfon's intricate history with foreign invaders, it remains the most Welsh-speaking town in the country. We local *Cofis* were traditionally defined as those born within the old town walls, but these days it just means anyone from Caernarfon in general. The *Cofi* accent and dialect are quite unique but, sadly, there are many words that we no longer use today, though we still stand out amongst fellow Welsh speakers.

Perhaps the most famous *Cofi* slang word, one that never fails to amuse people, is *cont.* Yes, as in the c-word. *Cofis* end most of their sentences with *cont*, especially when they've had a few to drink. It can be a term of endearment or an insult and there is even a feminine version for the ladies – *gont.* There is no link between that word and the name of our Roman fort, by the way.

Speaking of Segontium, I remember when attending secondary school here that the classes were divided into letters: S.A.N.T.P.E.B.L.G., which stood for the Welsh version of Saint Peblic, though they must not have had enough pupils for a *Dosbarth I*, it seems. Our class name would be allocated depending on what year you were in. For example, 7S, 8S, 9S and so on. I emailed Danny a couple of questions for the book a few weeks back. He signed the document he sent back: '"Danny Hanks, 7E." Hope it's alright, Mr Williams!'

Sant Peblig, also known as Publicus, was one of Magnus and Elen's sons. He built a church near Segontium that became the parish church of Llanbeblig.[10] Growing up, we would tell tales of the Pink Lady, who supposedly haunts the graveyard at Llanbeblig, but I can't find any information about her online.

I have lived away from Caernarfon for half of my life now, but the majority of my adult time here has been spent in the pubs, some of which also have a reputation for being haunted, including the one I once lived and worked at: The Black Boy Inn.

It was built around 1522, which makes it one of the oldest pubs in Wales. It is found just within the old town walls, on Northgate Street, or Stryd Pedwar-a-Chwech (which means Four-and-Six Street) in Welsh, which referred to the going rate for a girl, a bottle of gin and a room back when it was one of the biggest brothels in town.[11]

On my way through town, I pop in to see my old boss, John 'Black Boy' Evans. John adopts the names of his pubs wherever he goes. Building up pubs that have seen better days is his calling in life and the Black Boy is his pride and joy. Recently, he's been building a little Black Boy Empire within the old town, buying the playground off the council, turning a disused building into a restaurant and function room, making hotel rooms out of old town houses. Indeed, the Black Boy of today is a far cry from the Victorian brothel that it once was.

'*Iawn*, John?'

'I haven't got any work for you, sorry Russell.'

'Eh? Oh. No, I'm not here for that!'

I tell him my intentions and he agrees to help. John's been the owner of the Black Boy for about twenty years now, he should know a thing or two about its history. 'What can you tell me about the origin of the name?'

'Ah, see, now that isn't very clear. The classic story goes that it was named after a young Black man named Jack, the first Black person to be seen in Caernarfon, back in the mid-1700s. Jack reportedly married a local woman, fathered seven children and was buried at the churchyard in Ynyscynhaearn, near Criccieth.'

That's the story I've heard, but John tells me that the inn was actually named the Black Boy way before that.

'Another theory is that it was one of many Black Boy pubs found across the UK that was dedicated to King Charles II, whose mother nicknamed him "Black Boy". This would have been the late 1600s. Others say that the pub owes its name to a black "buoy" that used to guide ships into Caernarfon's harbour. There's a black buoy found outside the pub today.'

'In light of the recent political climate, have you had any complaints about the name?'

'We've had a few comments from both sides of the divide, but the majority of people seem to agree that we should keep it as it is a part of history, something we can learn from.'

'I heard you've got a few resident ghosts?'

'There are. We believe there are many ghosts here, though I have yet

193

to see one for myself. A few staff members have said that they have over the years, mind, and guests.'

This is true. I remember when I worked here, we had a group of Geordie workmen staying with us and one would flat-out refuse to stay in a certain room because he swore he had seen a woman sitting at the edge of his bed one night. Other guests had complained about this particular room previously. At one point, there was a convent situated round the back of the pub. Many guests have reported seeing the ghost of a nun wandering the halls of the old inn. People have also reported being choked by a 'phantom strangler'.[12] Not me, though; no phantom prostitute ever came up to see me in the night.

But my local, as it were, used to be the Anglesey Arms. The Anglesey sits on the seafront, looking out over the Menai Strait. Nothing beats a pint whilst sitting on the sea wall watching the sun setting over the Irish Sea, let me tell you.

The place was originally a Custom House, built around 1736. It became the Anglesey Arms Hotel sometime in the nineteenth century, when the Custom House moved to Porth-yr-Aur. The closest of the castle's towers to the pub was nicknamed the 'hanging tower' and was where the town's executions would be held.

In 1838, the area outside the pub became the stage of a very *Scooby-Doo*-esque scenario … locals had been too scared to go out at night as there were rumours of a phantom hearse going around that brought bad luck to all those who saw it. Then a local trader named Boaz Pritchard was arrested one day. When customs officers raided his warehouse, they found ninety-nine barrels of contraband brandy, a coffin and a hearse.

The Anglesey is said to be haunted by several mischievous ghosts who pick up glasses from off the shelves, hold them up in the air for a bit then smash them on the ground. People using the darts board have also reported darts flying off the board when no one was near them (a likely story – I've been there on darts nights, you can't blame ghosts for that!) and guests who have stayed in the rooms upstairs have reported hearing keys turning in locks late at night when no one was around. The most haunted room, by all accounts, is Room Three, where a ghostly figure has often been seen sitting on the edge of the bed.[13]

Growing up here, I had no idea I was exposed to so much rich history and folklore and I wonder what else I've missed … regardless, for now, with my journey nearly over, it's time for a well-deserved pint. As such, I take my place on the Anglesey wall and watch the sun set over Ynys Llanddwyn, my final destination.

31

Where the folk
is the 'Welsh Valentine's Day' from?

Santes Dwynwen is the Welsh patron saint of lovers ... and sick animals, for some reason. She is celebrated in Wales on 25 January each year; however, she is not officially recognised as a saint by the Catholic nor Anglican Churches, nor does she appear in the Roman Martyrology, the Church of Wales calendar or the Roman Catholic calendar for Wales. So, let's call her an indie saint for now. Despite this, she has regained popularity in recent years and now Welshmen get two shots a year at getting it right.

In the 1960s, a student at University College in Bangor named Vera Williams, in a bid to revive Dydd Santes Dwynwen, commissioned four designs for Saint Dwynwen's Day cards, pitching it as the 'Welsh Valentine's Day'. Since then, the celebration has steadily grown in popularity, although it's nowhere near as popular as Saint Valentine's Day just yet.[1]

In fact, the journey to becoming a recognised celebration wasn't an easy one for Dwynwen; a lot was accomplished in 2003, when the Welsh Language Board (WLB) teamed up with Tesco to distribute 50,000 free cards in forty-three of its Welsh stores. Inside one of those cards was a little heart, the finder of which won a big prize. The WLB also pushed for the use of concerts, singles nights, poetry nights and such to promote it.[2]

Along with this, Ynys Llanddwyn and Porthddwyn on Anglesey, as well as the church of Sen Adhwynn in Advent, Cornwall, are all dedicated to her, and yet she isn't officially recognised as a saint. Why is that, and what makes Saint Valentine so special?

San Valentino, or Valentinus, was a Roman saint and clergyman (either a priest or a bishop) who lived in the third century, over a hundred years before Dwynwen. He is best known as the saint of courtly love, but is also the saint of Terni, a city in central Italy, epilepsy and beekeeping, of all things.

It is rumoured that the use of the 'heart symbol' to represent love derives from something he used to do when helping Christian couples get secretly married and the husbands to escape conscription into the pagan army. In order to remind those men of their vow to God's love, he would give them cut-out hearts from parchment. The use of the heart symbol goes as far back as the Ancient Egyptians and was used to represent Silphium, a plant used for contraception (believed to have gone extinct due to its extensive use).

He is commemorated on 14 February because this was the day, in 269 (though other accounts have it down as 270 and 273), that he was imprisoned, tortured and martyred in Rome for helping out the Christians. Just before all this, Valentine wrote a letter to the woman he loved and signed it 'from your Valentine', which inspired the use of Valentine's Day cards in present day. Unlike Dwynwen, he is officially recognised as a saint by the Roman Catholic Church and features in the early martyrdoms.[3]

The details of Dwynwen's story, on the other hand, are a bit hazier and there are many different versions of it. Despite being associated with the small tidal island of Ynys Llanddwyn up on Anglesey, where she spent her remaining years, she actually hailed from Breconshire. She is believed to have been the daughter of Rigrawst and King Brychan Brycheiniog, who is said to have faced off against King Arthur. Rigrawst was daughter to Sevira, Macsen Wledig's daughter, and Gwrtheyrn.

Ynys Llanddwyn can be found at Newborough Warren, probably my favourite beach in the world (and I've lived in Australia!). From its golden dunes, you can enjoy excellent views of the Irish Sea, the Menai Strait, Pen Llŷn and the mountains of Eryri. Also, keep an eye out for red squirrels while you're there.

Visible from the beach and forming a part of the Newborough Warren National Nature Reserve, Ynys Llanddwyn isn't quite an island, more of a narrow strip of land that is separated from mainland Anglesey during high tides. During such times, Ynys Llanddwyn is inaccessible for a couple of hours or so.

I was going to end my journey in Caernarfon, but when Sophie told me that she was popping up for the final weekend of the trip, we arranged to go to Llanddwyn with Danny and his wife Mari. From the car park, it's a fifteen-minute-or-so walk to the 'island'. Mari is very excited that I'm covering Santes Dwynwen: she's a primary school teacher and had recently been teaching her pupils all about her.

'So you know the story pretty well, then?'

'Well, I know the "kiddy version" of the story. This is what I tell them: a long time ago, there was a beautiful princess called Dwynwen who lived with her father, King Brychan Brycheiniog. Her father wanted her to marry an important and wealthy prince, but she was already in love with Maelon Dafodrill, a common man from the neighbouring village.'

Remember that – Maelon Dafodrill, not 'Daffodil'.

'Dwynwen refused to marry the prince and was banished from the castle. She went to tell Maelon, but he was furious that she had disobeyed her father, so he dumped her. *Bechod*!'

I feel as though I need to react with an 'Aww!'

'Dwynwen was heartbroken. She ran off into the forest and cried herself to sleep. Then she had a dream, and in her dream, an angel appeared with two potions that would "ease her heartbreak". The first cup froze Maelon, as a punishment for being "cold hearted". But this didn't make Dwynwen feel any better, and so she drank the second potion.

'This one granted her three wishes. Her first wish was to thaw Maelon. Her second was for all the people of Wales to feel love and happiness. Her last wish was that she would never fall in love nor have to marry, as she never wanted to feel heartache again. And so, she became a nun and came up to Llanddwyn to build her own church. Many couples still visit the place today. It is also said that there used to be a "magical well" on the island that people used to drink from to help them with their heartache or something, but I don't know much about that part of the legend ...'

I think she's on about the well said to have contained sacred fish (or, in some versions, eels) whose movements could predict the future of people's relationships. More specifically, they revealed the faithfulness of a lover: should a woman first scatter breadcrumbs on the surface then lay her handkerchief on top, then if the eel disturbed it, then her lover would be faithful to her. If it left it untouched, then she needn't bother with him.

Dwynwen is said to have died of natural causes and was buried somewhere here on Llanddwyn. Her church became something of a holy shrine in the years that followed, but eventually fell into disrepair and the holy well was buried in sand. But as always, the romantic Victorians saved the day and helped revive Dwynwen's memory, erecting a cross on Llanddwyn to commemorate her.[4]

I ask Mari how she goes about teaching her pupils about Dwynwen's story.

'We make love spoons and such. I'll read them a story, do some arts and crafts like love potions, Santes Dwynwen cards ... I even bring science into the equation and conduct experiments based on the state of matter, like freezing and thawing. I once held a "chemical reaction" lesson in which I froze some white vinegar and lemon juice in heart-shaped moulds then sprinkled bicarb soda on top so they started frothing. The kids loved that!'

'What about you and Danny, do you guys celebrate it?'

'For sure! Danny will sometimes buy me a special gift, or we'll have a romantic date night. Mind you, this year it was reduced to flowers from a petrol station that he got on his way back from work, but it's the thought that counts, I guess. All the restaurants have a deal on, and most shops in Caernarfon decorate their shop windows.'

'So which is more important to you: Dwynwen or Valentine's?'

'Dwynwen! I'm Welsh, and it's important to our heritage and culture. Valentine's Day is celebrated in most Westernised countries, so it's nice to be able to have our own day to celebrate love.'

Danny and I hold back and let the girls walk ahead, as naturally happens when couples walk together. I ask him about Santes Dwynwen but he seems more interested in, and far more knowledgeable of, the maritime history of the place. Ynys Llanddwyn is located in the south-western corner of Anglesey, at the southern entrance of the Menai Strait. As such, it became an important place during the rise of the British Empire, when the shipping of slate from the ports of Bangor, Caernarfon and Port Dinorwig in Y Felinheli was in full swing.

'So what do you know about all that?'

'I know that the cottages were built to house the pilots who would board ships to navigate the Menai Strait. It's something I know a bit about due to having four generations of pilots in the family who still guide ships through to this day. The waters have proven to be treacherous, judging by records left by the lifeboat stationed on the island in 1852. In one week in December, they saved thirty-six sailors from three separate wrecks.'

A safety beacon was built on the island in 1824 in the form of Twr Mawr, which guided ships entering the Strait, and a second lighthouse replaced it in 1845. Ironically, the older lighthouse was then returned to service thanks to a modern light being placed in it and was still in use up until the 1970s.[5]

But the biggest attraction, for Mari and me, at least, is Dwynwen's church.

'Take a picture of me and Danny sitting in the window, Russ – there's a specific angle through which you get a view of both the cross and the lighthouse in the distance ...'

In 2011, archaeologists excavated the nave of Dwynwen's church. They believed that Llanddwyn, along with the other numerous tiny islands found off the coast of Anglesey, was something of a 'time capsule'. You see, Edward I's conquest of north Wales practically went as far as Beaumaris – there was no military advantage to invading the rest of the island – so the inhabitants were largely left to their own devices. In a nutshell, a lot of their stuff wasn't replaced by Saxon stuff.

Archaeological evidence suggests that the church was ransacked to provide building material for the two lighthouses and perhaps also the cottages, boat sheds and a large sea wall. Indeed, it seems that most, if not all of the structures on the island have remnants of the church in them.[6]

Back at the car park, we hug and part ways. It's a strange feeling, having gone on my final walk for the book. And, with that, my journey across Wales comes to an end. Tomorrow, we head back to Cardiff, where we shall return to our – *Buzz! Buzz!*

Who's this now? Dad …

'*Helo?*'

'*Iawn?* Was thinking, before you head off tomorrow, maybe there's time for one more place. I can drive you up, save some petrol for your journey back.'

32

Where the folk
did the cow jump over
the burial mound?

'Go on, take it. Quick!'

'Hold on, let me just …' I squat down as low as I can and tilt my phone to the side, trying to find the most flattering angle for the most unflattering boulder. The rock sits in the dirt in the middle of a field somewhere on Anglesey.

'That one's emptying its bladder, look – it's getting ready to charge!'

'What?' I look up at the herd of bullocks and see that one of them is staring right back at us with a ticked-off look on his face, head bowed and legs spread apart as a powerful jet of urine hits the ground beneath him.

'*Na*, he – oh yeah … yeah, he does look a bit … yeah … yeah, let's go …'

Edging away, trying to appear as calm as possible, we head for the lowest fence, just in case. 'C'mon …'

'*Moooooo!*'

'Go. Go!'

Picking up speed, we see Mam opening the gate for us, signalling for us to hurry up. The earth is rumbling behind us and I know that we are not the only ones charging towards that gate. A sudden rush of excitement picks us up, fear diminishing as we break out in nonsensical laughter as we catch glimpses of each other running with our knees kicking the air as we avoid treacherous holes and mounds of excrement. Well, avoiding most of it, at least.

Mam slams the gate shut behind us and we become the dominant species once more. 'Bloody idiots!'

We're at Elim, in the small community of Tref Alaw. Dad brought us here solely to snap a photo of that rock, for it marks the spot of Bedd Branwen, a Bronze Age funerary mound dating as far back as 2000 BC, to those mysterious days of henges and stone circles. It is what's known as a ring cairn, or ring bank enclosure, and was used by our ancestors to hold cremations (and some, later on, as gravesites).

I should say at this stage, by the way, that many of these places are on private land and although farmers are generally happy for people to go see them, don't make the same mistake we did – ask for permission first and certainly don't go if there's livestock about.

This place wasn't known as 'Branwen's Grave' until 1813, when an excavation of the site uncovered an urn full of human remains. Some believed that this was proof that Branwen from the Second Branch of the *Mabinogi* was in fact a real person.

According to legend, she died by suicide, blaming herself for a whole lot of death and destruction, and was buried along the banks of Afon Alaw, which flows nearby. Further research and a second excavation in the 1960s, however, uncovered several more urns at the site, which confirmed that the place wasn't reserved solely for Branwen, if that even was her. Indeed, most scholars and historians would still agree that Branwen was merely a fictional character. Nevertheless, the name stuck.[1]

As we all stand here laughing after our narrow escape, it gets me thinking about my journey and all that I've – hold up – am I seriously going to end this book with us all gathered around laughing like something out of *The Waltons*? Guess so ...

From underground lairs to sandy beaches, the tallest mountain and the chilliest rainforest to the towns, villages and cities we call home, these stories have infiltrated every nook and cranny of this land. People learn about them in school and, although most forget them, or at least keep only faint memories and give vague recollections, there are others who devote their entire lives to them.

They dress up as dead horses and dance in the moonlight collecting money for charity; they sneak into abandoned buildings in search of treasure and secret tunnels; they meticulously investigate them, building up cases that expose supposedly true events as false; they worship old deities, theme their weddings around them and dedicate real ales in their name. Universally, these stories have huge roles to play in our languages and metaphors, our sense of morality and in our understanding of the world and of life and death.

Finding the origins of these tales is impossible; there is never a clear answer, never a definitive version. Are they remnants of our ancestors' collective memories, tall tales invented to stop the next generation from making the same mistakes they did, or proposed theories to explain natural events? Are they meant to be taken seriously at all, or do they exist simply to entertain? Are some even just instruments of propaganda?

And what does the future hold for folktales? Most of the modern world explains the inexplicable with inexplicable (to the most of us) science and, aside for some indigenous communities, most of us don't sit around campfires telling stories any more; we tell them through the medium of books (guilty!), films and video games. They are also becoming censored, with sensitive topics such as rape and abuse often being left out so as to be more appropriate for a younger audience.

And what of the places associated with these stories? As we have seen on our journey across Wales, they themselves are under threat from rising sea levels, industrialisation, deforestation, vandalism, neglect, Anglicisation, weather damage, privatisation, you name it. Should we strive to preserve these places, to promote them and to protect old place-names?

Who the folk knows (sorry, I had to slip one in before I finished!)? But I do know that I've barely scratched the surface. With so many other places left to visit, this hero's journey has only just begun ... and if you fancy going on a Welsh adventure of your own one day, maybe I'll bump into you on top of some enchanted hill or creepy castle, or in a haunted pub, more likely. Until then, *hwyl fawr*!

In loving memory of
Dean Powell

Endnotes

Introduction

1. Sioned Davies, *The Mabinogion: A New Translation* (Oxford: Oxford World's Classics, 2007), pp. ix–xxi.

1 Where the folk's the party at?

1. *www.llamau.org.uk*, accessed 22 November 2022.

2. *www.ons.gov.uk*, accessed 23 December 2023.

3. Reem Ahmed, *The stories behind the most curious street names in Cardiff* (*www. walesonline.co.uk*, 2022), accessed 23 December 2023.

4. Ahmed, *The stories behind*.

5. Mark Hughes, *From slums and cholera to Cardiff's live music hub: the fascinating story of Womanby Street* (*www.walesonline.co.uk*, 2017), accessed 22 November 2022.

6. Dic Mortimer, *A–Z of Cardiff* (Stroud: Amberley Publishing, 2016), p. 35.

7. Literature Wales, *Rebels* (*www.landoflegends.wales*), accessed 22 November 2022.

8. Jack Davies, *10 things you probably didn't know about Tongwynlais* (*www. tongwynlais.com*, 2014), accessed 22 November 2022; *History* (*www.castellcoch. com*, 2022), accessed 22 November 2022; Shirin Biswas, *37 Castell Coch facts: history, significance and much more* (*www.kidadl.com*, 2022), accessed 22 November 2022.

9. *Fforest Fawr, near Caerphilly* (*www.naturalresources.wales*, 2022), accessed 22 November 2022.

2 Where the folk can I find a hungover ghost?

1. Peter Stevenson, *Welsh Folk Tales* (Cheltenham: The History Press, 2017), p.213; Marie Trevelyan, *Folk-lore and Folk-stories of Wales* (London: EP Publishing Ltd, Facsimile of 1909 edition, 1973), pp. 89–90.

2. *Garth Mountain, Mynydd y Garth – climbing, hiking and mountaineering information* (*www.mountain-forecast.com*, 2022), accessed 24 November 2022.

3. *The Englishman Who Went Up a Hill But Came Down a Mountain* (*www. festival-cannes.com*), accessed 24 November 2022.

3 Where the folk can I hear the scream of a banshee?

1. Editors of Encyclopaedia Britannica, *Caerphilly* (*www.britannica.com*), accessed 25 November 2022; Hywel Wyn Owen, *The Place-Names of Wales* (Cardiff: University of Wales Press, 2015), p. 22.

2. Andrew-Paul Shakespeare, *Monsters, ghosts and a head-munching banshee – the folklore of Caerphilly, Wales* (*www.medium.com*, 2017), accessed 25 November 2022.

3. Jeffrey L. Thomas, *Caerphilly Castle* (*www.castlewales.com*, 2009), accessed 25 November 2022.

4. *The Green Lady of Caerphilly Castle* (*www.astonishinglegends.com*, 2018), accessed 25 November 2022.

5. *Gwrach-y-Rhibyn* (*www.astonishinglegends.com*, 2019), accessed 25 November 2022.

6. Moonlight (Amanda), *The Gwrach-y-Rhibyn* (*www.vampires.com*), accessed 25 November 2022.

7. B. B. Wiffen, *Choice Notes from 'Notes and Queries'* (London: General Books, 2012), p. 32; Elias Owen, *Welsh Folk-Lore,* 1st edition (CreateSpace Independent Publishing Platform, 2015), pp. 4–153; Wirt Sikes, *British Goblins: Welsh Folklore, Fairy Mythology, Legends and Traditions: 2nd Edition* (London: Sampson Low, Marston, Searle & Rivington, 1880), pp. 216–19.

4.Where the folk can I travel back in time to catch witches, fairies and ghosts?

1. Taken from the entry ticket at Llancaiach Fawr Manor (2021).

2. *Llancaiach-fawr, Gelligaer* (*www.britishlistedbuildings.co.uk*), accessed 26 November 2022.

3. *Llancaiach Fawr Manor* (*www.visitcaerphilly.com*), accessed 26 November 2022; *Manor House and tours* (*www.llancaiachfawr.co.uk*), accessed 26 November 2022.

4. Richard Suggett, 'Witchcraft dynamics in early modern Wales', in Michael Roberts and Simone Clarke (eds), *Women and Gender in Early Modern Wales* (Cardiff: University of Wales Press, 2000), pp. 75–103.

5. Matthew Hopkins, 'The Welsh Witch Trials', *Caernarfon Herald*, 28 October (2020), accessed 26 November 2022.

6. Peter Stevenson, *Welsh Folk Tales* (Cheltenham: The History Press, 2017), pp. 56–64.

5 Where the folk can I find a genuine fairy-tale castle?

1. *Pennard Castle* (*www.crazyaboutcastles.com*), accessed 20 April 2024.

2. *Local Area Report – Pennard Parish (W04000587)* (Nomis. Office for National Statistics, 2011), accessed 28 November 2022.

3. Royal Commission on the Ancient and Historical Monuments of Wales, *An Inventory of the Ancient Monuments in Glamorgan: Volume III: Medieval Secular Monuments, the Early Castles from the Norman Conquest to 1217* (London: Stationery Office Books, 1991), pp. 69–295.

4. Walter Evans-Wentz, *The Fairy-Faith in Celtic Countries* (Oxford: Oxford University Press, 1911), p. 138.

5. Wirt Sikes, *British Goblins: Welsh Folklore, Fairy Mythology, Legends and Traditions* (London: Sampson Low, Marston, Searle & Rivington, 1880), pp. 12–17.

6. *Pennard Castle* (*www.landoflegends.wales/location/pennard-castle*), accessed 20 April 2024.

6 Where the folk is the propa' Lady of the Lake, 'en?

1. John Davies and Nigel Jenkins et al., *The Welsh Academy Encyclopaedia of Wales* (Cardiff: University of Wales Press, 2008), p. 570.

2. Mike Rowland, *Guto Nyth Bran*, BBC Online (*www.bbc.co.uk/wales/arts/yourvideo/media/pages/michael_rowland_01.shtml*), archived from the original in 2009, accessed 1 December 2022.

3. Peter Stevenson, *Welsh Folk Tales* (Cheltenham: The History Press, 2017), p. 24.

4. Pollyanna Jones, *Llyn-y-Forwyn* (*www.pollyanna-jones.co.uk*, 2013), accessed 1 December 2022.

5. *Llyn-y-Forwyn* (*www.ourparanormalworld.com/united-kingdom*), accessed 29 January 2021.

6. Stevenson, *Welsh Folk Tales*, pp. 22–4.

7. F. Jones, *An Approach to Welsh Genealogy* (Trans. of Hon. Soc. of Cymmrodorion, 1948), p. 400; P. Davies, *The Physicians of Myddfai revisited* (*www.botanicgarden.wales*), accessed 1 December 2022.

7 Where the folk can I get vampire furniture from?

1. Becky Little, *The bloody truth about vampires* (*www.nationalgeographic.com*, 2016), accessed 2 December 2022.

2. Peter Stevenson, *Welsh Folk Tales* (Cheltenham: The History Press, 2017), pp. 103–4.

3. Marie Trevelyan, *Folk-lore and Folk-stories of Wales* (London: EP Publishing Ltd; Facsimile of 1909 edition, 1973), pp. 54–5.

4. Stephen Miller, *Epidemics timeline* (*www.awfhs.org*, 2019), accessed 2 December 2022.

5. Stevenson, *Welsh Folk Tales*, pp. 102–3.

6. *Llanmaes House, Llan-Maes* (*www.britishlistedbuildings.co.uk*), accessed 2 December 2022.

7. Dr Lloyd Bowen, *Welsh History Month: Llantrithyd Place, Vale of Glamorgan* (*www.walesonline.co.uk*), accessed 2 December 2022.

8. *Christmas comes early for 'Westminster Abbey of Wales' thanks to HLF funding* (*www.heritagefund.org.uk*), accessed 25 March 2021.

8 Where the folk did the 'Mad Doctor' go to burn the baby Welsh messiah?

1. Mary Jones, *The life of St Illtud* (*www.maryjones.us*), accessed 3 December 2022.

2. Nathan Bevan, *Who was Dr William Price? He's the inspiration for Robert Downey Jr's Welsh accent in Dolittle* (*www.walesonline.co.uk*, 2020), accessed 3 December 2022.

10 Where the folk can I find a good, old-fashioned hero?

1. Hywel Wyn Jones, *The Place-Names of Wales* (Cardiff: University of Wales Press, 2005), p. 19.

2. J. A. Giles (ed.), *Six Old English Chronicles, Book 12* (1848), from *Historia Regum Britanniae* by Geoffrey of Monmouth.

3. Sioned Davies, 'Performing *Culhwch ac Olwen*', *Arthurian Literature*, 21/31 (2004), p. 30.

4. Sioned Davies, *The Mabinogion: A New Translation* (Oxford: Oxford World's Classics, 2007), pp. 179–214.

5. Joseph Campbell, *The Hero with a Thousand Faces*, 3rd edition (1949; Novato: New World Library, 2012), pp. 294–5.

6. Campbell, *The Hero with a Thousand Faces*, pp. 65–6.

7. Campbell, *The Hero with a Thousand Faces*, p. 213.

11 Who the folk dances with Mari?

1. Geoffrey Ashe, 'Geoffrey of Monmouth', in *The New Arthurian Encyclopaedia* (New York: Garland, 1996), pp. 179–82.

2. *Dinas Rock, near Neath* (*www.naturalresources.wales*), accessed 8 December 2022.

3. Tony Oldham and Keith Jones, *King Arthur's Cave, caves of the south eastern outcrop* (*www.showcaves.com*, 2003), accessed 8 December 2022.

4. Edmonds Flavell, *The Skeleton Found in King Arthur's Hall* (Transactions of the Woolhope Naturalists Field Club, 1874), pp. 28–31.

5. E. W. Allen, *The Antiquarian* (1871), p. 164, accessed 8 December 2022.

12 Where the folk can I find a good, old-fashioned hero?

1. Sioned Davies, *The Mabinogion: A New Translation* (Oxford: Oxford World's Classics, 2007), pp. ix–xxi.

2. Davies, *The Mabinogion*, pp. 3–22.

3. Bill DeMain, 'Fleetwood Mac: the Story behind Rhiannon', *Classic Rock Magazine* (2015), accessed 8 December 2022; *Stevie Nicks on Rhiannon* (*www. inherownwords.net*), accessed 8 December 2022.

4. *Llantarnam Abbey* (*www.britishlistedbuildings.co.uk*), accessed 8 December 2022.

13 Where the folk did everyone go?

1. Sioned Davies, *The Mabinogion: A New Translation* (Oxford: Oxford World's Classics, 2007), pp. 35–47.

2. John Davies and Nigel Jenkins, *The Welsh Academy Encyclopaedia of Wales* (Cardiff: University of Wales Press, 2008), p. 730.

3. Pembrokeshire County Council, *Narberth captures its castle* (*www.pembrokeshire. gov.uk*), accessed 16 December 2022.

4. *Gorsedd Arberth* (*www.indianajones.fandom.com*), accessed 16 December 2022.

14 Where the folk can I find a beautiful princess and the ghost of a killer ape?

1. B. G. Charles, *The Place-names of Pembrokeshire* (Aberystwyth: National Library of Wales, 1992), p. 395.

2. Gwenllian M. Awbery, *Cymraeg Sir Benfro/Pembrokeshire Welsh* (Llanrwst: Gwasg Carreg Gwalch, 1991).

3. Conor Gogarty, *Welsh ice cream maker apologises for 'little England beyond Wales' branding* (*www.walesonline.co.uk*, 2022), accessed 21 December 2022.

4. *Ghosts of Carew Castle* (*www.pembrokeshirecoast.wales*), accessed 21 December 2022.

5. *Carew Castle history* (*www.pembrokeshirecoast.wales*), accessed 21 December 2022.

6. Kitty Parsons, *Pembrokeshire legends: Skomar Oddy* (*www.pembrokeshire.online*, 2020), accessed 21 December 2022.

7. Taken from an information board at Carew Castle, 2022.

8. *About Carew Tidal Mill* (*www.pembrokeshirecoast.wales*), accessed 21 December 2022.

15 Where the folk can I find militant dancing fairies and a retired giant-beaver-monster-thingy?

1. Sioned Davies, *The Mabinogion: A New Translation* (Oxford: Oxford World's Classics, 2007), pp. 192–5.

2. Brian John, *The legend of Bedd-yr-Afanc* (*www.brian-mountainman.blogspot. com*, 2012), accessed 22 December 2022.

3. Ian, *Bedd-yr-Afanc* (*www.mysteriousbritain.co.uk*, 2008), accessed 22 December 2022.

4. David Ward, *Eisteddfod's stone circles may be made from fibreglass* (*www. theguardian.com*, 2004), accessed 22 December 2022.

5. *The legend of Stonehenge* (*www.preselijewellery.co.uk/pages/about-us*), accessed 22 December 2022.

6. *Pentre Ifan chambered tomb, near Nevern* (*www.coflein.gov.uk*), accessed 22 December 2022.

7. Vicki Cummings and Colin Richards, *The Essence of the Dolmen: the Architecture of Megalithic Construction; Functions, Uses and Representations of Space in the Monumental Graves of Neolithic Europe* (published 20 October 2014), (*www.academia.edu/10011202/Cummings_V_and_Richards_C_2014_ The_essence_of_the_dolmen_the_architecture_of_megalithic_construction_ Pr%C3%A9histoires_M%C3%A9diterran%C3%A9ennes_2014*), accessed 22 December 2022.

8. *Pentre Ifan – portal tomb in Wales in Pembrokeshire* (*www.megalithic.co.uk*), accessed 22 December 2022.

9. Taken from information board at Pentre Ifan.

10. Pembrokeshire Coast National Park, *Pentre Ifan Fairies (Pembrokeshire: Land of Legends)* (*www.youtube.com*, 5 May 2017), accessed 22 December 2022.

11. Peter Stevenson, *Welsh Folk Tales* (Cheltenham: The History Press, 2017), pp. 177–8.

12. F. Sirois, 'Perspectives on epidemic hysteria', in M. J. Colligan, J. W. Pennebaker and L. R. Murphy (eds), *Mass Psychogenic Illness: A Social Psychological Analysis* (Hillsdale: Erlbaum, 1982), pp. 217–36.

13. D. M. Schullian, 'The Dancing Pilgrims at Muelebeek', *Journal of the History of Medicine and Allied Sciences* (Oxford: Oxford University Press, 1977), pp. 315–19.

14. Kevin Hetherington and Rolland Munro, *Ideas of Difference* (Hoboken: Wiley-Blackwell, 1997).

16 Where the folk is the only patron saint in the village?

1. *Llanddewi-Brefi signs 'for sale'* (*http://news.bbc.co.uk/1/hi/wales/mid/4278513. stm*, 2005), accessed 22 December 2022.

2. Ben Johnson, *The leek – national emblem of the Welsh* (*www.historic-uk.com*), accessed 22 December 2022.

3. BBC, *Saint David: the early life of David* (*www.bbc.co.uk/wales/history/sites/ themes/figures/saint_david.shtml*), accessed 22 December 2022.

4. Marcus Hughes, *This is the reason why the daffodil and the leek have become iconic symbols of Wales* (*www.walesonline.co.uk*, 2019), accessed 22 December 2022.

5. Huw Rees and Sian Kilcoyne, *Wales on This Day* (Cardiff: Calon, University of Wales Press, 2022), pp. 55–8.

6. Bronwen Weatherby, *Welsh council grants workers a day off for St David's Day* (*www.walesonline.co.uk*, 2022), accessed 22 December 2022.

7. Jacob Milnestein, *The Welsh corpse candles of St David* (*www.spookyisles.com*, 2013), accessed 22 December 2022.

8. Sue Vincent, *Going West: The Talking Stone* (*www.franceandvincent.com*, 2022), accessed 22 December 2022.

9. Oliver Davies, *The Life of St. David by Rhigyfarch, Celtic Spirituality* (Mahwah: Paulist Press, 1999), pp. 191–212.

17 Where the folk can I find a pirate-fighting monk?

1. *St Govan and the pirates* (*www.pembrokeshirecoast.wales*), accessed 22 December 2022.

2. David Owens, *The amazing (and huge) hidden cave hidden beneath one of Wales' most popular coastal walks* (*www.walesonline.co.uk*, 2019), accessed 22 December 2022.

3. *The legend of St Govan's Chapel* (*www.kingarthursknights.com*), accessed 22 December 2022.

18 Where the folk can I find a talking seal and an angry Welsh lady?

1. Visit Wales, *Welcome to Fishguard* (*www.fishguard-wales.com*, 2013), accessed 3 January 2023.

2. Coastal Cottages of Pembrokeshire, *Jemima Nicholas, a Fishguard heroine* (*www.coastalcottages.co.uk*), accessed 3 January 2023.

3. *The last invasion of Britain, 1797* (*www.fishguardonline.com*, 2021), accessed 3 January 2023.

4. Peter Stevenson, *Welsh Folk Tales* (Cheltenham: The History Press, 2017), pp. 44–5.

5. Stevenson, *Welsh Folk Tales*, p. 38.

6. Riley Winters, *Legends of the Selkies, hidden gems of sea mythology* (*www.ancient-origins.net*, 2016), accessed 3 January 2023.

19 Where the folk is the 'Welsh Atlantis'?

1. *Cantre'r Gwaelod – the lost land of Wales* (*www.bbc.co.uk*), accessed 3 January 2023.

2. Neil Prior, *Map may show evidence of Wales' Atlantis off Ceredigion* (*www.bbc. co.uk*, 2022), accessed 3 January 2023.

3. Anna Lewis, *The stunning ancient forest on a Welsh beach that's more visible than it's been in thousands of years* (*www.walesonline.co.uk*, 2019), accessed 3 January 2023; Chris Griffiths, *How a storm revealed a Welsh kingdom* (*www.bbc.com*, 2020), accessed 3 January 2023.

1. *The legend* (*www.devilsbridgefalls.co.uk*, 2023), accessed 4 January 2023.

2. *About* (*www.elanvalley.org.uk*), accessed 4 January 2023.

3. *Devil's Bridge, Ceredigion* (*www.stayinwales.co.uk*, 2021), accessed 4 January 2023.

4. *Devil's Bridge* (*www.historypoints.org*), accessed 4 January 2023.

5. *Local history* (*www.devilsbridgefalls.co.uk*, 2023), accessed 4 January 2023.

6. Jon Kaneko-James, *Who was Jack o' Kent, the Welsh Doctor Faustus?* (*www. spookyisles.com*, 2014), accessed 4 January 2023.

21 Where the folk did the flower-faced girl go?

1. Christopher R. Fee, *Gods, Heroes and Kings: The Battle for Mythic Britain* (Oxford: Oxford University Press, 2004), p. 68.

2. Sioned Davies, *The Mabinogion: A New Translation* (Oxford: Oxford World's Classics, 2007), pp. 179–214.

3. Davies, *The Mabinogion*, pp. 47–65.

4. Baz, *The Stone of Goronwy: holed stone in Gwynedd* (*www.megalithic.co.uk*), accessed 6 January 2023.

5. *The Owl Service* (*www.literaryatlas.wales*), accessed 6 January 2023.

6. *Tomen y Mur* (*www.welshslatewaterfeatures.co.uk*), accessed 6 January 2023; *Tomen y Mur* (*www.snowdonia.gov.wales*), accessed 6 January 2023.

1. Sioned Davies, *The Mabinogion: A New Translation* (Oxford: Oxford World's Classics, 2007), pp. 47–65.

2. Remy Dean, *How to foil the devil: the tale of the Maentwrog standing stone* (*www.folklorethursday.com*, 2016), accessed 8 January 2023.

3. Ian, *Maentwrog (Twrog's Stone)* (*www.mysteriousbritain.co.uk*, 2018), accessed 8 January 2023.

4. Woodland Trust Wood Group, *Coed Felenrhyd & Llennyrch* (*www. woodlandtrust.org.uk*), accessed 8 January 2023.

5. Remy Dean, *Black arts and talismans: Huw Llwyd, the real Welsh wizard* (*www. folklorethursday.com*, 2017), accessed 8 January 2023.

23 Where the folk can I listen to talking starlings and a Welsh banger?

1. *Places mentioned in the Second Branch of the Mabinogi (www.nantlle.com)*, accessed 9 January 2023.
2. *What does Baile Átha Cliath mean in English? (www.ilovelanguages.com)*, accessed 9 January 2023.
3. Sioned Davies, *The Mabinogion: A New Translation* (Oxford: Oxford World's Classics, 2007), pp. 22–35.
4. Mark Cartwright, *Harlech Castle (www.worldhistory.org*, 2019), accessed 9 January 2023.

24 Where the folk do skeleton brides, disgraced kings and Nazi spies go to hide?

1. *Nant Gwrtheyrn folk tales: Rhys a Meinir (www.nantgwrtheyrn.org)*, accessed 10 January 2023.
2. *The history of Nant Gwrtheyrn (www.nantgwrtheyrn.org)*, accessed 10 January 2023.
3. *Nant Gwrtheyrn folk tales: The Story of Gwrtheyrn (www.nantgwrtheyrn.org)*, accessed 10 January 2023.
4. *Nant Gwrtheyrn folk tales: The Three Curses (www.nantgwrtheyrn.org)*, accessed 10 January 2023.
5. *Nant Gwrtheyrn folk tales: Elis Bach (www.nantgwrtheyrn.org)*, accessed 10 January 2023.
6. *Nant Gwrtheyrn folk tales: A German Spy? (www.nantgwrtheyrn.org)*, accessed 10 January 2023.
7. Jim Krawiecki, *Yr Eifl – The hills of the northern Lleyn (www.thebmc.co.uk*, 2008), accessed 10 January 2023.
8. *Tre'r Ceiri – hillfort (www.medievalheritage.eu)*, accessed 10 January 2023.
9. *St Beuno's Church, Clynnog Fawr (www.historypoints.org)*, accessed 10 January 2023; *St Beuno (www.catholic.org)*, accessed 10 January 2023.
1. *Home (www.bragdylleu.cymru)*, accessed 12 January 2023.
2. John Owen Huws, *Straeon Gwerin Ardal Eryri, Cyfrol 1–3* (Llanrwst: Gwasg Carreg Gwalch, 2008).
3. Iestyn Hughes, *Darwin and Moel Tryfan – Diluvialists v Glacialists (https://web.archive.org/web/20160810000037/http:/www.atgof.co/daarwin-a-moel-tryfan/*, 2012), accessed 12 January 2023.
4. Julie Brominicks, *Llyn y Dywarchen, Gwynedd (www.countryfile.com*, 2021), accessed 12 January 2023.

5. *Nantlle Railway* (*www.nantlle.com*), accessed 12 January 2023.

6. *Dinas Dinlle Iron Age fort saved from erosion* (*http://news.bbc.co.uk/local/ northwestwales/hi/people_and_places/history/newsid_9369000/9369294.stm*, 2011), accessed 12 January 2023.

7. *Caer Arianrhod* (*https://earthwisdomearthscience.com/tag/caer-arianrhod/*, 2020), accessed 12 January 2023.

8. *Dinas Dinlle Iron Age fort saved from erosion.*

26 Where the folk can I find space rock and a martyred mongoose?

1. *Rupert Bear and Beddgelert* (*www.beddgelerttourism.com*), accessed 16 January 2023.

2. Katrin Raynor, *Beddgelert meteorite: big find in a small village* (*www. skyatnightmagazine.com*), accessed 16 January 2023.

3. *The legend of Gelert* (*www.beddgelerttourism.com*), accessed 16 January 2023.

4. Ben Johnson, *The legend of Gelert the dog* (*www.historic-uk.com*), accessed 16 January 2023.

5. Ian, *Royal Goat Hotel, Beddgelert* (*www.mysteriousbritain.co.uk*, 2009), accessed 16 January 2023.

6. *The mongoose and the Brahmin's wife* (*www.culturalindia.net*), accessed 16 January 2023.

7. Rudyard Kipling, *The Jungle Book* (London: Macmillan Publication, 1894).

8. Huw Rees and Sian Kilcoyne, *Wales on This Day* (Cardiff: Calon, University of Wales Press, 2022), pp. 172–3.

9. Gergely Lajtai-Szabó, *St Gellért – The first Christian martyr of Hungary* (*www. dailynewshungary.com*, 2017), accessed 16 January 2023.

27 Where the folk did the Welsh get their flag from?

1. Jaymelouise Hudspith, *The Welsh flag has been voted the coolest looking flag in the world* (*www.dailypost.co.uk*, 2021), accessed 19 January 2023.

2. *Dinas Emrys – Merlin & the dragons* (*www.sacredsiteswales.co.uk*, 2017), accessed 19 January 2023.

3. Sioned Davies, *The Mabinogion: A New Translation* (Oxford: Oxford World's Classics, 2007), pp. 111–16.

4. James MacKillop, *Dictionary of Celtic Mythology* (Oxford: Oxford University Press, 1998), p. 349.

5. Prof. Geller, *The Wild Hunt* (*www.mythology.net*, 2017), accessed 19 January 2023.

6. *Wales history: why is the red dragon on the Welsh flag?* (*www.bbc.co.uk*, 2019), accessed 19 January 2023.

7. *Act of Union* (*www.britannica.com*), accessed 19 January 2023.

8. *Union Jack* (*www.royal.uk*), accessed 19 January 2023.

28 Where the folk can I find a relocated giant-beaver-monster-thingy?

1. Ben Johnson, *The legend of the River Conwy Afanc* (*www.historic-uk.com*), accessed 20 January 2023.

2. *Moel Siabod – a stunning walk in Snowdonia National Park* (*www.10adventures.com*), accessed 20 January 2023.

3. *Horse-drawn coach, Capel Curig* (*www.historypoints.org*), accessed 20 January 2023.

4. *Tŷ Hyll history* (*www.snowdonia-society.org.uk*), accessed 20 January 2023.

5. James McCarthy, *Beavers could return to Wales within weeks* (*www.bbc.co.uk*, 2021), accessed 20 January 2023.

29 Where the folk is the highest story in Wales?

1. *Yr Wyddfa* (*www.snowdonia.gov.wales*), accessed 23 January 2023.

2. *Car i lawr o gopa'r Wyddfa* [Car down from the summit of Yr Wyddfa] (*http://news.bbc.co.uk/welsh/hi/newsid_9580000/newsid_9584500/9584550.stm*, 2011), accessed 23 January 2023.

3. *Snowdon: park to use mountain's Welsh name Yr Wyddfa* (*www.bbc.co.uk*, 2022), accessed 23 January 2023.

4. *Rhitta Gawr* (*www.legendsofwales.com*, 2017), accessed 23 January 2023.

5. Terry Marsh, *The Summits of Snowdonia* (London: Robert Hale Publishing, 1984), pp. 178–83; Geraint Roberts, *The Lakes of Eryri* (Llanrwst: Gwasg Carreg Gwalch, 1995), pp. 145–8.

6. Roberts, *The Lakes of Eryri*, pp. 143–5.

7. Roberts, *The Lakes of Eryri*, pp. 100–1.

8. Matthew Trask, *The legends of Cadair Idris* (*www.medium.com*, 2018), accessed 23 January 2023.

9. *The story of Ceridwen* (*www.ceridwencentre.co.uk*), accessed 23 January 2023.

10. *The life of Taliesin the bard* (*www.bbc.co.uk*), accessed 23 January 2023.

30 Where the folk is the girl of my dreams, cont?

1. Carly Silver, *Meet Magnus Maximus, the Roman usurper-turned-Welsh hero who inspired King Arthur* (*www.ancient-origins.net*, 2016), accessed 23 January 2023.

2. Sioned Davies, *The Mabinogion: A New Translation* (Oxford: Oxford World's Classics, 2007), pp. 103–8.

3. *Elen ferch Eudaf Hen* (*www.geni.com*, 2022), accessed 23 January 2023.

4. Davies, *The Mabinogion*, p. 108.

5. *Segontium Roman Fort* (*www.cadw.gov.wales*), accessed 23 January 2023.

6. Davies, *The Mabinogion*, pp. 103–10.

7. Reginald Allen Brown, *The Architecture of Castles: A Visual Guide* (London: B. T. Batsford, 1984), p. 88; *Caernarfon Castle* (*www.cadw.gov.wales*), accessed 23 January 202.

8. Richard Jones, *Ghosts of Caernarfon Castle* (*www.great-castles.com*), accessed 23 January 2023.

9. *The prince in the tower* (*www.cadw.gov.wales*), accessed 23 January 2023.

10. Sarah Woodbury, *St. Peblig's Church* (*www.sarahwoodbury.com*, 2021), accessed 23 January 2023.

11. *Our story* (*www.black-boy-inn.com*), accessed 23 January 2023.

12. *Say hello to the Black Boy Inn's ghosts!* (*www.black-boy-inn.com*, 2022), accessed 23 January 2023.

13. Eryl Crump, *Spooky connection between two North Wales pubs with the same name* (*www.dailypost.co.uk*, 2021), accessed 23 January 2023.

31 Where the folk is the 'Welsh Valentine's Day' from?

1. Catrin Stevens, *Santes Dwynwen/Saint Dwynwen* (Llandysul: Gomer Press, 2005).

2. BBC News Wales, *Cards for rival love saint* (*http://news.bbc.co.uk/1/hi/wales/2683117.stm*, 2003), accessed 26 January 2023.

3. Leonardo Palacios-Sánchez, Luisa María Díaz-Galindo and Juan Sebastián Botero-Meneses, *Saint Valentine: patron saint of lovers and epilepsy* (*www.sciencedirect.com*, 2017), accessed 26 January 2023.

4. David Hughes, *What is Dydd Santes Dwynwen? The meaning behind Welsh Valentine's Day explained and what St Dwynwen did* (*www.inews.co.uk*, 2023), accessed 26 January 2023.

5. *Llanddwyn Island* (*www.anglesey-history.co.uk*), accessed 26 January 2023.

6. Neil Prior, *Llanddwyn Island: archaeologists unearth building remains* (*www.bbc.co.uk*, 2021), accessed 26 January 2023.

32 Where the folk did the cow jump over the burial mound?

1. sunbright57, *Bedd Branwen, Glanalaw, Treffynon, Anglesey* (*www.thejournalofantiquities.com*, 2014), accessed 26 January 2023.

Bibliography

Allen, E. W., *The Antiquarian* (1871).

Ashe, G., 'Geoffrey of Monmouth', in *The New Arthurian Encyclopaedia* (New York: Garland, 1996).

Awbery, G. M., *Cymraeg Sir Benfro/Pembrokeshire Welsh* (Llanrwst: Gwasg Carreg Gwalch, 1991).

Barber, R., *Myths and Legends of the British Isles* (Martlesham: The Boydell Press, 1999).

Billing, J. (ed.), *The Hidden Places of North Wales: Including Snowdonia and Anglesey* (Plymouth: Travel Publishing Ltd, 1998).

Black Book of Carmarthen (Llyfr Du Caerfyrddin) (Aberystwyth: National Library of Wales, NLW Peniarth MS 1, *c*.1250).

Bord, J. and Bord, C., *Atlas of Magical Britain* (London: Guild Publishing, 1990).

Boucicault, D., *La Dame de Pique, or The Vampire, a Phantasm Related in Three Dramas* (1852).

Brown, R. A., *The Architecture of Castles: A Visual Guide* (London: B. T. Batsford, 1984).

Campbell, J., *The Hero with a Thousand Faces*, 3rd edition (1949; Novato: New World Library, 2012).

Charles, B. G., *The Placenames of Pembrokeshire* (Aberystwyth: National Library of Wales, 1992).

Colligan, M. J., Pennebaker, J. W and Murphy, L. R. (eds), *Mass Psychogenic Illness: A Social Psychological Analysis* (Hillsdale: Erlbaum, 1982).

Davies, J. et al., *The Welsh Academy Encyclopaedia of Wales* (Cardiff: University of Wales Press, 2008).

Davies, O., *The Life of St. David by Rhigyfarch, Celtic Spirituality* (Mahwah: Paulist Press, 1999).

Davies, S., 'Performing *Culhwch ac Olwen*', *Arthurian Literature*, 21/31 (2004).

Davies, S., *The Mabinogion: A New Translation* (Oxford: Oxford World's Classics, 2007).

Evans-Wentz, W., *The Fairy-Faith in Celtic Countries* (Oxford: Oxford University Press, 1911).

Fee, C. R., *Gods, Heroes and Kings: The Battle for Mythic Britain* (Oxford: Oxford University Press, 2004).

Fishlock, T., *Wales and the Welsh* (London: Cassell and Company Ltd, 1972).

Gater, D., *The Battles of Wales* (Llanrwst: Gwasg Carreg Gwalch, 1991).

Giles, J. A. (ed.), *Six Old English Chronicles, Book 12* (1848), from *Historia Regum Britanniae* by Geoffrey of Monmouth.

Guest, Lady C., *The Mabinogion* (Llandovery: Tonn Press; London: Longmans, 1826–1845).

Hetherington, K. and Munro, R., *Ideas of Difference* (Hoboken: Wiley-Blackwell, 1997).

Huws, J. O., *Straeon Gwerin Ardal Eryri, Cyfrol 1–3* (Llanrwst: Gwasg Carreg Gwalch, 2008).

Jones, F., *An Approach to Welsh Genealogy* (Trans. of Hon. Soc. of Cymmrodorion, 1948).

Jones, H. W., *The Place-Names of Wales* (Cardiff: University of Wales Press, 2005).

Jones, W. H., *Old Karnarvon: A Historical Account of the Town of Carnarvon, with Notices of the Parish Churches of Llanbeblig and Llanfaglan* (H. Humphries, 1882).

Kipling, R., *The Jungle Book* (London: Macmillan Publication, 1894).

MacKillop, J., *Dictionary of Celtic Mythology* (Oxford: Oxford University Press, 1998).

Marsh, T., *The Summits of Snowdonia* (London: Robert Hale Publishing, 1984).

Miller, H. H., *The Realms of Arthur* (London: Peter Davies, 1970).

Monger, C., *The Englishman Who Went Up a Hill But Came Down a Mountain* (London: Miramax/Corgi, 1995).

Mortimer, D., *A–Z of Cardiff* (Stroud: Amberley Publishing, 2016).

Owen, A. (ed.), *Writers' and Artists' Yearbook 2021* (London: Bloomsbury Yearbooks, 2020).

Owen, E., *Welsh Folk-Lore*, 1st edition (CreateSpace Independent Publishing Platform, 2015).

Owen, H. W., *The Place-Names of Wales* (Cardiff: University of Wales Press, 2015).

Powell, D., *Dr William Price: Wales's First Radical* (Stroud: Amberley Publishing, 2012).

Powell, D., *Llantrisant: An Historic Hilltop Town* (London: Pitkin Publishing, 2017).

Red Book of Hergest (*Llyfr Coch Hergest*) (Oxford: Bodleian Library MS Jesus College III, 1382–1410).

Rees, H. and Kilcoyne, S., *Wales on This Day* (Cardiff: Calon, University of Wales Press, 2022).

Roberts, G., *The Lakes of Eryri* (Llanrwst: Gwasg Carreg Gwalch, 1995).

Ross, D., *Wales: History of a Nation* (Glasgow: Geddes and Grosset, 2015).

Royal Commission on the Ancient and Historical Monuments of Wales, *An Inventory of the Ancient Monuments in Glamorgan: Volume III: Medieval Secular Monuments, the Early Castles from the Norman Conquest to 1217* (London: Stationery Office Books, 1991).

Schullian, D. M., 'The Dancing Pilgrims at Muelebeek', *Journal of the History of Medicine and Allied Sciences* (Oxford: Oxford University Press, 1977).

Sikes, W., *British Goblins: Welsh Folk-lore, Fairy Mythology, Legends and Traditions: 2nd Edition* (London: Sampson Low, Marston, Searle & Rivington, 1880).

Stevens, C., *Santes Dwynwen/Saint Dwynwen* (Llandysul: Gomer Press, 2005).

Stevenson, P., *Welsh Folk Tales* (Cheltenham: The History Press, 2017).

Stoker, B., *Dracula* (Edinburgh: Archibald Constable and Company, 1897).

Suggett, R., 'Witchcraft dynamics in early modern Wales', in M. Roberts and S. Clarke (eds), *Women and Gender in Early Modern Wales* (Cardiff: University of Wales Press, 2000).

Trevelyan, M., *Folk-lore and Folk-stories of Wales* (London: EP Publishing Ltd; Facsimile of 1909 edition, 1973).

White Book of Rhydderch (*Llyfr Gwyn Rhydderch*) (Aberystwyth: National Library of Wales, NLW Peniarth MS 4–5, *c*.1350).

Wiffen, B. B., *Choice Notes from 'Notes and Queries'* (London: General Books, 2012).

About the Author

Russ Williams was raised in the predominantly Welsh-speaking town of Caernarfon in north Wales. He now resides in Cardiff, where he continues to write. As a member of Roath Writers, a Cardiff-based writing group, he published his first short story, 'Press 2 for English', via the group's annual anthology in 2015. He also has two active blogs, *Brawd Autistico* and *Where the Folk*.

His short piece 'When Hats are Life' appears in Helen Bucke's *Bearing Untold Stories: Life on (and off) the Autism Spectrum. Where the Folk* is his first traditionally published book.